MORE
DARRELL
SIFFORD

MORE DARRELL SIFFORD

Columns From The Philadelphia Inquirer, 1981-1992

by Darrell Sifford

with a foreword by
Marilyn Sifford

ANDREWS and McMEEL
A Universal Press Syndicate Company
Kansas City

Library of Congress Cataloging-in-Publication Data

Sifford, Darrell, 1931-1992
    More Darrell Sifford :   columns from the Philadelphia inquirer,
  1981-1992 /   by Darrell Sifford ; with an introduction by Marilyn
  Sifford.
      p. cm.
    Includes bibliographical references.
    ISBN 0-8362-8095-4
    1. Marriage—United States. 2. Family—United States. 3. Par-
  ent and child—United States. I. Sifford, Marilyn. II. Philadelphia
  inquirer (Philadelphia, Pa. : 1969) III. Title.
  HQ536.S496   1994   94-32873
  306.8'0973—dc20   CIP

Designed by Barrie Maguire

Dedication

To Darrell. You are remembered.

And to Gene Roberts, executive editor of The Philadelphia Inquirer *from 1972 to 1990, who recognized Darrell's unique gift and provided the opportunity for him to come to the* Inquirer *as a full-time columnist in 1976.*

Acknowledgments

On the last full day of winter 1994, I attended the Book and the Cook Fair, an annual Philadelphia event, at the Pennsylvania Convention Center. There I unexpectedly encountered Ken Bookman, an *Inquirer* editor who was there as one of the fair's participating cookbook authors. In 1992, Ken and I had worked together on *What Do You Think? The 100 Best Columns of Darrell Sifford*, and it seemed like a good time for me to mention to him something that I had had on my mind for a few weeks.

So I asked Ken whether anyone at the *Inquirer* had given any thought to publishing a second book of Darrell's columns.

"It's interesting you would ask," he replied. Just a couple of days before, he said, that very possibility had been discussed by Ken and his boss at the *Inquirer*, Bob Greenberg. Ken asked what I thought of the idea.

I told him that I would love to preserve more of Darrell's work. The reception generated by *What Do You Think?* was phenomenal, and the letters and comments I received reinforced my belief that there were a lot of readers old and new who would love to have a second collection.

From there, things moved pretty quickly. Andrews and McMeel, which had published several other books with the *Inquirer*, quickly expressed interest in this one, and it was scheduled for publication in the fall of 1994.

To Ken, Bob, and Max King, who helped to bring about the publication of this book, I wish to extend my sincere thanks and gratitude.

To readers of Darrell's column and of *What Do You Think?* I want you to know that without you, this second book would not have happened. Many of you bought multiple copies for friends and loved ones. And the letters and comments I continue to receive about the book and about Darrell's work in general are testimony to his legacy and to the unusual bond he had with you, his readers. Thank you for making this possible.

I wish to again acknowledge the University of Missouri Journalism School, *The Philadelphia Inquirer*, and particularly Max King and John V.R. Bull for setting up the Darrell Sifford Memorial Prize in journalism. I extend my deepest appreciation to all of you who have remembered Darrell with your gifts to the fund. This fund will preserve Darrell's legacy by encouraging similar work by other journalists.

To Abe Schwartz, who made a sculpture of Darrell for me as a gift, my heartfelt thanks to you for remembering Darrell and me in such a loving way.

To Betsi Smith-Higgins, who gave to me a "sea creature" that Darrell had made from clay in her Kindergarten for Adults, my deepest thanks.

Betsi fired it later and but for her I would not have known of its existence. I had it made in bronze for Jay and Grant, Darrell's sons. And finally, my thanks to all those who contributed to Darrell's work as part of his network of resources and friends. Those who have contributed to the columns in this book are listed below:

Ray Adams, Lynn Atwater, Rosara Berman, Manny Bertin, Robert Bly, Philip Bobrove, John L. Bulette, Isaac H. "Quartie" Clothier, Erich Coché, Sidney J. Cohen, Sidney M. DeAngelis, Gayle DeLaney, John D. Erdlen, H. Bruce Ewart, Ed Fish, Carol Gantman, Dave Garroway, Matti Gershenfeld, Frances Graboskey, David Grady, Victor Gruhn, Rev. James W. Haney, Lee Hausner, Irwin Hyman, and Neil Izenberg.

Also, Wallace R. Johnson, Edward Kuljian, Marvin Kanefield, Melvin Kinder, Murray Klein, Ned Klumph, Arlene Kramer, George S. Layne, Bill Liberi, Daniel Lieberman, Harold Lief, Cynthia Livingston, Marilyn Machlowitz, Leo Madow, Edward Mazze, Layton McCurdy, Alan Loy McGinnis, Richard McKnight, Richard Moscotti, Jane Norman, Anna Polcino, Maurice Prout, Robert Reath, John Reckless, Arnold S. Relman, David Rice, David Rich, and Helen Rosen.

Also, Alice G. Sargent, Harvey Schwartz, Charles W. Scott, Susan F. Scott, G. Pirooz Sholevar, Thelma Shtasel, Peter E. Sifneos, Marvin Silverman, Clara Simpson, Enos Slaughter, Julian Slowinski, Lewis B. Smedes, Betsi Smith-Higgins, Jean G. Spaulding, Alan Summers, Rev. Lynwood Swanson, John A. Talbot, Don Tashjan, Phyllis Taylor, Stephen R. Treat, Ralph Undewager, Burton L. White, Linda Wingate, Peter C. Whybrow, Gardner Yenawine, and Arnold Zenker.

Contents

Foreword

Since Darrell Sifford's accidental death on March 6, 1992, my journey through grief to new beginnings has been an emotional and spiritual one, a journey of learning and transformation. I have been changed in profound ways. Here is some of what I learned:

•

I now know I can survive life's darkest hours and emerge intact—somehow stronger, wiser, and more humble. When Darrell died, I felt as though my life force had gone with him. During those first months, it took all my energy and more to take some control of my daily existence, to continue my work, to follow through with things I needed to do to honor Darrell's life and legacy. When I look back, I am amazed at the decisions I made and what I was able to do. It was as though I had a guardian angel or perhaps several, helping me through this period. One day I said to a close friend, "I know I have to go through this grief in order to heal." My friend's reply was, "Yes, you have to go through it— but you don't have to give in to it." That reply resonated with me and has helped me monitor how I was feeling and when I needed to help myself or to seek help from others.

I have gained increased respect for my own inner resource of judgment and a deeper trust in my own instincts about what is right for me. My appreciation for life in all forms is deeper, my sense of what is really important is keener, my awareness of how much good is in the world is broader, my ability to live in the moment is much greater, my humility about what I can control relative to the future is increased.

•

Healing after a loss has its own timetable. We can help it or stall it by our own awareness and willingness to work through the pain and grief. If one pathway is blocked, the pain will find another way to surface. It will not be forever suppressed or erased or wished away or avoided. Understanding this helped me accept and honor the whole range of feelings and behavior I experienced without judging myself too harshly.

•

I now know there is a spiritual world beyond this world. On the morning of the first anniversary of Darrell's death, I dreamed that a very important mentor of mine who lived in New York had died. I had thought about contacting him during that first year, but I kept putting it off.

I decided when I got up that morning I would not put it off any longer. I called several times and there was no answer. A few days later, a woman answered.

"May I speak to Sydney?" I asked.

"Oh, I guess you didn't read the paper," she said.

"No, I don't read the New York paper, I live in Philadelphia," I replied. "What happened?"

The woman then confirmed what I already knew. Sydney had died the day before I had the dream. I believe that Sydney had come to me in the dream to tell me that he had died. His spirit survived his physical death. And while I had other experiences that reinforced my belief in "another world," this one really got my attention.

I am much more open-minded now about what is possible and not so quick to discount things I can't explain.

•

It is possible to find meaning and happiness in a new relationship. One day, I was working in my office at home when the phone rang: It was Karol. Karol, Ginny, and Alina, my closest friends, and my sister Joan had met me at the airport on March 8, 1992, when I returned from that ill-fated trip.

"Marilyn, I don't want to be intrusive," Karol said, "but I have a brother-in-law who is going through a divorce and he would like to meet someone who would enjoy doing some things but who doesn't want to get involved."

Without asking any questions, I answered, "Karol, if that's what he's looking for, that's perfect for me." I didn't have any interest in "dating," but I had just reached the point where I felt I needed to come out of my cocoon of grief and work. A few days later, Bob Butera called and invited me to come with him to Longwood Gardens and Winterthur, about an hour's drive from Philadelphia. It was exactly the kind of day I needed. The beauty of nature has always been a healing tonic for me—and Bob's ease, his lack of pretense, his considerate nature, his openness all made it very comfortable to be with him. The following week, we went to Valley Green in a Philadelphia park for a picnic. Though neither of us felt ready for a relationship, by the end of that first week we both knew there was potential for a special relationship.

On May 29, 1994, we were married at a very special ceremony in the Sarah P. Duke flower gardens in North Carolina with our families and a few close friends present. I wanted my family members, who had shared the hard times, to also share our joy in this new beginning. It was a very special day for all of us.

●

The most powerful force for healing is love. Love and support have come to me in countless ways:

In conversation, letters, walks in the park, breakfasts, lunches, dinners, and many other gestures of friends.

In letters from strangers.

In long drives, visits, and phone calls from my family.

In a video of photos set to music from a 24-year-old niece, and in a little white barking dog from a 6-year-old niece.

In summer drives in the country with Bob, and in delicious bowls of pasta with fresh tomato sauce that we made together.

In the warmth and enthusiasm with which Bob's mother, Ann, his daughter, Nina, his son, Bobby, and his entire family made me one of them.

In parties given by friends to celebrate our new beginning.

I could go on.

My close friend Susan lost her husband, Rick, to cancer a few months after Darrell's death. Susan and I have shared our journeys, which have been different and yet the same. In one of our many conversations, Susan said something that resonated with me as a universal truth: "We have to witness each other's pain."

There is enormous comfort and validation and healing in knowing that another human being can see and feel your pain. Susan and I have been each other's witnesses and soulmates on this journey. It has gotten me over some tough spots where I could have gotten stuck.

●

In March 1992, I wrote a tribute for Darrell's memorial celebration. Since that time, I sent out hundreds of copies to readers who made contributions to his memorial fund. I received so many warm and appreciative responses that I would like to share it here.

●

One day, Darrell and I were walking along the beach talking about our dreams, our fears, and our plans, and I asked Darrell how he would most like to be remembered. He said:

"I would like to be remembered as someone who lived a life that mattered. As someone who had touched people's lives in a positive way —who helped people see that they have choices and that they are not alone."

You, his readers, friends, and colleagues, have given Darrell this gift—both when he was here physically and now as his spirit, his words, his voice, and his life continue to touch our spirits, our words, our voices, and our lives and the lives of those we care about.

There are so many things I love and cherish about Darrell—many of which are the same things that you, his readers, have grown to love.

I love his rare ability to share his life: the joy and the pain, the struggle and the triumph, the vulnerability and the strength, the curiosity and the compassion, the humor and the humanity.

I love his courage: Among the many things I admire about Darrell's work was his freedom of mind and thought. When considering whether or not to do a column, he *always, always* asked the question: "Is there something in this story that would benefit readers?" That was his acid test. And he never worried too much about criticism. He didn't expect everyone to agree with what he wrote. When writing about a controversial subject, he felt he had gotten it about right if he received similar amounts of praise and criticism. And always, constructive feedback from readers fueled his curiosity, leading to more questions, more ideas, more exploration, and more understanding. Frequently, he brought home letters from readers that he wanted to share with me. He never stopped being amazed and touched by the way people shared their lives and wisdom with him.

I love the father: Darrell loved his sons, Jay and Grant, deeply. He worked hard to be the kind of father with whom they could relate—their accomplishments and disappointments, their life struggles, and their fears. He wanted to know them and he wanted them to know him.

I loved his friendship and companionship. Our time together was special: long walks, long talks, music, the ocean, our cat B.G., Hershey's Mill, laughter, tears, plans, and dreams. Being together multiplied the joy of good times and lightened the pain of hard times.

And I loved the husband and partner: Darrell and I, like many of you, lived some of the life struggles that he wrote about. He committed himself to face the growing pains of creating a vibrant and rich and deep relationship based on a kind of partnership between a man and a woman that is still quite rare. He told me on several occasions during his last year that this was the accomplishment of which he was most proud.

Darrell appreciated the life journeys of others more as he continued his own.

I have one thing to ask of you and a promise to leave with you.

The way we can honor Darrell the most is to live our lives fully, to be true and good to ourselves and the people we love, and to do and say the things we feel to the important people in our lives. He modeled this well for all of us.

My promise to Darrell and you is this:

Darrell had already planned to publish a book of his columns and this was one of the projects he worked on while we were away. He sat on the beach one day . . . and selected his hundred favorite columns from a preselected group of about three hundred. I am working with *The Philadelphia Inquirer* to prepare this book for publication.

I came home from Belize to find a beautiful, silvery mourning dove on a nest with two eggs in an English ivy planter by our front door. The dove is a symbol of peace and love and the holy spirit. I named her Darrell and she has brought me a measure of comfort.

Darrell has been with me during these very difficult and painful days. I have gained strength from his love, from rich and beautiful memories of the 16 years we shared as partners, from his legacy, and from the many wonderful stories and expressions of affection and admiration from you—the people who valued his work and who thought of him as a friend.

From the heart, I thank you for your loyalty, your friendship, and for sharing yourself with "our very special Darrell."

•

The book I referred to above was published by the *Inquirer* about six months after his death, entitled *What Do You Think? The 100 Best Columns of Darrell Sifford*. About 20,000 copies are now in circulation.

That number of copies confirms the bond that existed between Darrell and you, his readers, and has directly led to the book you are now holding. This collection comprises another 100 columns, which, like the first group, was chosen by Darrell shortly before his death.

For me, and I hope for you too, they help strengthen the bond between us and his memory.

—Marilyn Sifford
July 1994

Getting ready: A death talk
February 22, 1981

They sat in a paneled study that for a day had become a television studio, and they talked about living and dying and the not-so-great gulf that sometimes divides the two.

The man, who was dying and knew it, described how on the day before surgery to diminish his brain tumor he had called into his room his five grown children, one at a time, and embraced them, cried with them and "got a lot of things straightened out." In a sense, he said, it was counseling at its best. He explained what each child meant to him, and it was, both for father and each child, "a special time."

His oldest son, he recalled, "put his arms around me and kissed me. I was very touched by that."

No, he said, there was no unfinished business in his life. He had said what he wanted to say to the people he loved. His will was the way he wanted it, and he had completed his financial planning. This, he said, is "why a person should be told" that death's footsteps are right outside the door.

He was as ready, he said, as it was possible for him to be.

The man's wife, seated on his right, said that in the beginning she had asked repeatedly: "Why is this happening to us?" But now she didn't ask any more. She was thankful, she said, "for what we have," although at times she still was "angry for what we're not going to have." After the diagnosis 16 months ago that his brain tumor would be fatal, life never again was the same. But that change, in itself, was the "beginning of the resurrection," the first tottering steps toward accepting death's inevitability.

The dying man is Robert Reath, 55, a former Philadelphia resident whose home now is in Weems, Va., and whose brother, Henry Reath, is a Philadelphia lawyer. He volunteered for a filmed interview because he "wanted to share the experience. I think we've handled this reasonably well ... and the interview helps us to find out." But more than that, he said, the purpose in preserving a discussion of his impending death was that it might help others—those who are dying and medical people who work with the dying. Purpose is important at this point in his life, he said.

"I have no hope of recovery, but I hope I can be useful."

Reath came to Philadelphia to tape the interview with Dr. Perry Black, professor and chairman of neurosurgery at Hahnemann Medical College, and Black's wife, Phyllis, who has a doctoral degree in social work. Black has not been involved with Reath as a physician, but he agreed to arrange the interview after Reath's brother, who is a neighbor, approached him about it last summer.

In addition to Reath's wife, two of his children participated in the interview, the result of which is a 57-minute color film that, Black said, eventually will become a training film for physicians.

One morning not long ago, Black, his wife, Henry Reath, and a handful of other people assembled in a room on the 14th floor of a Hahnemann Medical College building to view the film for the first time, and before the lights went out Black and Henry Reath provided this background information:

Robert Reath, a former products manager for SmithKline, the pharmaceutical giant, left Philadelphia a dozen years ago and eventually settled in Austin, Texas, where he developed and sold pension programs, primarily to medical people.

Gradually he reached the decision that it was time to realize his life's dream—to return to school, get a doctoral degree and go into private practice as a counseling psychologist. So he sold his business and used the money to complete his education. After that he moved his family to Virginia, built a house, and got ready to begin life as a therapist.

But then tragedy struck. At first, the warning signs were subtle: He bumped into things; he had difficulty judging where he was stepping; he had tremors that were manifestations of mini-seizures. Rapidly, the signs became blatant: His peripheral vision deserted him; his left hand refused to obey his mind's commands when he played the piano; he fell in the water as he attempted to hop from his boat onto a dock.

He consulted specialists, and the medical diagnosis was immediate and jarring: He had a fast-growing type of malignant tumor that originated at the junction of the part of his brain that controls memory and the part that controls vision. Without surgical intervention he surely would be dead within six months. With surgery and good fortune, his life might be extended up to two years.

Now, here Robert Reath was, with his wife, Nancy, in the television film, a healthy-looking man in a gray suit, blue shirt, and red necktie with gray stripes. He was on "borrowed time," Perry Black said, but "reasonably intact ... and not typical of these patients at this stage." Gradually he would fade away, and eventually he would go into a coma and die, Black said, but the death process, even after hospitalization, might stretch into weeks or even months.

It is not a pretty prospect, and Robert Reath is fully aware of that.

Perhaps this is why the film is so starkly dramatic. He is looking death squarely in the eyes and, even as he flinches, he says:

"All of us can come to grips with death if we have to."

And then in the next breath he says that physicians can make this easier or tougher, and it hinges on acceptance of their own mortality.

If a physician hasn't "come to grips with his own death, then he's the one who'll give an extra pint of chemotherapy" and try to stave off death—instead of allowing nature to follow its merciful course.

In the film, Reath says that "yes, absolutely," he wants his family to pull the plug and not keep him alive mechanically when he sinks into the coma from which there is no hope of return. But then he smiles and cautions a daughter: "Don't pull it out too soon."

The key to satisfaction in the final months is to "find a mark you made in life, amplify it, and appreciate it," he says. He is savoring his degree in counseling and he continues to see a few clients and to work in a clinic a day or two each week.

In the beginning, he says, he "hopped from denial, anger, depression, acceptance, bargaining, and back to acceptance." What else could he do but accept that what would be was going to be? "I have no choice ... but I'm angry at that darn tumor."

He continues to lose "some small motor dexterity" but this upsets him now less than it first did—back when he tried to put up a towel rack a month after surgery. "It would have taken me 30 seconds before ... but now I couldn't do it. I was so frustrated. I went downstairs and bawled like a baby."

Reath, who is an Episcopalian, is no longer undergoing chemotherapy, he says, because of the danger of developing lung fibrosis. "It's up to my defenses now to handle it ... One of these days, the tumor will start growing and that'll be it ... I try to live life a day at a time, positively. I've added 16 months to my life by doing things positively."

Belief in life after death has helped quiet his fears, he says, although "I think about dying all the time."

Mrs. Reath, asked if she has any advice on coping in a soul-bending crisis, says that it's important to recognize the "emotionality" that will be present and to accept it as normal—not try to suppress it.

She says that the emotional distress is one reason that people have difficulty understanding what physicians are trying to explain to them.

"We had to be told over and over. Doctors may not realize this ... because they're accustomed to this. But it's new for us. We ask the same things over and over ... and they have to respond again and again. This is what divides doctors from true physicians. [True physicians] take the time" to explain and explain and explain.

When the wife's career skyrockets

April 27, 1981

Career turbulence—both hers and her husband's—can be a substantial factor in a woman's midlife crisis. The turbulence can result from success that is less than was hoped for, from one spouse's moving ahead more rapidly than the other, from a disparity in salary.

In the words of psychologist Thelma Shtasel: "If the woman is making more money than the man, the man often has trouble with that. Our culture is not tuned to a woman's making more ... and many men can't accept it. They're not happy with the extra money; they regard it as a personal defeat."

Yet, said Shtasel, who is married to a physician, there are some husbands who aren't threatened—no matter how much success, fame, and financial fortune are heaped on their wives. What separates these men from the many who are driven up the wall if they can't be No. 1, who feel emasculated and resentful if the wife's career eclipses theirs?

There is no doubt, Shtasel said, that the husbands "who handle the wife's career best are those who feel confident and secure in their own identity in what they do. They like their work. They get enough recognition, money, power, and control ... and this frees them to enjoy their partner's success. But if they're feeling that they've not made it, then the wife's success is going to be terribly threatening."

As she said that, I thought back to a man I had sought out at a cocktail party a number of years ago. His wife had decided to go to work after their children were old enough to fend for themselves. But what could she do? Well, how about selling real estate? That's a good job for a wife and mother, isn't it?

So she found a job as a salesperson in an established company—and her husband encouraged her because "she needed something to do." When her commissions totaled just a few thousand dollars the first year, he symbolically patted her on the head and told her to keep trying—because the "real" world was a tough nut to crack.

She kept plugging along and then, for reasons that nobody—including her and her husband—can isolate, she caught fire. She sold and sold and became convinced that real estate was so profitable that she ought to go into business for herself. Why make money for somebody else when she could make it all for herself?

Her husband agreed, and a company was formed with her as president and chief salesperson. I interviewed her a few years later after she had sold and listed millions and millions of dollars worth of property in a single year—more than anybody in the history of the real estate board in her city. How much money was she earning? When I asked, she just

4

smiled. But it was a bunch—far more than was brought home by her husband, who was a business consultant.

To many people he became known not as himself but as her husband. It didn't seem to faze him. He'd stand back, smile, and appear to savor the attention that invariably would be showered on his wife—especially after word got out in the newspaper about her sales record.

His reaction, quite frankly, surprised me. At that time, I'd never met anybody who seemed so pleased by somebody else's success. So that night at the cocktail party, I asked if he didn't feel threatened—just a little bit—by the money she made and the renown she attained.

His answer: No, not at all. He was successful in his career, and he was adequately paid. The people with whom he came in contact professionally knew that he was talented. They respected him. His wife respected him, too. After all, a husband was good for more than a paycheck, wasn't he? A husband still could provide the things that his wife needed even if she earned more than he, couldn't he?

No, he said, he was her greatest fan, and his hope was that she'd rake in all the money there was. Dollars, he said, never could shatter their relationship.

I mulled over that story as Thelma Shtasel continued to talk about careers and marital crises, and then I interrupted to ask: Do husbands often agree to leave their jobs and accompany their wives when the wives are transferred to better jobs in other cities?

A lot is written about that, Shtasel said, and if you believe what you read, it's possible that you could think that husbands all over America are pulling up stakes and moving wherever their wives' careers take them. "But I'm not sure much of that really is happening. It's hip to talk that way, but the decision to give up a job always is difficult—like giving up a name. That's something a woman did when she married, but I don't have a sense that men, generally, are giving up their jobs."

Nobody knows for sure, she said, because women haven't been a big factor in the upper-level work force long enough "for us to get a chance to look at it" on a broad scale.

But there has been more than ample time to recognize the numbers of husbands who haven't coped with their wives' professional success. This is because the husbands, wives, or both have tracked into therapists' offices and asked for help.

Here's an example of the kind of thing that could bend a relationship out of shape, Shtasel said:

"Husband and wife are lawyers in Washington. She skyrockets to assistant attorney general, but he's still with the law firm. He's making $150,000 a year, but he's not an assistant attorney general." It's more than he can stand, and their marriage becomes a 15-round fight.

Another example: "Their careers take them along different pathways, and the wife gets more publicity than the husband. She has long

TV interviews, and she becomes a mini-celebrity. The husband feels shorted by that, and a crisis results." She has treated a couple with precisely this problem, she said.

Is there anything a woman can do to help her husband feel better about his career—so that he perhaps will feel better about her career, too?

That's an interesting question ... and we'll get to it one of these days. But in the meantime—what do you think?

Having kids, making choices
May 3, 1981

It was five o'clock on a late summer morning, and Maurice Prout, coffee cup in hand, was waiting for the sun to climb out of the silvery Atlantic Ocean, which formed the horizon as he stood on the porch of a house that he and his wife had rented for a week on Long Beach Island, off the South Jersey coast.

Now the cup was empty, and he walked into the kitchen for more coffee. What was that noise? Would anybody else be up so early? Why, yes, there was Christopher, toddling around in his diapers, searching for his father.

Prout picked up his son and carried him to the porch, where, wrapped against the chill in the same blanket, they sat and watched the sun come up.

Later Prout would say of this moment: "There's no word I could pick to describe it. It goes beyond 'peaceful.' There was a profound sense of great satisfaction, a fullness that I felt because he was with me. It was just the two of us, and there he was—a piece of me, but different."

My wife, Marilyn, and I were offering a Sunday morning presentation at the Unitarian Church in Cherry Hill on the give and take of marriage, on communicating and achieving intimacy. The congregation responded with questions and opinions and, when the formal program was finished, a number of people continued the discussion with us.

More than a few of them talked about the effects of children on marriage and about the changes that new parents must make in their established lifestyles. Was it really possible, some asked, to have the same level of husband-wife intimacy after children as before children?

A businessman wondered if it would be possible for him to pursue his career with the same intensity that he had sustained before his child was born. After all, he said, his wife expected him to be home more now, to be an active father, to share fully in the tasks of parenting. Did that mean that he'd have to back off from his work, to come in late sometimes and leave early sometimes? If he did that, what would happen to a career that he had nurtured for these many years? Did being a parent mean that he would have to settle for only a piece of his grand dream?

Psychologist Maurice Prout is 34, head of the behavioral therapies section of Hahnemann Medical College and the father of two boys, Christopher, who now is almost 3, and Jeremy, who is 1 year old. He seemed a logical person to respond to the questions about marital intimacy and occupational achievement.

Is it possible to be a star both at home with the children and at the office with the career? Does the presence of children automatically slice into the quality of husband-wife intimacy?

Here is some of what he said:

"We have to make difficult choices. Society doesn't give a whole lot of credit for being a good father. This may change somewhat because of *Kramer vs. Kramer* and what followed it, but by and large a man's status is derived from his occupation, from his hard work. The image of self generally is based on what we do in the outside world. There is little external reinforcement" for accomplishments as a father.

The price of parenting can be high, Prout said.

"... If you're going to spend time with the kids, you have to give up your goal of being chairman of a clinical psychology department by the time you're 40. You're not going to work as hard and, even if you try, you still need to be home for dinner by seven.

"It's a choice between being a good father and developing a sense of yourself in your career. I'm not sure I know what to do about that. You have to choose your loss. If it's career, the loss is immediate because ambitions necessarily must be bridled. If you don't modify your career goals, there is another loss, later on, with the children. When they're in their teens or in early adulthood, there's a sense of distance, of acting out. You talk with a friend about his relationship with his kids, and you sense that you don't have it. Why not? Because you weren't there."

In terms of the marriage relationship and husband-wife intimacy, Prout said, children do extract a toll. "By definition, they have to—if parents are going to allow their children to grow in a healthy way. Statistics show that if there is no change in the relationship, if parents live primarily for themselves, the children are not going to grow up well as adults. They will not function well. There will be a sense of their being cheated, owed, entitled.

"I try to avoid talking about shoulds, but there should be a rechanneling of energy and resources into the children. If that happens, then there's not the same amount of time for each other and for career."

When career-minded couples are childless, Prout said, they probably are going out several nights a week because they're earning "fairly good money and they're able to invest most of their energy in themselves and their careers. Then they decide it's about time to have a child. What happens? Well, the child comes in and, if you're there for the birth, it's quite a joyful experience. But the rest of parenting really is bittersweet."

The sweetness, Prout said, comes from watching the child grow and develop and in sharing golden moments—like watching the sun come up over the Atlantic Ocean. The bitterness is the other side of the coin. "The baby is crying, and you're up at 3:38 A.M. You know that you have a 7 A.M. patient and that you're booked fully for the day. You change the diaper, give him a glass of water, and quiet him down. Then he goes back to sleep, but you don't—because by now you're fully awake."

This is the dark side of parenting, Prout said, and there are many others—such as when the child grows into "the Terrible Two stage. He's in touch with his independence, his sense of authority. You make a request and whether he wants to comply or not, he answers 'no.'" Anybody who can manage that without grinding his teeth in dismay is more than a little unusual, he said.

While there are consequences to the children if their needs are not given priority, there also is bad news for the marital relationship if parents don't pay enough attention to each other.

"It's important to take time to talk during the day, to schedule a babysitter once a week or more, if possible, for quiet time away from the children. The notion of time alone is so critical that it should be scheduled in and taken care of—because children are all-pervasive from 6 A.M. to 8 P.M."

Prout said that what he sees "from statistics and from patients is that if the relationship is not managed well, if there is no private time, all sorts of things can happen," one of which is divorce. "What is the divorce rate now—about 45 percent? I don't know if the relationship wears out or if it fails because there are too many stresses on it—career, children, perhaps caring for aged parents. All of these sap resources.

"People in their 20s didn't have these things going on. Their stars were rising and they had more energy for their own narcissism. But now these things are going on, and they take more and more time and energy away from the relationship. Eventually, the relationship goes stale, gets crusty ... and a new partner is sought."

He is not sure, Prout said, that children are the major problem. Perhaps it can be traced to "the seasons of a man's life ... and the sense of fallibility" that strikes most of us in one way or another. This is a time when extramarital affairs are not uncommon—as partners "try to recapture what the relationship once had but which it no longer has. It's a negative playout."

But the positive side to parenting should not be downgraded, Prout said. "In my own case, my children are two very delightful people ...

even if they're sometimes up at 3:38. They're delightful to be with. I come home and they're excited. They tell me to pick them up. They hug me and kiss me. When I leave, I look up at the window, and there they are, with Helen, and I have a sense of solace and great fullness."

Having a child changes the marriage

May 4, 1981

It was my first telephone call of the day, before 9 A.M., and the man said that he had begun to question the validity of the American road to happiness—a home in the suburbs, children, and a station wagon.

He had nothing against suburban living and station wagons, he said, but he was distressed that society seemed to think that happiness was not possible without children. He and his wife are childless by choice, he said, and the price they pay is that they often are called selfish by those who are knee-deep in babies.

"There's not enough of anything to go around these days," the man said. "People ought to be more sober about having children. I don't think that enough people consider the consequences of becoming parents—the stresses and everything else."

I told him that it was ironic that he had telephoned on the very morning that I was writing a story that addressed some of his concerns.

There is no doubt, said psychologist Maurice Prout, that the texture of marriage changes when a child arrives. Husband and wife have less energy "for their own narcissism" and they must, if they want their child to grow in a healthy way, rechannel their resources away from themselves and into the child.

Career, which previously might have been pursued with tunnel vision, now needs to surrender center stage to the child. The result of that change is fairly obvious, Prout said: The glorious dreams of yesteryear probably aren't going to come true, and somebody who wanted to head a department by age 40 now must get his goals in line with the realities of responsible parenting.

It is critically important, he said, for parents to have a reasonable amount of time with their children. "You don't have to spend eight or 10 hours a day with them, but you must have some time together—meaningful, quality time."

Do people tend to consider adequately the consequences of parenting before they become parents?

No, not in his opinion, Prout said, and maybe it's not even possible to do so. "It's difficult to assess the responsibilities of parenting without experience. You can talk about it intellectually, but it's different when your child wakes you up at 3:38 in the morning and you can't go back to sleep."

Even though husband and wife understand that they'll have to change their lives when they become parents, they sometimes have great difficulty making the changes, Prout said.

"You take a hard-driving professional guy. His career is another piece of him and he wants to see it grow and develop, too. Work, like his child, is an extension of himself, and it's difficult to keep things in balance" at the office and at home.

"Most people probably don't fully appreciate how much the relationship will change," said Prout, 34, who is the father of two young boys. "But if the relationship doesn't change, I suspect that the kids will not fare well. If the family unit is too exclusive, if husband and wife continue to live for themselves, then the children's subsequent behavior will reflect it."

This, he said, amounts to a mandate for responsible parents to pay attention to their children when their children need attention. It's a fact, Prout said, that parents can't make up later for what they didn't do earlier. Many have tried, but few, if any, have succeeded.

One of the payoffs for responsible parenting, he said, is that the parent can benefit as much as the child.

"Kids offer us a way to regain or make up for something that we feel we missed in life as a child. As we give to our children, we can change a legacy, change a way of being. If you had a distant father, you can make a choice not to be distant to your own children. This is not to benefit the children; it's to benefit you, the giver.

"This represents a rare opportunity to change the course of events— when you realize that you don't have to be distant with your children, as your father was with you. You make an active choice to be this way even though this is not what would be expected of you, considering your background."

It is, Prout said, "an interesting way of healing oneself. I am aware of it in my own life—that it is a unique opportunity for me."

Because it's not possible for a parent to give top priority to both child and career, one necessarily must take a backseat to the other. And, Prout said, no matter which choice you make, you win some and lose some. "If you don't invest in your career, it comes back on you. It's the same with a child. If you're not around, there's a behavioral playout in the teens ... when the child may be into drugs, truancy, bad grades, whatever—flags to indicate some disturbance."

In the past, Prout said, the focus was on the mother's nurturing of the child. If the child had problems, it was because the mother had problems. But nowadays, increased attention is being given to the father's role, and "clearly there are costs to be had when the son's father is not there.... You take a driving father whose son becomes a lifeguard—not because he's happy with the job but because it's a way to irritate the old man. This is acting out in the extreme."

It is possible that this son, as an adult, could follow in his father's footsteps and "invest in work as a child. But there are choices to be made and, if you're a product of that, you can change and invest in your biological child" and help both the child and yourself.

But this is perceived by some as a difficult choice because there's not much outside reinforcement for being a good father, Prout said. "Even women are saying now that there's not much reinforcement for being a good mother." This may be one reason why women, apparently in increasing numbers, are returning to work quickly after childbirth.

Prout's wife, Helen, left her job as executive director of a senior citizens' organization to become a full-time mother, and she's happy with her decision, "but I'm not sure that everybody has that option, considering the state of the economy."

The money problem can't be overemphasized these days by couples who are pondering the wisdom of having children, he said. "You have two incomes, and then one income drops out. Unless the lifestyle is altered, the husband may be absent more than before because he'll have to work doubly hard."

"How can anyone go through that?"

June 29, 1981

Sheila Scanlon first dated George Ewalt in 1969—even though her brother, who was married to Ewalt's sister, had warned her against it.

"I don't want you to go out with him," her brother said. "He's crazy; he acts strange."

But they dated anyway and, Sheila Scanlon would say, "at times he was strange, but I thought he was fun. He didn't want to be serious about anything. He just wanted to have fun."

She could understand that because, after all, he had been to Vietnam. They dated and dated, and within a year they were married.

Ewalt sometimes was moody, his wife would say, but more often he was happy-go-lucky. Then he began to change. "Three or four years after we were married, he started to quiet down in a strange way, in a way that didn't fit his personality. He was a very outgoing person, but he withdrew. And he'd go into fits of anger ... over nothing. Our daughter would spill a glass of milk, and he'd fly into a rage."

The marriage began to creak at the seams, and steadily the gap between them widened. In November, the breaking point was reached. George Ewalt's wife screamed at him: "I'm fed up! George, what the hell's wrong with you? I value this marriage, but we can't go on like this. We've got to get help."

Ewalt knew that she was right. He contacted the Veterans Administration and began a series of weekly meetings with a psychiatrist. There, in the privacy of the doctor-patient relationship, he fell apart, cried, and regurgitated horror stories that he had buried for years—stories about men who had been killed, men who had killed themselves because they couldn't tolerate the war and the jungle any longer, men who had killed women and children, men who had slaughtered ... and slaughtered ... and slaughtered.

At home, Sheila Ewalt didn't know what was going on, but she was certain that she didn't see any improvement in her husband's condition. What made him alternately withdraw and then erupt into such fury that he sometimes punched the wall and screamed?

One day, at the psychiatrist's suggestion, she accompanied her husband to a therapy session. There, the psychiatrist instructed Ewalt to "tell her a story, George, one story."

Ewalt told a story, and later Sheila would describe her reaction this way: "I became hysterical. I was crying, almost blind with tears. Oh, my God, how can anybody go through that? They go over there and then they become different people. They set aside a part of the brain ... so they can do things that don't synchronize with their personalities. They're taught, like everybody, not to kill, but then they go over there and kill and come back and have to hide it all. My God, if I can't handle this one story, just listening to it, what would I be like if I had been there? I'm surprised there weren't mass suicides."

Her husband, former infantry corporal George W. Ewalt, Jr., told her that there had been mass suicides.

Not long ago, I interviewed Philadelphia psychiatrist Harvey J. Schwartz, who in working with Vietnam veterans at an outpatient clinic had concluded that many of them had lost the ability to have intimate relationships with their wives and children. Much of that, Schwartz said, could be traced to the unusual nature of the war, in which it sometimes was impossible to identify the enemy.

Soldiers, he said, "were exposed to women and children ... and a beautiful child could be a walking land mine. Later this can bring a problem with the soldier's own children. His baby cries ... and his feelings surface—when he was frightened of beautiful children or when he killed them."

As they killed, Schwartz said, soldiers blocked their consciences. "They were numb at the time. But then later, back with their families, they get in intimate situations when numbness doesn't work, and the horrors of war come out. There is a conscious revival of the horrors ... Many of them have developed underlying feelings of terribleness about themselves."

On the day that the Schwartz interview was printed, my telephone almost danced off the desk. The calls seemed without end.

There was an Army officer who had spent his Vietnam tour in Saigon, who complained that the interview made it appear as if "everybody over there was murdering women and children."

There was a combat officer who had become a pacifist during the war, who said that he was surprised to read that many veterans had developed psychological problems because he felt that many of them already had problems when they went to Vietnam. "Many of them wanted to be there," he said. "For them it was hunting, and they enjoyed it." And he said that their craziness had been fertilized by commanders who offered three-day passes to soldiers who brought back ears that they had cut from the enemy dead.

There were former soldiers who agreed that what Schwartz had said was absolutely on target. They, too, found it difficult to be intimate with their wives. They, too, felt walled off from their children.

And then there was a call from Sheila Ewalt, who said that she worked for a metals brokerage firm in Bala Cynwyd, Pa. Her husband, George, had looked war straight in the face, and the two of them and their daughter, Tara, still were paying the price. It was much worse than the psychiatrist had told me, she said. Not only was her husband scarred emotionally, but he also had developed skin cancer and nerve disorders as a result, she said, of his exposure to Agent Orange, a chemical defoliant used extensively in the central highlands of Vietnam, where he had spent most of a year.

Nobody seemed to remember, she said, and nobody, including the government, seemed to care. They were struggling alone, the three of them, and sometimes the odds against them seemed overwhelming.

Scanlon's Saloon is located on a corner of the 4200 block of Manayunk Avenue in a working-class section of northwest Philadelphia.

It's a place where George Ewalt, 33, can go alone—near his home—and not worry that somebody will say or do something that will send him into an unbridled frenzy of anger. His brother-in-law owns the saloon, and everybody knows him there. He can sit and sip his ginger ale through a straw out of a tall glass, and people will leave him alone.

On this day, he's in the dining room, behind the bar, his full beard neatly trimmed. He's wearing jeans and a plaid madras shirt, the open collar of which reveals a bone necklace.

He walks with a cane because a kneecap that was weakened by shrapnel in Vietnam was shattered in an accident at Fort Hood, Texas, where he put in the final months of his Army life after he returned from Vietnam, in early 1968. His limp is obvious, and, yes, it's sometimes difficult for him to function as a telephone company lineman who lays underground cable. But everything considered, he's done OK on the job—for 11 years.

His wife is with him. She is a pretty, fair-skinned, red-haired woman who once a month accompanies George to therapy and then goes to her own therapy, too, because she accepts the reality that she needs help to deal with what's going on.

Once when daughter Tara was acting out her frustrations, the three of them booked into family therapy, and right away George told the therapist: "I was in Vietnam, and sometimes that causes me problems." The therapist's reply was: "Don't worry about Vietnam; that's in the past."

The heartache of alienation
August 16, 1981

As boys, we were wounded by our fathers, Victor Gruhn was saying, and the fathers "had to wound us. They wanted to bring up the boy to be a man. In the process of putting steel in our blood" the fathers became, in the eyes of their sons, people who scarcely were human. "We hated our fathers ... We didn't really know why, but it was as if we'd been forced into it."

The coming back together of fathers and sons is possible only when the sons discover the truth of what the fathers had told them all along: "This hurts me more than it hurts you." At that point, when the sons see and feel the humanity of their fathers, when the tears flow like water, the doors are open to absolute reconciliation.

And, said Gruhn, it's never too late for this to happen. Never.

The letter was from a Philadelphia-area woman who reminded me that I had written many times in my column "about the pain and devastation of alienation from a child. I always admired your candor, and I am asking for any help that you can give my husband and me with a child whom we hope we have only temporarily lost."

Here is part of what the letter said:

"Peter is 25, the older of our two children. When he was in his last year of college, he told us that he had become a Christian. My husband and I are non-observant Jews, considering ourselves to be Jewish more in the ethnic sense than in the religious. We were not thrilled with Peter's announcement, and at first we argued, but we accepted it eventually....

"Knowing that we did not really approve, Peter was quiet about his beliefs. He went to some services of the Messianic Jews, but did not join any church or organization. He also told us—and this is still true—that he also considers himself to be a Jew.

"Three years ago he left our home and went to California, where he married a young Jewish woman, Judy, he had met in college.... In the summer of 1979, Peter and Judy went to live on a kibbutz in Israel—to work and to learn the Hebrew language—with the intention of perhaps remaining there. On the kibbutz, Peter met a born-again Christian couple, not ethnically Jewish, who persuaded him to leave Judy because she was not a believer. Peter returned to the United States without Judy, and since then it has been all downhill.

"... Peter's personality changed completely. From the boy who was easygoing, charming, and bright and who had a hundred friends, he turned into a silent, lonely young fundamentalist who accepted every word in the Bible as literally applicable to life, a religious fanatic.... He dropped out of college in his senior year, and from time to time he would go to Canada, where the couple he had met in Israel lived, and who had become his personal gurus.... He could not hold a job or apply himself to anything but the Bible. He lost every one of his friends and made no new ones.

"My husband and I were bewildered. We visited two psychiatrists, without Peter, because he refused to go. The psychiatrists seemed as puzzled as we were.... During all of this time, we were in communication with Peter, even when he did not live at home.... Finally, we got angry and quarreled, and Peter left. We have no idea where he is. Probably we could locate him, but the question is: What do we do with him after we have found him?

"... Judy explained to us that Peter had spent a very large amount of concentrated time with Albert, the Canadian, on the kibbutz, and we think that in that faraway, strange atmosphere a certain amount of mind control might have taken place. Peter agrees with everything Albert believes and has kept in touch with him.... I will not claim that Peter does not have emotional problems, perhaps very deep ones. But we always got along with him before his conversion.... Certainly there were some resentments against us, which he never communicated...."

The woman ended her letter by asking whether I could direct them to somebody who might be helpful in their understanding what had happened and why and who might offer them some insight into resolving their dilemma. I suggested that they contact the Rev. Victor Gruhn, pastor of

Resurrection Lutheran Church in Horsham, Pa., because in interviews with him I had found him to be not only wise but also compassionate.

Gruhn was telling me that most of us, as boys, had been wounded by our fathers in their efforts to assure our passage into manhood. The greatest wound of all, he said, was that we never saw the flesh-and-blood side of our fathers.

"My father brought me up that way," Gruhn said, "to achieve, to learn. Anything that offered growth, I would get. But there was very little love shown ... because he didn't perceive that he had to give me love in the way that he gave love to my sister...."

Gruhn said that the only time he ever saw the soft side of his father was "when my sister died.... He was a clergyman, and all through it, he was the Rock of Gibraltar. The day of her funeral was his birthday. We came back from the funeral ... and I still had one more duty to perform. Duty, you know, is all-important to a man. I didn't question if in doing my duty I would wound him, because the heart is second class. I had to greet him, as he came home, and I said to him in German: 'God bless you on your birthday.' He broke down on my shoulder and cried. It was the only time I ever saw his tenderness."

But, said Gruhn, one time was enough. It usually takes only one glimpse of the father's humanity to begin melting the son's hostility toward the father. Just one.

What he was saying, he said, was that Peter, perhaps, had not yet found that humanity in his father and was looking for another father. Through excessive involvement in religion, he perhaps was seeking the warmth that he felt he had missed at home.

I told Gruhn that I could identify with the family's pain because I once had felt that my older son, Jay, was so deeply involved in his religion that he was smothering his personal growth. I told Gruhn that I also could identify with what he was saying about the father-son relationship. "It hurts me to say this," I said, "but I think that's what Jay was looking for, too—warmth, love, and acceptance from another father."

Gruhn picked up on that. I had been wounded, and I had acknowledged it in a variety of ways, including, "It hurts me to say this...."

It is the wounding of ourselves that is our redemption, Gruhn said. "We have to be wounded to achieve our humanity ... because in the sterility of the technology of the world in which we live, we don't have to show love. We can marry our jobs."

He said that he hoped Peter would return to his family. "But before he can come back, he has to see the wound."

Entering into risk-taking
September 27, 1981

Do you have trouble getting to sleep on Sunday nights? Would you rather climb into a bag and accept a beating than enter the office on Monday mornings? Does anticipation of the weekend make Friday your best day of the week?

Ah, yes, I can tell by your expression that I'm getting close to where you live. Would you like to chuck your job and get into something that you really want to do—something that could warm your stomach rather than tie it in a knot?

OK, what's keeping you where you are? Oh, I see, the anchor is money, or prestige, or responsibility. After all, nobody walks away from money, prestige, or responsibility. Isn't that what we've been taught all our lives?

Well, keep on reading, because you're about to meet somebody who could become worth his weight in gold to you as a role model, somebody who admittedly took the first risk of his life and who now is cashing in.

No, he's not cashing in with money. Psychologist Philip Bobrove estimates that it's costing him $10,000 a year to do what he wants to do, but "being my own man is worth more to me than money. Having time to talk with my wife before 11 P.M. is worth more to me than money."

Not too many months ago, Bobrove was just like some of you—a sleepless wreck on Sunday nights because he dreaded Monday mornings and the mounds of paperwork that he sometimes likened to "a Rube Goldberg machine that has lots of movement but that does zero."

Back then, Bobrove was clinical director of the geriatrics division of Jefferson Medical College's department of psychiatry and human behavior. He was, in his words, "Peter Principled in my administrative ability. I reached a certain point and it was obvious that I didn't have the drive to continue. I enjoyed the clinical work, but what needed to be done administratively—the writing of grant applications and things like that—didn't interest me. I wanted to get out."

Bobrove got out, all right, but he took an unusual route. He did something, he said, that "most people don't have an opportunity to do: I hired my own replacement and shaped my new job.... I could have continued where I was. I really had a choice. My boss, being the good fellow that he is, always has been supportive of me. He would have made it easy for me to continue ... but I couldn't. For myself, I needed a change."

Bobrove exited from his cage by arranging to work half-time at Jefferson and by expanding his limited private practice and buying an old house in Haddonfield, N.J., where he has set up his office and is renting out the rest of the space.

"Yes, it's a risk. I am an economic idiot. If I balance my checkbook, I feel like a genius. I was very insulated from all of that at Jefferson. My salary came in regularly; I knew how much I would earn; I didn't have to worry about repairs because the big daddy in the sky took care of all of that." But the zing had gone out of his life.

"In a sense it's a midlife crisis," said Bobrove, who is 45, married and the father of three teenage boys. "I bought a car—a Z car—and my oldest boy, who's 18, said: 'Dad, you're at the point in your midlife crisis when you're supposed to have this kind of car.' I said something fatherly like 'Oh, go to hell,' but there is something of the midlife crisis, although I don't like to call it that because it cheapens it—like if I identify it, it will go away. I'm not saying I'm going to run off with a 26-year-old blonde, but I know what I can do and what I want to do. I know my skills."

The midlife crisis, Bobrove said, comes when we arrive at the point at which we seriously ask ourselves what life is really worth. "I now have less time to live than I've already lived. I wasn't happy with my life. I knew that I'd probably die of a heart attack or cholesterol poisoning before I was 50. I saw others in full-time private practice. I read a couple of books, which told me what I already knew. There was the realization that this was what I wanted to do, that I was really good. I felt competent, and I was moving from a position where I felt mediocre as an administrator."

Like everybody else, Bobrove said, he wanted a guarantee that he wouldn't fail in his new venture. "But there are no guarantees, and I decided to try anyway. It just felt right"—even though he annually would forfeit $10,000 in benefits, including $2,200 a year in college tuition aid for each of his children.

"Hell, no, I can't afford to give up $10,000. Who can? But my response is that a lot of good money will do me if I'm fertilizing crabgrass."

Never in his whole life had he taken a chance, Bobrove said. "From high school, I went to a college education that was paid for. Then I went to graduate school with a scholarship. After that, I was into jobs in large institutions that took care of me. I got married. There was no risk because I married somebody with the same interests, somebody from the same class. I had children because I was supposed to have children. Yes, this is my first risk, but you know what? It's time to see what I can do, and it's not like I'm giving up my whole career."

He has entered his risk-taking rather gently, he said, and this is what he advises for others who are contemplating significant life changes. "A big risk would have been to hock everything, open a huge clinic, and hire people. I'm not willing to risk that much, but I am willing to halve my income to double my life."

It is not prudent, Bobrove said, for anybody to take a risk as major as his "unless the unhappiness is pervasive in everything you do, unless you have a burning desire to do this new thing. Otherwise, you can ride out the unhappiness until you get over the midlife crisis," and by then things may not look so dark. "But if you're where I was—at the point where the work no longer is meaningful or rewarding—then you've got to weigh the risks of continuing the work and dropping dead of boredom ... or running out on your wife, smashing yourself up, or drinking too much. If you're going to do that, then it's better to try to channel yourself into something constructive"—like a new job.

Risk-taking, Bobrove said, is "easier when it's done in groups. The larger the group, the more risk-taking. It's hard to do it alone. Don't take a risk without talking to somebody to check out the rational aspects. If a business selling moustache wax in Vermont seems right for you, find out what the demand is. Then if it looks like you can do it, go ahead. But not without checking it out—not in today's world."

Midlife, he said, is when recognized lack of time "pressures you into looking at options open to you. In the process of examining the options, you check out what other people have done. This is how you find out that you're not alone. This is what helps give you the courage to make a change."

It's important to recognize that a certain amount of luck is involved in successfully negotiating most changes, Bobrove said. But it's not luck in the sense that "a bundle of cash drops out of a truck, and you pick it up. No, luck is being around and taking advantage of things that happen.

"People say to me: 'Gee, Phil, you were lucky to find a replacement so you could work half time.' Yes, I was lucky, but I'd had my eye out for somebody who could come in and do what needed to be done. People say I'm lucky that the house came on the market when I needed it, but I'd been looking for a house just like it."

In other words, Bobrove said, he helped make his own luck—and that's the best kind.

It's apparent to him, he said, that most of us have far more control over our lives than we often think. "It may be true that we're like a leaf blowing in the wind, but we can change direction ... a little anyway. We're not helpless victims of destiny."

Bobrove's advice: "Find out what it is that you have—and then hone it. ... A perceived value of what you're going to do makes change attractive" and less frightening.

How has Bobrove's wife, Elaine, reacted? "She told me: 'I'm very scared, but if you want to do it, do it. You need it to survive.'" He couldn't have said it better himself, Bobrove said.

Infidelity and trust

October 12, 1981

The letter from the suburban woman was not unlike many that I have received over the years:

"… For many months I've been living in a kind of hell, watching my marriage disintegrate. While it is impossible for me to summarize in anything short of a book the problems leading to my separation, I would be very grateful if, through your interviews, you could offer some suggestions on handling infidelity in a spouse. Specifically, can there ever again be trust and faith in the relationship?

"My husband seems to think that despite all the lies in the past, I should simply take his word that the affair is over. How do you go about building that trust? How do you get your mind off the other woman, especially if their work brings them together and if they sometimes, as my husband says, must have business lunches and drinks and possibly travel together?

"My husband has offered me little consolation, and he has no empathy. I have little hope for the success of this marriage, and I am not sure that I could live with such an insensitive person. But, more than that, I am afraid that I never will be able to trust another man.

"Please write something on this. Your other columns on surviving in this sometimes cold and cruel world have helped me tremendously."

Well, what do you think?

I took the letter with me to an interview with Marvin Kanefield, who is chief of staff and senior attending psychiatrist at Philadelphia's Friends Hospital. What, I asked him, would he advise the woman to do if she had confronted him face to face with the problem outlined in the letter? I told him that I didn't see how a husband, if he felt anything for his wife, could fail to offer more reassurance than this husband apparently had.

Kanefield's response—"Yes, that's the key phrase, all right: 'If he felt anything for his wife'"—seemed to leave little doubt that he surmised that the marriage might be in big, big trouble.

In his psychiatric practice, he has encountered several situations that seem somewhat similar to this one, he said—situations in which husbands had not supported and had not reassured their wives. Many times, he said, "the guy wants his wife to throw him out. He doesn't want to walk away from the marriage. He thinks of his kids and his reputation, and he doesn't want to be the heavy. He doesn't want to be the initiator. He wants his wife to throw him out so that he doesn't have to take responsibility for leaving."

In other words, Kanefield said, the husband can create an intolerable situation and then announce to the world: "I didn't end this marriage. It was her idea."

When this strategy is adopted, he said, there's little hope of turning things around because the husband obviously has on his mind something other than perpetuating the marriage. Until that changes, the limits of what can be done are rather firmly fixed.

What about sexual relationships outside marriage? Do they usually mean that the game is over?

"Some people believe in fidelity; some don't. People should find out where each other stand and never cross-match in marriage."

Kanefield grinned as he said that, but it obviously wasn't because he thought that he'd coined something funny.

No, he said, infidelity is only as bad as people make it. The choice is theirs.

"If you take away the cultural and religious thoughts, then [infidelity] is a matter of personal choice. I don't want people to burn a cross on my lawn for saying this, but two people in a marriage must decide what they want to do.

"I think that if my wife felt she needed an affair to fulfill her life, if she really wanted it, well ... if I could be spared the pain of knowing, I believe that I'd tell her to go ahead. Some people couldn't tolerate this, but I think I could. But I couldn't tolerate it if affairs were a continuing thing or if she had an affair out of anger at me. I'd feel bad about that."

What about trust? Can it ever be established again after it has been breached?

"I trust everybody and nobody. I trust people until they betray the trust, and I don't give back the trust to them until a series of events and behaviors indicate to me that things are going satisfactorily.... But I don't think that this woman [who wrote the letter] is ever going to trust her husband again. She's looking for a formula, and there is no formula.... People tend to want a formula; they tend not to want to experience life and write their own formula.

"What does she want from me? Should I tell her how he should live? I can't do that. I can give her some options for how she can live, but the two of them have to work it out or not work it out ... The husband seems to be rubbing her nose in the aftermath of the affair. If he and the other woman really have to be together in business, I believe that I'd lie about it if I didn't want to hurt my wife. The husband seems very hostile in his behavior toward his wife."

While infidelity is a way of life for some people, Kanefield said, it is possible that other people who are by nature faithful can "still do a whole series of affairs"—not because they've grown horns but because they become locked into habit-forming behavior.

"If you have a problem in life, you may find yourself doing the same thing over and over again to satisfy your internal needs. After a while it becomes habitual. You take a 14-year-old boy who masturbates. He may swear to God that he'll never do it again—until he gets that internal feeling. Then he'll promise to do it just one more time.

"For myself, I can say that I'll eat no more ice cream, but I wouldn't want you to be around when I get that feeling for ice cream. Then I want one more cone. It can be the same with affairs ... We can have affairs out of our hostility for the other person or for our own reasons. If we need to be told that women still find us attractive, then the next time a woman finds us attractive," we're back in the sack—whether that's our plan or not.

But, said Kanefield, one mistake or even a series of mistakes doesn't necessarily mean that somebody can't ever again be trusted.

"The first time I meet you, I give you 100 points of trust. You either maintain them or lose them by what you do. You're entitled to mess up, but you've got to earn the trust back. If negative acts take away trust, then positive acts have to earn back trust. All of us, at some time, lie and fudge. It's part of the human condition. We're all caught with our hands in the cookie jar, but we don't have to live or die by that—if we're honest about it.

"But the behavior of this guy [the husband of the letter writer] seems to me to say to the wife: 'You have no rights; your only option is to listen to me and believe me.' That's no marriage contract. That's a one-way contract" that reasonable people wouldn't propose or buy into.

Overvalued children
November 1, 1981

Over the years, they have streamed into his office, troubled parents and their troubled children, and one of the cases forever is lodged in the memory of psychiatrist G. Pirooz Sholevar. Let's listen as he talks about it:

"The father had manual jobs—three of them in fact.... One during the day, one at night, and another on weekends. He was working to send his daughter to a prestigious school, one of the most expensive in the country. At school, the daughter spent money like she was a member of the jet set. Nobody ever would have guessed her father's status.

"But it backfired ... the whole thing. The daughter associated with people who, when they found out about her father, looked down on him ... and she became ashamed of him. It was one of the most painful experiences I ever had, as a therapist. The father sacrificed himself for her, and she walked away from him. It was heartbreaking."

The daughter is representative of what Sholevar terms "an overvalued child," and by any name, these children are in trouble—and so are their parents. The reason: "You can't talk about an overvalued child without talking about an undervalued parent," said Sholevar, who is clinical professor of psychiatry and human behavior at Jefferson Medical College in Philadelphia and director of its division of child, adolescent, and family psychiatry.

It's not difficult to identify those who are overvalued and undervalued when they walk through the door, he said. "The mother wears what looks like a hand-me-down dress from her mother, while the daughter is in designer clothes.... There's a father who sends his son to the finest medical facilities in the country but who, himself, stands in line at a clinic. There's a father who never takes a vacation but who finances his daughter's trip to Europe, where she lives lavishly."

The common denominator in parents who put their children one-up and themselves one-down is that they are divorced and, for a mile-long list of reasons, they are trying frantically to be good parents and to help their children. In reality, said Sholevar, they are failing on both counts.

"Normal parents tell their children that they can't afford certain things. But if parents feel guilty, then they buy whatever the children ask for"—anything from a $350 dirt bike to a $10,000-a-year private school.

Overvalued children, Sholevar said, come in two varieties. On the one hand, there is the child who was valued before divorce, but "later a parent makes a tremendous increase in the emotional investment in the child." On the other hand, there is the child "who was kind of ignored until the divorce and then one parent who'd never showed much interest all of a sudden shows tremendous interest."

After any divorce, Sholevar said, there always is a "readjustment of investment in the child. It's a normal process and it's understandable. Let's say that a child plays baseball and for whatever reason the father can't come to a game. But the mother attends, and the child does OK and she says: 'Your daddy will be so proud of you.' Then the father comes home and maybe he spends two minutes talking to the child: 'Hey, I hear you hit a home run. I'm proud of you.' The father can delegate a lot of interest and investment through the spouse when he's married. But when he's divorced, he can't delegate"—and his interest and investment often become more personal and more intense.

It is apparent, Sholevar said, that there are three reasons that couples give for divorcing:
- "One spouse says the other is a lousy spouse."
- "One spouse says the other is a lousy father or mother."
- "One spouse says that there's nothing wrong with the other but he

or she just doesn't want to be married any more."

In a large number of cases, Sholevar said, "the underlying implication behind divorce is that one thinks the other is a lousy parent. So you examine that parent and you find that he's trying to make up for being a bad parent by trying harder now to be an extra-good parent. You take a typical middle-class father. Often he didn't spend so much time with the child. He was overly concerned with his career, and he wasn't with the child when he was needed most—when the child was very young. So there's a tremendous amount of guilt about neglecting the child. After the divorce, it's understandable that the father will try to make up for what he didn't do earlier."

Here are some of the other reasons given by Sholevar for parents' tending to overvalue children:

• Hostility toward the divorced spouse. "If you felt shortchanged in the relationship, you can increase your investment in the child and try to steal the child away from the other spouse—as a way to hurt the other spouse."

• Compensation for loneliness. This, Sholevar said, is a "dynamic that is not well known," but here is what it amounts to: After divorce ends even a terrible marriage there inevitably are feelings of loss—loss of spouse and relationship. The child becomes a "hold-on" and is over-valued "as a way to un-do the loss." In successful divorces, the loss is acknowledged and mourned. In unsuccessful divorces, "people feel loss but they don't acknowledge it and they don't mourn it. They try to find a way to get around it ... and they hold onto the child as a representative of the lost spouse."

• Identification as an adult. After divorce, Sholevar said, there often is a tendency for grandparents "to become reinvolved with the divorced person ... and they start to treat him like a little child. When he was married, the parents treated him as a married man, a husband, and a father. But when he's divorced, they treat him like a boy again. It's very threatening ... and he feels that he's losing status. So he holds onto the child to maintain his position as a parent and as a grownup."

• A place to hide. The ground is fertile for overinvestment in the child if the divorced parent has no life of his own. "With no social, sexual, or work life, the parent tends to concentrate on taking care of the child," Sholevar said. "It's a defensive investment ... because the parent feels safe with the child but afraid of developing relationships on the outside."

• Compensation for perceived failure. The child can become over-valued, Sholevar said, if the parent feels that divorce represents failure and that the only way to make up for failure is to succeed gloriously in parenting. It's amazing, he said, that the "concept of divorce as a significant failure still prevails" to such an extent. "Many still feel that there is no successful divorce—only failed marriage."

Divorced men are as prone as divorced women to overvalue children and undervalue themselves, Sholevar said, and in fact "men can fall victim more readily ... because they don't have a good standard on how to deal with children. A middle-aged man may treat his daughter in ways that are very inappropriate, as if they're on the same level. There is a tendency for divorced middle-aged men to date younger women, and often the daughter and the girlfriend are no more than three or five years apart in age." The result: rampant confusion.

How can a divorced parent tell if he—or she—is on the expressway to exaggerating a child's value and creating problems on top of problems?

Here are three questions, Sholevar said, that need to be asked:
• What are the needs of the parent?
• What are the needs of the child?
• To what extent are the needs of both being satisfied?

If there is an imbalance in satisfying needs, it's obvious that a problem is building, Sholevar said. "If the bulk of energy and financial means goes to satisfy the child and if there is little for the parent, then you know that the parent has overvalued the child and undervalued himself. You can figure it out. At the end of the year, the parent finds that he's spent $100 on clothes for himself and $5,000 for the child. The parent's medical bills are $75 and the child's medical bills are $8,000. It's the same for recreation ... and for everything else.

"After divorce, there is a tremendous tendency by almost everybody to feel failure, and so we punish ourselves through undervaluing ourselves. We pay a penalty to the child by self-neglect, and the child collects the payment."

In the process of paying, the parent sets himself up for what may be a lifetime of misery, Sholevar said. In the process of collecting, "the child's total development gets distorted." Clearly, everybody loses.

A distorted self-image
November 2, 1981

The tragedy that can cripple a child who is overvalued by a divorced parent is that the child's total development is distorted.

This happens, said psychiatrist G. Pirooz Sholevar, because the child "doesn't develop a realistic sense of self. On the one hand, the child feels that he should be treated like nobility" forever, because he has become accustomed to getting everything he asks for. But on the other hand, the child "lacks a basic sense of self-confidence" and, as a result, feels rotten about himself.

"We get our sense of self from trying things and finding out what we can do," said Sholevar, who is clinical professor of psychiatry and human behavior at Jefferson Medical College in Philadelphia and director of its division of child, adolescent, and family psychiatry. "But the overvalued child doesn't try. He doesn't have to try ... because everything is given to him.

"Most of us learn that we must earn what we get, that there are no handouts, but the overvalued child doesn't learn this.... So we have a child who wants everything, but feels he doesn't deserve anything. It's the worst possible combination. The less the child feels he deserves, the more he asks for, and the more he feels that he's not getting the right things."

One result is obvious: An unhappy, confused child who likely will develop into an unhappy, confused adult.

Another result can be that the child forever will feel indebted to the parent who overvalued him and will feel obligated to pay back the parent—at the expense of his own life.

"We see this in people who are in their 50s and 60s, whose parents are in their 70s and 80s," Sholevar said. "They try to pay back their parents by devoting their lives to them, and they miss their own opportunities. Some don't develop marital relationships. Others don't invest in careers. They remain with their parents ... to try to repay them."

It is not uncommon for divorced parents to deal with children in a perverse way that has the effect of forcing them to grow up before their time and depriving them of childhood, Sholevar said.

Here is one example of that:

"A significant number of divorced people become depressed—or more significantly depressed. Maybe 20 to 40 percent will become symptomatically or clinically depressed after divorce. Some withdraw; some attempt suicide. Depressed parents don't dare go outside. So they stay home and invest in the child, and the result of this can be that the child becomes the caretaker of the parent. There is a reversal of roles, and we have what is known as the 'parental child'—a reversal of generational lines. The child becomes the parent.

"The earliest I ever saw this happen was at age 9. There was a 9-year-old girl whose divorced mother was very depressed and suicidal. At 11 o'clock one night, the girl held her younger brother by the hand and brought her mother to the hospital. The mother had not eaten in three days. It was the most exaggerated case of role reversal I've known ... and things like this amount to gross exploitation of the child. The child's needs are not tended to—because the parent's needs are put first."

After most divorces, Sholevar said, there is a tendency "to treat the child as an equal partner," regardless of the child's age. "Very frequently you find a mother asking a child: 'How does my hair look? What about my clothes? Do you like my lipstick? Is this gown cut too low?' These are questions that one spouse usually asks the other spouse, but after divorce the parent asks the child. And it may be too heavy to ask a 10-year-old girl to give her opinion about her mother's low-cut gown."

Divorced men are every bit as guilty as divorced women of this "equalization of status between parent and child," Sholevar said. A not uncommon trap into which middle-aged men fall is treating a daughter in almost the same way that they treat a girlfriend who is not much older than the daughter. What happens is that the daughter feels that she no longer has a father figure.

While the overvalued child is hurt by parents who give too much and ask too little, the undervalued parent is hurt, too, Sholevar said. In some ways, the damage to the parent may be even more extreme. Here are some reasons why:

The child who is cared for with every ounce of the parent's energy limits the parent's possibility of dating and re-establishing a new social life.

Even if the parent dates, the focus may be on finding a mate who will be a good foster parent "instead of somebody who will be a good spouse."

The overvalued child interferes with a parent's investing appropriately in a career or advancing an education.

It is also possible, and often happens, that overvaluing a child, even for a brief period, can cause a parent to miss connections that will be felt for a lifetime. "Divorce occurs mostly when people are in their 40s," Sholevar said, "when they're at the height of ability and physical attractiveness. If they overinvest in the child for only three or five years, it can make a significant difference in their lives ... because attractiveness may change in a few years. Self-esteem can drop" and what might have been never materializes.

"For a few years of overvaluing their children, parents may suffer for 25 years to come," Sholevar said.

It is not unusual, he said, for divorced parents eventually "to express a fantasy wish that they had no children so that their future chances won't be jeopardized. A question that often is asked is: 'Who would want to marry somebody with three children?' It's a fantasy ... and generally parents won't tell you. In treatment, we usually have to bring it up," but then parents often say that, yes, their children are a burden.

This acknowledgment is critical, Sholevar said, because it helps give the parent a realistic basis for deciding to jump off the merry-go-round of overvaluing the child. He is amazed, he said, by how often the child picks up the parent's attitude change and rather quickly adopts new behavior.

A problem child not infrequently ceases to be such a problem, Sholevar said, because he recognizes that he no longer can get away with it.

This is the point at which everybody begins to win.

Where lonely people flock

November 26, 1981

In the heart of Center City Philadelphia, just a chip shot away from City Hall, stands Arch Street United Methodist Church, which has posted a sign that announces to those who walk past that the church's "chapel of prayer" is open daily for meditation from 9 to 5.

You can stand inside the door—as I did the other day—and watch a steady stream of people come in off the sidewalk, enter the chapel, and pray. They tend to look pretty much like everyday people, no more troubled than the rest of us, but it's absolutely amazing, the Rev. James W. Haney said, how many people over the years "have stopped by on their way to the bridge" from which they intended to jump to end lives that they perceived as not worth continuing.

Why? How can life be so bad as to be without value?

The common denominator tends to be loneliness, Haney said—crushing loneliness that carries such terrible pain that people are convinced that nobody cares about them.

Haney, who has been in the ministry for 40 years, 18 of them at the Arch Street church, where he now is senior minister, said that Center City "breeds loneliness" because it is a place where people tend to mind their own business and not to share themselves with others as they might in the suburbs, where people barbecue in their back yards and chatter over their fences.

In shoulder-to-shoulder urban living, he said, there are few barbecues and not many casual conversations.

His church is without a single member who "graduated up from Sunday School." Everybody moved in from somewhere else, and some of them came to church originally out of loneliness, because they had nowhere else to go. "I try to start where the person is," Haney said. "I try to find out how lonely they are and if they have anybody. I try to see if they can relate to somebody where they live or to somebody on the phone. I assure them that we and God care. That sounds trite, I suppose, but it's a starting point. Some of them think that nobody cares."

Haney's church 10 years ago founded and financially supported Contact, a telephone-counseling service that dealt to a large extent with the problems of the lonely. Impetus for this sprang primarily from one lonely person about whom Haney never has stopped thinking.

"He was a graduate of MIT, a bright young man with a good job, apparently a late bloomer. All of his friends had married, and he felt alone. He came in for counseling, but he assured me that he was OK, that he was going to make it. He was seeing a psychiatrist, and I felt that he'd be all right. But when he left my office, I forgot to tell him something. I should have told him: 'If you need me, don't hesitate to call—regardless of the hour.' I thought it, but I didn't say it, and at 2 o'clock that night he jumped out of his apartment window. Why? Because he thought that nobody really cared."

How can anybody become so desperate?

"You can get so deeply within yourself that you think that you're stuck, stuck in your habits, in drugs, in things you've done that you think are so terrible that they can't be corrected. You think that others don't like you. You feel so alienated that there seems to be no way to handle life. So you end it all—by going off the bridge or out the window."

Does embracing theology that preaches God's love tend to soften the impact of loneliness?

Yes, it does, Haney said, and he cited this personal example: "My first experience of being accepted and loved was from my grandmother. When she died, I turned to Jesus Christ. Through my teen years, my greatest relationship was with Jesus Christ. As long as I knew that He was my friend and accepted me as I was, it didn't matter what others thought of me."

But, Haney said, that didn't guarantee that he would forever walk in the warmth of the relationship. "You have the love of Jesus, but you can lose it—if you become preoccupied with other things. When you're trying to keep the stones [of the church] together and keep the insurance paid, it's possible to lose sight of Jesus unless you remember why you're trying to keep the stones together."

That amounts to a mandate to keep our priorities straight, Haney said. Otherwise, it's not difficult to slip back into our old ways—which for some can mean merely drabness but for others can trigger thoughts of a trip to the bridge.

Does he ever encounter people who are lonely even when they are not alone—even when they are surrounded by others?

Yes, he does, and these are people who generally have such low opinions of themselves that they lack any significant self-love. "Usually, they've not been given any sense of worth. They don't feel lovable—and so they can't be loved. This is one of the most pathetic things—to be lonely in the presence of others."

Often a solution is to help these people get involved with others so that they "take the focus off themselves. If they lose themselves in others, do for others instead of trying to receive all of the time, then their loneliness tends to abate ... I don't see lonely people who have a strong sense of themselves, who really like themselves to the extent that they can get involved with others. Lonely people constantly seem to think of themselves—their illnesses, their uncertain futures, their [perceived] lack of people who care for them."

The terrible irony, Haney said, is that "in that frame of mind it's hard for anybody to like them ... and it becomes a self-fulfilling prophecy.

They think that they are unloved and they often are—because they behave in ways that are not very lovable."

Holding on instead of letting go

December 14, 1981

A few years ago, Neil Izenberg was driving to the 10th reunion of his high-school class along with what he described as a "carload of friends who'd gone their own ways, too—a couple of physicians and a writer."

As the miles buzzed past, Izenberg found himself thinking: "I can't understand this. I'm nervous about going back to the reunion. I've presented papers all over the country, but I'm nervous about this." His friends shared his feelings, and one said, "I've changed shirts five times already." Everybody, said Izenberg, was "equally excited and disturbed."

What was causing these unsettling feelings?

Well, the feelings probably resulted from unresolved conflicts that went on during the teenage years, said Izenberg, who today is section head of adolescent medicine at Albert Einstein Medical Center, Northern Division. And no amount of rational thought, even by high-powered adult minds, can wipe them out.

What happened to him, his friends, and the rest of us during adolescence produced essentially the "same conflicts as in the rest of life—except that something gives them greater power during adolescence ... developing sexual identity, separation from parents, fears of dependence, the uncertainties of independence."

There is no question, said Izenberg, 31, that the adolescent years are tough for most children and their parents, but parents not infrequently make things even tougher because they "tend to forget the crises that went on in their own adolescence. This is why people, including doctors, often find it difficult to deal with adolescents."

Izenberg, who also is assistant professor of pediatrics at Temple University's medical school, said adolescent medicine had blossomed as a specialty because of the critical need for somebody to be tuned in to the turbulence of the teenage years.

"A scenario I see repeated so often in my office is that a parent brings in a child, who sits far from me ... and exhibits body language that indicates separation from what's happening. I ask the child why he's here, and the parent usually answers. The parent will give a list of reasons, but the final thing always is attitude ... and its impact on behavior. It happens so frequently that it's really striking.

"The parent brings in the child because the parent wants to talk about behavior, and the way it's presented, you know this is the most important thing."

What is the behavior that parents of adolescents find so troubling? The answer to that question is contained in a single word—rebellion—that is keyed to the teenager's pulling away from the family and that many times is compounded by the family's near-frantic holding on.

"I once had an anthropology course in which somebody defined the family as a unit of structure whose purpose is to fall apart. The fact is that this moving away by young people is rooted in American culture, but it's often difficult for parents to tolerate this inevitable separation of the child from themselves.... Frequently, this produces an overgrasping by parents and an over-moving away by teenagers."

The problem, said Izenberg, is that often the parents aren't aware of what's happening. They only know that their teenagers have changed and that their once-happy family isn't so happy any more.

"This blatant holding on can be seen by observers who are clued into it—because the behavior is pretty overt. But the family can be oblivious to it," Izenberg said. "Some therapists call it the 'enmeshed' family. One person answers for another. Sometimes they seem to share symptoms. They'll talk about 'our' headache or what 'we' want to do. It seems to be an act of disloyalty to the family to try one's own wings."

The price that is extracted by this kind of tugging can be enormous. "The legacy that is left to the children frequently is a constellation of psychosomatic symptoms ... and behavioral symptoms, but the real issues often are avoided [by the family] and substitute issues take their places. It's more acceptable to argue about irrelevant behavior like eating habits or disobedience—rather than tackle the whole complex of family problems."

Is there a road map to guide families through this perilous period? "The secret of success in negotiating adolescence together is to set up rules of behavior beforehand: It's OK to communicate within the family, whether it has to do with a difficult emotion, fear of failure, or the joy of success. It's OK for children to have healthy opinions about sexuality.

"When parents use euphemisms for sexual organs or acts, what does that mean? It means that parents are unable to talk about them, not that the children are unable to talk about them"—but the message that clearly is transmitted is that it's not OK to talk openly about sex in this family. That sets up a lot of young people for a lifetime of hard knocks, Izenberg said.

It's important, he said, to discuss things that matter—risk, change, and commitment as well as sex. The family that is able to have meaningful conversation in many areas usually has "no particular problem with sex." And it works the other way, too, he said. "For a family to be able to talk meaningfully about sex and not about other things would be very unusual."

What is behind the many suicide attempts by teenagers? After all, it's widely reported that suicide is the third leading cause of adolescent deaths—behind accidents and tumors—and it's believed that many of the accidents may be unreported suicide attempts.

Izenberg: "The vast majority of suicide attempts are pleas for better communication. Only a tiny fraction were meant to be successful, but they miscalculate and become successful.... A suicide attempt often is a distorted effort to contact the family because the teenager feels out of control and not heard.

"This is why I feel such sadness about the demise of the extended family with the uncles, aunts, and grandparents. Children had alternate behaviors that they could observe—parental figures who weren't involved in discipline" and who would listen to them even if their parents wouldn't listen.

"But when the family is isolated, this pattern of not listening becomes entrapment," and the adolescent sometimes feels that he must do something drastic to merit attention.

And that, Izenberg said, can have tragic consequences.

Female managers, male behavior
February 9, 1982

A few years ago, management consultant Alice G. Sargent discovered the truth about what happened to women as they climbed in male-dominated business organizations:

They quickly were socialized into male behaviors. "They put on the uniform and dressed for success. They stopped crying and began to express anger as men do"—by pounding the desk and gritting their teeth. They were determined to prove that anything men could do, they could do better—and they honed to a fine edge their rational, analytical thinking and competitiveness.

And then were they happy and successful? No, as a matter of fact, said Sargent, they were sick. Before they knew it, they were "supporting gastro-intestinal specialists and suffering from lower-back pain. They had developed all the symptoms that men traditionally have had."

But while women were changing, men were not, Sargent observed. Nowhere in American society—especially not in business, heaven forbid—was there any institution that tended to socialize men into some of the traditional female behaviors—relationship-oriented skills such as helpfulness, understanding, awareness of others' feelings, valuing interdependence and collaboration. Without question, what was happening was that American business was drifting more and more toward the macho end of the spectrum—and everybody, bosses and subordinates alike, was paying a terrible price.

It occurred to Sargent—as it had to others—that the best of all possible business worlds could be realized if traditional male and female behaviors somehow were blended together to achieve the best of both and weed out the worst of each.

That was the beginning of Sargent's romance with androgyny, and it led her to write her first popular book, *Beyond Sex Roles*, in 1977 and her second, *The Androgynous Manager*, which has just been published.

Sargent, who lives nine months of the year in Washington, D.C., and the other three months at her home in La Jolla, Calif., where she writes, is a consultant for a number of Philadelphia-area corporations, including INA, Sun Co., and DuPont. In an interview, she said that consciousness-raising groups had been helpful in leading men and women toward androgyny and away from their traditional behaviors.

In men's groups, she said, men tended to discover quickly that they had no idea what it meant to be a man—"just as whites don't know what it means to be white. Men had been socialized to fill organizational roles, and they didn't know the price they were paying."

You can examine literature until your eyes burn, she said, and you won't find anything that dwells on "emotionally sustaining relationships among men. Men are emotionally illiterate. The culture doesn't provide much language for men to express feelings to each other. Anger is the only acceptable emotion. Men are able to acknowledge their vulnerability only with women, and they need women to validate their masculinity."

On the other hand, Sargent said, women's groups tend to draw women into becoming more assertive and expressing anger more openly. That's the good news. The bad news is that many women these days seem to think that they have to become "like men" to be competent in business, and they view competence as "something that is in competition with femininity." The result: Down with femininity. "Women are trying so hard to be competent now and to tell them to hang on to their femininity and to be nurturing, well, that behavior is not totally where women are at today."

More bad news, according to Sargent: "Men and women are exiting from consciousness-raising groups and missing each other coming in and going out the door. Why? Because men want to be intimate and women want to be assertive."

While androgynous management is still trying to get a foothold, Sargent said, there's no question that "highly macho, old-style management is out of it now. I'm talking about the can-do style, where you give the boss whatever he wants, whenever he wants it—even if it means staying up all night and missing your son's graduation. What I see now is management that can acknowledge some vulnerability and that puts some value on interdependence."

As a group, engineers seem to be closer than most in achieving a sizable measure of androgyny, Sargent said, especially aerospace engineers. "They're in short projects that require a lot of teamwork, and they understand that technical competence is only a small part of it, that interpersonal skills are needed, too."

How can people determine how far along they are on the androgyny scale? Sargent presented separate lists of questions for men and women. First, for men she asked: Do you usually:

• Hide feelings of vulnerability and dependence when that's exactly what you're experiencing?

• Insist on an independent approach to problem-solving even though you might be helped by input from co-workers?

• Let your desire for career advancement overpower all other goals and life needs?

• Insist on competition when collaboration would be more effective and appropriate?

And now these questions for women. Is it normal for you to:

• Rely on the suggestions of others at the expense of your own creativity?

• Quickly back down in arguments for fear that others won't agree with you?

• Spend too much time counseling and sympathizing with others about their personal problems?

• Feel reluctant to act forcefully when accomplishing tasks because you're afraid that co-workers might find your approach too aggressive?

If you answered "yes" to any of these questions, you've got some growing to do before you can claim a healthy portion of androgyny, Sargent said. What do you have to do to stimulate growth? Well, first you get into a consciousness-raising group, and then ...

A downright upright love story
March 4, 1982

If you are sometimes convinced that the world is crazy, that nothing makes sense, that not enough good things happen to good people, then this is a column that will make your day. I've been waiting almost two years to write this column—and it's with unbridled jubilation that I share it with you.

It all began in the spring of 1980, when I prepared a column that went like this:

You've seen the ad on television: The woman is on the telephone, explaining to her girlfriend a graceful way to invite a man over for a glass of sherry. Then the doorbell rings, and the woman puts down the phone and welcomes her boyfriend into the apartment, saying that it's "downright upright" for a woman to ask a man to sip her sherry.

I absolutely adore that ad—perhaps because it's nice, every now and then, to escape from reality. What do you think?

His name is Bill. He's 30, a psychologist who has been separated from his wife for two years. During that time, he has been swamped by friends who have given him telephone numbers of women who might be right for him. But not one woman ever has called him, and "it's just not fair. Why does the man always have to call?"

Then he answers his own question: "The simple truth is that there aren't many Harvey's Bristol Cream women around. It takes time to change behavior patterns."

Her name is Linda. She's 29, a career woman whose long-term relationship with a man recently ended. Now she's trying to get back into circulation. And it's rough. Just the other night, she and some girlfriends went out, and, quite by accident, her eyes focused across the room on a man, who returned her gaze. He was attractive, and he seemed interested in her. But he didn't walk over to her.

Linda wanted very much to approach him, to introduce herself, to find out his name. But "I couldn't do it." It was as if something held her back.

Is there a way that the Lindas of the world ever will feel comfortable taking the initiative with the Bills of the world? Or is the woman with the sherry forever a fantasy?

That's what I asked psychologist Thelma Shtasel, who, believe it or not, teaches clients behavior patterns to help them meet people and overcome fears of rejection.

Two things must happen, Shtasel said, before women can be as relaxed as Miss Sherry when they approach men:

Women must encourage themselves to take the first step and banish into dark corners the old-fashioned notion that "good girls don't call boys."

Women must educate themselves to the stark—and perhaps surprising—reality that many men would turn cartwheels of joy if a woman invited them out to dinner or to the theater.

Women, said Shtasel, are hesitant to take the first step, and it's almost as if they fear that they would "shift to the masculine gender. They fear that men won't like them if they're not cuddly dolls. They are terrified that they will not be 'marketable.' But women need to recognize that this is not true" in most cases.

Women, like men, tend to be fearful of rejection, and this is a factor in their reluctance to approach men. But for women, the problem is more acute because society, except in sherry commercials, hasn't told them that it's all right to be bold.

The column then began discussion of a series of strategies that women could employ to feel reasonably comfortable about taking the first step and approaching men. The column received enormous response, and I wrote some of the response into a later column. But what I never wrote, until now, is what happened to Linda and Bill.

At the time, Linda worked for the same corporation as Marilyn, my wife, and after the column appeared, she asked Marilyn: "Hey, what does Darrell think about that guy Bill?" Through Marilyn, I told Linda that my impression of Bill was that he was a solid fellow, somebody with whom I thought I could develop a genuine friendship.

The next question was: "How can I get in touch with him?" I provided the telephone number for an office out of which he worked in Philadelphia. Was she really going to call him? Well, maybe, Linda said. She just might dial him sometime and announce that she was Miss Harvey's Bristol Cream, and how about meeting for a drink?

I called Bill's office and spoke to the recording device: "Hey, Bill, a woman named Linda may be getting in touch with you. I didn't want it to come as a surprise."

Linda did call Bill, all right, and the first few times, she never made contact. He was out when she telephoned, and she was out when he returned her calls. But they finally bridged the gap, and one evening, at Linda's suggestion, they met for a drink at the piano bar of the Commissary on Sansom Street in Philadelphia. No, Linda didn't order sherry—although she had threatened to. What she did order she doesn't remember, but Bill recalls that it was Pear William, a pear liqueur imported from France. He can't remember what he ordered, but he does remember that it was a first-class evening with a first-class woman.

Linda was not reluctant to admit that she thought Bill was a first-class guy, and a romance flickered and eventually ripened. A few Saturdays ago, Marilyn and I were invited to the home of a friend where a Common Pleas Court judge married Linda and Bill, and where the host lifted his champagne glass in a toast not to sherry, which surely would have been appropriate, but to good times and good health:

"May all your pains be champagnes."

After that they left for a week in Jamaica, two beautiful, deliciously happy people.

I felt good all over—and I still do. In fact I feel better than good, especially now that I've shared the story with you.

Don't embarrass your kids
March 18, 1982

Here's a question for every parent: How many times have you done things that embarrassed your children?

Well, if you can believe a survey that purports to capture the feelings of 160,000 American teenagers, you may be dishing out more embarrassment than you think. High on the list of things that teenagers wish their parents wouldn't do is—you guessed it—not embarrass them in front of their friends.

In the book *The Private Life of the American Teenager*, co-author Jane Norman of Bala Cynwyd, Pa., writes that parental attitudes and behavior about inflicting embarrassment "have an enormous impact on the quality of the parent-child relationship. If we embarrass our children ... there is very little chance for a positive relationship to flourish."

What are the no-no rules with which parents should be familiar? Here, according to teenagers, are some of them:

• Don't reprimand in front of friends. This, said Norman, is the "ultimate humiliation and one that caring parents will go to great lengths to avoid." In the book, she quotes a 15-year-old girl: "My father hit me a lot when I was younger. It really scared me, but I thought everyone got hit with belts. But my mother hit me once in front of my brother's friends, and I hated that the most. One time, I corrected her English in front of her friends, and she got mad. When I asked her how come she could hit me in front of my brother's friends, but I couldn't correct her in front of her friends, she said: 'I can do it because I'm your mother.'"

• Don't criticize or praise in front of friends, family, or strangers. Norman quotes a 15-year-old boy: "... I hate it when they say stuff in front of their friends. Like how wonderful you are or what you've done. It's so embarrassing."

• Don't make scenes in public. Although teenagers are sensitive to this, Norman said, there are times when parents have to stand up for their rights—such as when service is super-bad at a super-expensive restaurant. Teenagers may be embarrassed, but no harm is done if parents will discuss it with their teenagers and explain why they acted as they did. But other public displays are less legitimate. She quotes a 17-year-old boy: "In public places, my dad will yell at us or he'll put my mother down in front of guests. That's one of the most embarrassing things to do. And my mom, she started yelling at me in the middle of the hospital when I had a motorcycle accident. She yelled in the emergency room: 'You shouldn't be on a motorcycle at all!' It was embarrassing."

• Don't treat teenagers as if they're babies. This is one of the things that teenagers most dislike, said Norman, who quotes a 13-year-old girl: "Do you believe in a restaurant my father still orders for me? I keep telling him I can order for myself, but he does it anyway. The waitress must think I'm 2 years old." A 16-year-old boy: "My mother will take me by the hand and show me off to her friends when she has a party. She displays me like a pet dog. I hate that."

• Don't pry into the lives of their friends. Teenagers, said Norman, "guard their friendships tenaciously, and they resent parents who intrude or subject friends to a probing third degree." She quotes a 15-year-old girl: "I nearly died when my mother asked my friend whether her parents were still together or if they had split. It was none of her business.... My dad pries, too. He always asks my friends what their fathers do for a living, and it's so embarrassing. He's always checking up on my friends and I hate it."

• Don't show affection in public. Here's a quote from Dennis, 13: "Every time we go somewhere, my mother fixes my hair and adjusts my clothes. She pushes my hair out of my eyes and straightens my shirt. It's so stupid. And she even kisses me sometimes in front of my friends. God, it's embarrassing. I even hate it when she kisses me and there's nobody around."

• Don't initiate discussions about private matters. If teenagers want to discuss intimate issues, they'll come to us, Norman said. Here is a quote from Betsy, 16: "I wanted to kill my mother. I mean it—kill her. I was so embarrassed when she told my aunt that I finally got my period. It was none of her damn business." A sensible rule for parents to follow, Norman said, is to consider their teenagers as friends. "You wouldn't tell intimate things about a friend, so why would you tell them about your teenager?"

• Don't act inappropriately. Remember that you're a parent—and not a teenager, Norman said. She quotes Arlene, 16: "Sometimes my mom will come down in the basement when we're listening to records and she'll start dancing and singing, and she makes a general fool out of herself. My friends start laughing, but my mom doesn't realize they're laughing at her."

How does Norman, who has an 18-year-old son, think that teenagers should handle the embarrassment issue? "The best way would be for them to say to their parents: 'You embarrassed me when you did that, and here's why...' But it's difficult for many teenagers to do this because parents take it personally and get so uptight."

Has Norman ever embarrassed her son? Does a big wheel roll? She told this story: "I like to sing along with the car radio, and one day my son was in the car with two friends, and I was singing. He handled it well, I thought. He didn't say anything to me until his friends had left, but then he said: 'Mom, I hope I don't hurt your feelings and it's not that you have a bad voice, but please don't sing when my friends are in the car.' How could I get mad about that?"

Many times parents don't know when they are embarrassing their children, Norman said, and this is why it's so necessary for parents to encourage their children to identify the sources of embarrassment. But it's then incumbent on parents not to get angry or defensive. As parents, are we up to the task? What do you think?

Making a marriage work
April 5, 1982

A while back I printed a letter from a man who, after 12 years of marriage, had left his wife and two children. He talked unflinchingly about the agony of coming to terms with himself, with the future, and with the social forces and role definitions that he said had contributed to the whole mess, not only for him but also for many other men and women.

The column attracted many letters but none more haunting than the one that follows—haunting in the sense that the writer is aware even before he's married that doomsday could be stalking him already. Here are parts of the letter:

As a 26-year-old single man who plans on marriage in a year, it seems to me that every time I turn around another marriage is going down the tube. The reasons are as different and varied as the people who are involved in these unhappy couplings.

In the letter that you printed, the writer said that "romanticism is not enough; there must be more." Maybe I am naive about the ways of marriage, but would somebody please explain to me how to make one work?

Not enough romance, too much romance; not enough freedom, too much freedom ...

I love my fiancée deeply; is that not enough? Should we read every book and marriage manual that ever came down the pike? Will I be a different person because I'm married—or because people change anyway?

There are so many questions, yet not so many answers.... I want very much to avoid the pain that your letter writer and so many others have experienced. Yet I know that life offers no such guarantees. But maybe with a little advance knowledge my odds for failure would be lower. What do you think makes a good marriage? Your opinions please.

I decided to try to answer some of the young man's questions—not because I'm an expert, which I'm not, but because I'm in a position to evaluate what I think are some of the worst and some of the best of marriage: my own two marriages, the first of which failed dismally in so many ways, the second of which is succeeding joyously in so many ways.

I want to talk about my feelings—and go a step beyond. I shared the young man's letter with Marilyn, my wife, and asked if she also would respond. She agreed, and her opinions, which she wrote at home on a rainy Sunday, follow mine.

What I've learned about marriage—and I passionately believe in the validity of my experience—can be telescoped basically into five areas:

• Don't put every single one of your eggs in the marital basket. A psychologist once told me that marriage should be the most important thing in life but not the only important thing. I think that ought to be chiseled in stone somewhere. It's important to have outside interests—within reason—and to achieve a balance between the extremes of having no outside interests and having so many that the marriage is neglected. With a reasonable balance we can bring to marriage an energy that is diminished neither by the fatigue that can spring from devoting too much time to it nor by the indifference that can accumulate from devoting too little time to it.

• Build a mutual respect for each other. I'm talking about a respect that stems from the other person's being accepted as an equal, a full-fledged partner with the same rights and responsibilities as you have ... and the same feelings, too. The very best love and sex, too, I think, are tied in with this mutual respect, which is best explained as a desire to give each other equal treatment. In a simplistic way, you could say that it's offering the other person a half of the sandwich that's at least as big as your half.

• Fuzz with all your might the traditional role responsibilities. The best possible situation, I think, is for people to do what needs to be done when either of them has the time to do it. The worst possible situation may be to set aside one area exclusively for the man, another area exclusively for the woman. The problem is that this kind of arbitrary division seems to produce two solo acts—rather than one duet.

• Recognize the value of communication. Nothing works like sharing what's on your mind—as long as it's shared in the context of your having respect for the other person.

• Recognize, also, the value of silence. At times you can be so distraught that it's virtually impossible to communicate with respect—because you're hurting and you want to hurt the other person. This is the time to be silent for a while, until you're able to share in a constructive way what's on your mind, even if what you're sharing is negative. Once you've hurt somebody with your words, you seldom can make up for it, totally, with an apology. It's like a judge's instructing a jury to disregard a remark. After it's said, it's not possible to pretend that it wasn't.

OK, that's what I have to say. Now, here's Marilyn:

I'm not an expert on what makes marriage work, but I know that Darrell and I have a good one, and I can talk about that.

Our relationship is built on a foundation of mutual love, respect, consideration, open expression of feelings, and support to be ourselves and to develop and grow in ways we choose for ourselves. Is that enough? I don't think so. Even the strongest foundation can be shaken under certain circumstances.

For us, there are two other very important ingredients. One is that we both place the highest priority on our relationship. The other has to do with demonstrating this priority in our daily lives.

From the very beginning, Darrell and I had a strong relationship, but it's far richer now—and this hasn't happened by chance. We cause it to happen by doing things that nourish the relationship. What kinds of things? Here are some:

• A day never goes by that we don't tell and show that we love each other. This may be a kiss and an "I love you" as we leave for work, or a 30-second call in the middle of the day to say "I was thinking about you."

• We have many long talks about what each of us is experiencing professionally and personally. This means going beyond the superficial "What did you do today?" to discussing how we felt then and now. It means a willingness to be vulnerable and it requires that each of us be receptive. It sometimes means expressing opinion without giving uninvited advice.

• We make big deals out of ordinary occasions as well as important occasions. We can find something to celebrate almost every day. Some of our recent celebrations include: My return from my monthly weekend at American University in Washington, where I'm in a graduate program; Darrell's first successful attempt at making stuffed mushrooms; getting our carpet cleaned; Friday; coming home from work; Monday.

• We acknowledge the inevitability of differences in viewpoints and the importance of expressing them and the feelings that accompany them. We have learned to do this fairly rationally most of the time. We usually end up surrendering our need to be right and reaffirming our rights to our differences.

• We are best friends. We make certain that we have time together. We have long talks while perched on the kitchen counter. We take long walks in the city. We watch late-night movies. We silently read our separate books. We share life.

Troubled marriages: The children's role
April 22, 1982

Not long ago I interviewed psychiatrist G. Pirooz Sholevar for a series of stories on what happens when divorced parents overvalue their children.

At one point, Sholevar, who is director of Jefferson Medical College's division of child, adolescent, and family psychiatry, said that divorce typically caused parents to begin to treat their children as equal partners— almost without regard for the children's ages.

I wrote the stories without elaborating on that, but I didn't want to leave the impression that it's necessarily wrong for parent-child relationships to evolve toward equality. So I asked Sholevar to discuss at length the whole area of changing relationships as children grow older. That is correct, isn't it, doctor, that it's healthy and necessary for the nature of relationships to change?

Yes, it is, Sholevar said—in spades. "The child should not always remain the same, and the relationship should not remain the same— with the parent one-up and the child one-down." But it's a sad fact that in what Sholevar called "disturbed" families, these changes don't occur and the parents forever remain "always right."

It's healthy, he said, for children to have "early on some areas of equality" with their parents. "A child of 10 is more knowledgeable about baseball than most parents. I learned my baseball from my son, who is 9. In normal families, there always are some areas of expertise for the child, areas in which the child is equal or superior."

While these areas are limited when the child is young and the relationship remains one-sided in favor of the parents, the swing toward equalization becomes pronounced when the child is in college, Sholevar said. By the time the child marries or enters into some kind of significant partnership, the relationship with parents normally is equal—and parents can benefit from this as much as children.

"When children marry, they often are exposed to different families with different lives, and there should be a healthy give and take with their parents. I know a boy who came from a family where nobody ever took a vacation. The traditional wisdom was that you always saved your money for bad days. He married a girl who came from a family where all of the money was spent on vacations.

"After marriage, the couple was in a position to educate the families. The son asked his parents: 'Why do you save everything? You've never had a good day in your lives.' The daughter told her parents: 'You're spending all of your money and later on you'll be like paupers if you don't change.'"

The equality of relationship normally extends until later in life "when the parents are older and the child is at the height of life. Then a clear reversal occurs. The child advises the parents on what to do ... except in disturbed families where we find that the parents are always right—to the very end. But in normal families, the children should become the leaders."

Is it difficult for most parents to accept the changing roles and to embrace their grownup children as equals?

"Parents always have difficulty in acknowledging that their children are growing up ... and getting better than the parents are in many areas. In the movie *The Great Santini*, a Marine colonel always plays basketball with his son. One day, the son beats the father in a game, and the father stays up all night shooting baskets, practicing for the next game. The father couldn't accept that the son was better than he was."

In part, Sholevar said, this denial of reality is "related to our concept of mortality. If we accept that a child has grown up, we also have to accept that we are getting older and deteriorating.... No parent likes to surrender the upper hand to a child, but the difference is that the normal parent is relaxed enough not to inhibit the child. After the child succeeds, the parent can enjoy the success. The parent is not in competition with the child, and he can sit back" and savor the child's good fortune.

But parents who "view themselves as very incapable, who feel that they can do nothing right ... these parents tend to hold the child down as a way not to face their feelings of inadequacy. You take a parent whose educational goals were curtailed, a father who dropped out of college, and you'll often find that he holds back his child, that his child either drops out, too, or has great difficulty going to college. It's as if there's an unwritten code: Dad didn't do it and the child shouldn't do it either—or else Dad will look bad."

This also holds true in marriage, Sholevar said. "If the parents have a bad marriage, the code is that the children had better not have a good marriage. There's a kind of intergenerational loyalty, a conspiracy for the child's marriage to fail, too, so that the parents won't look bad."

It's an identical story in career. "You take parents who are capable, but some tragedy caused their careers to end. The children feel that the parents didn't achieve even though they were capable and that it would be selfish for them, the children, to get ahead. And so they don't. Often parents who were hurt in their careers will push a child into a good education, but the education won't be translated by the child into a good career. A son graduates from Harvard Law School, but he's not successful as a lawyer—so as not to surpass his parents."

All of this, of course, happens on an unconscious level, Sholevar said, and the vicious cycle can be snapped by bringing it to consciousness. "The father can say to a child: 'When I dropped out of college, it looked OK, but now I'm sorry. I hope you won't make the same mistake.' It's like removing a curse ... and the child moves forward"—not only in education but also in marriage and career.

The woman's midlife crisis

April 26, 1982

The man's letter began this way: "I now find myself in the middle of what is referred to as the midlife crisis. I am at the part where a marriage is dissolving."

As I continued to read, I was surprised to find that the man was referring not to his crisis but to his wife's—and that as her life changed, his life necessarily changed, too.

She had left him for another man after almost 20 years of marriage, and he was devastated. "Because I have been so surprised about what happened to me, I would forever reject any thought of involvement" with a woman who had not already gone through her crisis, he wrote. "It panics me. I don't need to become close to someone who is going to go through large and perhaps unpredictable personal change."

Then the man mentioned that he had read the column that "you proudly wrote on your wife's career success. You indicated that she is 32 and you are in your 40s.... Are you concerned or apprehensive about the impact of her midlife crisis, which has not yet begun but which most certainly will occur? What will happen to your relationship with her? Have you thought about that?"

After that letter, I didn't need a third cup of coffee to get my eyes open. I was wide awake, not out of fright but out of the realization that the man had provided a vehicle for what surely could be a column that would interest many people. The questions that demanded to be answered were these:

What are the components of midlife crisis in women? Is crisis inevitable? Are some women less affected than others? If so, why?

I directed my questions to psychologist Thelma Shtasel of Bala Cynwyd, Pa., not only because she's a member of the midlife club but also because she is directing group sessions for couples who are grappling with crises—not necessarily those that threaten marriage but those that make life less pleasant than it ought to be.

Shtasel said that a woman's crisis sometimes is ignited by the children's leaving home—as many have suggested—but she said that her experience has been that "most women are really delighted" when they finally get the children out from under their feet.

"You take a woman who's a traditional homemaker. For years, she's always served others—as the person who cooked, chauffeured, did the laundry, went to school plays and PTA meetings, and made the appointments with the orthodontist. She always was second, if not third or fourth, in line. Suddenly, she has freedom. The kids are out of the house, and she can feel attractive again, spend more time on her needs. No, I don't think the kids' leaving is a primary cause of crisis" in most women.

Major factors, she said, could be divided into three categories:
- Marital disruption—either by death, divorce, or separation.
- Career turbulence—either hers or her husband's.
- Lack of personal identity.

Divorce, said Shtasel, triggers "a terrible crisis for women, especially traditional women in traditional marriages. They may feel that they can't exist in the absence of a strong emotional bond. They can't be a person or do their own thing because, they believe, they don't have a helluva lot going for them. They don't know how to get along on their own without the structure of marriage."

One by-product of divorce, she said, is a "terribly shattered ego. A woman looks at herself in the mirror without her clothes and asks: 'Oh, who would want this old body now?' I'm seeing a woman who's 39 and divorced and living with a man. Her anxiety is high—he's already seeing other women. She said: 'I look at my little flabby breasts, and I know that he's not interested in them anymore. He'll never marry me.' And I'll tell you something: He won't."

The road to happiness for women whose marriages have ended is paved with their learning to do things for themselves and realizing that they don't have to have a man to be fulfilled.

Career women who are married may face a different kind of crisis, which is based on what Shtasel called "a certain competitiveness" with their husbands. "Which one is making it better? This is something that comes up at this time in life, when people have to come to terms with the reality that where they are between 40 and 55 is pretty much where they're going to be. They're not going to blow the world away—if they haven't already."

The competition also can center on salary. "If the man's making more and the woman feels that she's worth it, this can cause tremendous unhappiness. If the woman is making more, the man often has trouble with that. Our culture is not tuned to a woman's making more than a man, and many men can't accept it. They're not happy with the extra money; they regard it as a personal defeat."

The career woman often is faced with another nagging question, Shtasel said: Should she have children? "She knows that if she takes off 10 years, she can't make that up when she goes back to her career. If she has children, she may be resentful" over the rungs that have been kicked out of her career ladder. If she doesn't have children, "she may feel guilty later and think that she made a bad decision." Either way, Shtasel said, a crisis can develop.

Lack of personal identity and the frantic search that can result are factors that can disrupt the lives of all women, Shtasel said. The often-asked question "Who am I?" can emerge from any number of things—including the children's leaving home, the husband's having an extramarital affair or "conversely, by a woman's looking at her husband, seeing his pot belly and six-pack of beer as he sits in front of the tube, and wondering: 'Is this all there is to my life? What's in it for me?'"

At this point, Shtasel said, a woman can be "like an adolescent again, trying to figure out what she wants." Questions bite at her: "Can I make a contribution that anybody will care about? Does my mortality rest only on my children? Will anybody remember that I was here? Will anybody even come to my funeral?"

Trying to establish identity often can rock the marriage. "The woman decides that she has to do something, but when she tries, her husband may tell her that she can't do it. The relationship with him isn't very exciting, but it may be better than no relationship at all." So she may back off and mourn.

Or, said Shtasel, she may get involved sexually with another man as a way to say that she has identity "if only as a sexually attractive object. But it becomes harder for her to find partners if she's not in her 30s. And the partners she finds may not look like Robert Redford—and that's not too flattering."

Is midlife crisis inevitable for all women? Yes, generally speaking—although the severity and duration can vary greatly. The women who do best, Shtasel said, tend to be those who have an "emotional configuration" that allows them to roll with life's punches and not be flattened.

There are some people, she said, "who don't get depressed easily, who are not subject to wide mood swings, who are more stable. They do much better. They bounce back from the blows."

There are other people, she said, whose realistic expectations cushion them against crushing defeat and depression. "They expect to have some dreary days and, when these days arrive, they're OK. They can handle them. They don't get so depressed—and depression can contribute to crisis at any age."

It's not unrealistic to think that the front line of defense against disabling crisis is a solid support system, Shtasel said. This can include spouse, family, and friends.

"Women in the traditional role have a better support system than men, but in a career role they have a worse support system. The traditional woman is active in her church or synagogue and she has friends and keeps in touch with her family. The career woman suffers from lack of peers. Men have this support, but women don't have it yet."

The surviving child's guilt
April 27, 1982

It was 1964. Today's 32-year-old woman was then 14 when her brother, who was 21, was killed in a car accident.

She recalled her feelings, and the words gushed out—as if they'd been held back for an eternity, which they had been. "After the initial horror I felt tremendous guilt ... because of all the times I'd wished him dead or gone when I was angry at him. I also felt overwhelmed with an obligation to be 'good' for my parents. There also was the guilt of being the surviving child and the need to justify my living....

"There was a gap in the emotional aspect of our family. My brother's death was carefully avoided in discussions, as was anything that would mention his name in conversation.... There was great discomfort in discussing the death of any young person.... This created a stiff atmosphere at times—and to this day there exists a huge gap between my father and me on a demonstrative level. He seems to have closed off this part of his life....

"I feel more comfortable about the loss now, but I still feel a sense of obligation to my parents, being the only surviving child."

The problem, she said, was that nobody appeared to be concerned about her feelings, about her struggles. "Often it seems that sibling loss is treated as an afterthought once the parents are consoled."

•

She was 12 when her 3-year-old sister died of pneumonia 40 years ago, and, she said, "as the only remaining child, I felt completely isolated. While my parents still were mourning, I wanted them to hold me. I remember being rebuffed and my father saying: 'Don't think you're going to be spoiled now that you're the only one.' I felt as if the wrong one of us had died.

"I accepted the guilt for my sister's death and was petrified that one of my own children might die. I am sure that I was overprotective of them because of this ...

"I don't know for sure, but I believe somehow that I expected to be punished by the death of one of my children. I had a large family—four children—so that if something like this would happen to me, my child would not be alone."

•

You've just read parts of interviews with two women who are participating in a study of the impact of sibling loss in childhood—a study that is being conducted by Dr. Helen Rosen, assistant professor in the social work department at the Camden campus of Rutgers, the state university of New Jersey.

Little work has been done in this area, she said in an interview, but it always has been of special interest to her because when she was 13, she herself lost an older sister.

"It was devastating to me. At that age, I was beginning to feel more autonomous, but I became quite frightened.... It became harder for me to leave home and harder for my parents to let me go."

So far in the year-long project, Rosen has interviewed by questionnaire adults in six states, and she hopes to wrap up work by summer, when she will present some of her findings at an international pediatric conference in Chicago.

"We need to be aware that the loss of a sibling in childhood is an important event in life. We forget that children remember things ... and we need to help our children verbalize their feelings at an early age so they don't have to carry them around for 25 years."

One woman who responded, Rosen said, described how at 8 she was jealous of the attention that her sibling received after death. "The parents grieved and mourned, and she felt that if she died, her parents wouldn't grieve so much. Then she felt guilty about feeling jealous. What we need to stress is that these are normal feelings. We need to let people know that it's OK to feel these things."

As a rule, she said, it seems that 6- to 12-year-old children have the most problems with self-esteem when a sibling dies. "Under age 5, they don't really understand death very much, and their responses are detached. But by 6 or 7, they generally start to view death as a man who comes to take away a bad child. Death becomes personalized ... and suggests to them that they're bad in some way because this happened to them."

Many of these children, as adults, reported that they later had to work on regaining self-esteem.

About half of those in the study have been in therapy, Rosen said, "not necessarily because of sibling loss, but eventually it comes up. It is one of many things that they work out. One woman told us that, as a child, she felt elevated to special status after her sibling's death. Then she felt guilty that she had gotten a gain out of the loss.... Guilt feelings always affect self-esteem."

Here are some of the other preliminary findings in her study:

• Fathers seem to be affected differently. "The mothers grieve and get over it, but some fathers withdraw." Some physically leave home or begin to drink heavily. This dramatic impact may be caused, Rosen said, by a feeling that the loss of a child reflects negatively on their ability to care for their families.

• It seems that children from 13 to 16 find that their lives are most heavily impacted by siblings because they are "at the beginning of adolescence and starting to pull away from their families. But they become more anxious about leaving. The world is not seen as a safe place any more."

• As adults, these children may have especially strong desires to stay close to their parents and to be super-successful so that their parents will be proud of them.

The pull of the class reunion

May 6, 1982

Well, by golly, it came in the mail a couple of months ago—a notice about your high school class reunion this spring. Of course, you decided to attend. Or did you?

It's too good to miss. Or is it?

It'll be nice to see all those people again. But what's the point of it? After all, that was long ago and far away, and this is the here and now. People wouldn't be the same anyway.

Is that the level of ambivalence that you're feeling? Well, you've got company. Lots of folks are in the same boat, says Philadelphia psychologist Edward B. Fish, who not long ago went back to his native Boston to attend a reunion of his Depression-era boys' social club and who admits that he gets sentimental with old friends.

But it's a fact, he says, that not everybody wants to take a sentimental journey. Why not? Well, that's part of what Fish is going to talk about—the reasons people go or don't go to all kinds of reunions, but particularly to high school reunions, which, he says, take us back to a crucial time that was "tied up with our adolescence and formative years."

Reunions, says Fish, are significant because "in our rootless society they provide an opportunity for us to go back to our own roots ... and they can be a reference point for us—a way of comparing ourselves with everybody else."

A basic reason for going to a reunion, Fish says, is curiosity, "to see what happened to other people. It's a chance to show people what we've done and achieved, to reshape our images, to surprise people. Mostly the people who go to reunions are those with something to show. If you've not achieved a great deal, you'll probably not go ...

"To me the most important thing is nostalgia, but not all of us have the capacity for nostalgia. If you're cynical, bitter, gloomy, you probably won't go. You need the capacity to look back and dwell on things ... and you need a sense of humor, too."

It's obvious that reunions hold no attraction for many people, Fish says, because "as many people don't go as do go. An attendance of 40 percent is considered very good," and this suggests strongly that "many people have little to show or else they had painful experiences with the high school group. For many people, high school was an unhappy time."

Because a high school reunion offers a way of marking our progress, Fish likes to compare it with a marathon.

"You take a five-year reunion, and everybody is pretty much bunched together—like at the start of a race. It's like a get-together ... and the main differentiation is between those who went to college and those who didn't."

By the 10th year, "enough time has elapsed for a spread in terms of achievement and careers, but the 25th year probably is the most significant. The field is really spread out, and a lot has happened ... in careers and personally, too. You meet somebody you haven't seen for 25 years, and there have been so many changes. Gee, all the guys look so much older ... and who are those elderly women they're with?"

The 50th reunion, if there is one, tends to be marked by mellowness, Fish says. "You're just happy to be there."

If you go to a reunion, you can expect yourself and others to revert, to some extent, to high school behavior. "There was one guy at my reunion, and now he was a successful businessman, but in high school he'd been a loser, and everybody always ridiculed him. Right away, the ridicule resumed, but he said: 'Hey, you can't talk to me this way—I own my own business and I'm doing well.' But soon he fell back into his high school role, and others were ridiculing him and he was responding to it just as he did as a boy."

It seems, Fish says, that it's more difficult for single women to go back to reunions than single men.

"This is especially true if they graduated before 1965 or so ... because these women tend to be judged by whether or not they're married. I know a woman who has a master's degree in counseling and who is very involved in the women's movement. She was on the committee to organize the reunion, but she was not going to attend. Why? Because at 35, she was not married, and she knew that she would judged by that, she said. She could win a Nobel Prize, but people would want to know how many kids she had and what her husband did."

Women who were graduated within the last 10 or 15 years tend to be judged less by marital status. It's still a factor, Fish says, "but they're also judged now by what they've done career-wise. There's not as much stigma attached to not being married."

As a rule, career success—and not marital status—is the yardstick by which people judge men.

Sometimes people go back to reunions because they want to change everybody's image of them. "I knew this fellow who in high school was skinny and shy, and girls laughed if he asked for a date. He went to his 25th reunion to show people that he wasn't the same skinny, scared kid. This is a therapeutic value of going ... because you can see by the way others react that you're no longer a scared, skinny kid. Otherwise, you could go through life viewing yourself the way people viewed you in high school. But most people like this don't go back"—because the memories are too painful.

One thing that often surprises people at reunions is that they don't have very much to talk about ... even after so many years.

The difficulty, says Fish, is this: "What do you say to a guy you haven't seen for 25 years? What things do you recall? Often you'll focus on something that the other person doesn't even remember.

"We tend to see people the way we last saw them. If somebody was funny then, we expect him to tell jokes now. It's the same if he was a prankster, an intellectual, or an athlete. How do we zero in on where a person is now? We try to relate as we used to, and if this doesn't work, we don't know what to say. If the best dancer in the class doesn't dance now, what do you talk about?"

It's not unusual, Fish says, for most people to find that conversation dries up in about 30 minutes. "Nostalgia only can carry you so far—and then there's nothing else to talk about." If reunions lasted two days, the second day probably wouldn't be nearly as good as the first—and it surely would be a lot quieter.

Coping with a "bad therapist"
May 9, 1982

The woman had made an appointment to see me, and now she was sitting across from my desk and telling me a story that, unfortunately, sounded tragically similar to others that I have heard over the years. The thrust of her story: She felt that she had been wounded by her therapist, in her words "destroyed, stripped of self-esteem and confidence. I felt that I couldn't do anything."

She and her husband had been married for 25 years and, with the children grown and gone, she was prepared to leave the marriage, which had slumped from grim to awful, she said, because of her husband's bad feelings about himself—feelings that "filtered through everything and hurt the relationship."

But before she left, she decided to give the marriage one more shot, so she accepted the recommendation of a friend who had been helped by short-term therapy with a psychologist at a major Philadelphia-area institution. She and her husband began to see the psychologist—and that's where her troubles really started, she said.

"We were in marriage counseling for a year. The psychologist seemed to help my husband, who related to him, but with me the psychologist seemed defensive, antagonistic, and demeaning.... It was so bad at one point that I thought the purpose of marriage counseling must be to wreck one person and make her so defenseless and helpless that she couldn't leave the marriage."

After their year with the psychologist, she and her husband agreed that their relationship was much improved. "It's really good now," she said, "because he feels so much better about himself. But I was destroyed," and last fall she began to see a psychiatrist, who is "helping me unravel what happened, helping me to understand that it wasn't my fault, helping me rebuild my confidence and feel better."

The problem, she said, wasn't that the psychologist was incompetent. "But he recently had been divorced, and I must have tapped into his feelings with what I did or said, and he started playing old tapes. He seemed to have been trained in the school of psychologist that sometimes calls for confrontation with patients, being demeaning and antagonistic. If he'd been like this all the time, I'd have thought he was crazy and left therapy. But most of the time he was pleasant, although he never was as supportive of me as [of] my husband.

"He has good credentials and works for a place that wouldn't have a crazy psychologist on staff, a place with a good reputation. But people really should know about the dangers of going to a bad therapist."

•

What are the dangers of going to a "bad therapist"? How can you tell if the therapist really is bad—or if it's a warped perception on your part? Is it wise to pull out of therapy after you've invested six months or a year in it—especially if the other person seems to be finding help?

I took my questions to psychiatrist Levon D. (Don) Tashjian, who is director of college psychiatric counseling and adult services at Horsham Clinic, a private psychiatric hospital near Philadelphia. Here is some of what he said:

"As she presents the story, the couple got very bad treatment" from the psychologist. "One was helped to feel 'better' at another person's expense, and that's wrong. The goal of couples therapy should be to try to help two people iron out their conflicts—and not favor one side against the other.... A lot of so-called couples therapy really is not couples therapy at all. One is brought in to aid in treatment of the other, usually with not very good results. How can the husband feel better if the wife feels worse?"

The whole matter, Tashjian said, raises once again the wisdom of seeking a second opinion if somebody is dissatisfied with the way therapy is going. "Increasingly, second opinion is becoming a part of psychiatric treatment—as it now is in most other medical treatments. If the patient has any doubts, the patient ought to request and get a second opinion."

The second opinion, Tashjian said, can come from somebody who is recommended by the present therapist or from somebody who is chosen solely by the patient. What is important is that there exists "an understanding with the person delivering the second opinion that he never will assume treatment of the patient."

Why?

Because this removes any possibility that the person giving the second opinion can enter the case in an unhealthy way—either because he pushes or because the patient clutches.

"As a fresh person, if I'm giving a second opinion, I'm liable to dazzle you and give you a distorted image of me ... just because I'm fresh. You may think I'm better than I am because I'm different from the person you've been seeing."

An immediate red flag surfaces in any patient-therapist encounter if they seem to dislike each other, Tashjian said, and it's wise to consider getting out and finding somebody else. But it's important to know that what may seem like dislike actually can be normal "resistance" that is encountered in treatment.

"Let's say that you've been slogging along in treatment for six months. You feel you're getting nowhere, but you're dealing with difficult personality problems ... and you've got to work through this phase of resistance to get well." At first glance, this resistance can be misinterpreted as not getting along with the therapist, and it needs to be explored and clarified before any decision is made, Tashjian said. It is possible to differentiate between the two, he said. "A lot of mismatches exist in treatment, but sometimes resistance is misperceived as a mismatch."

In this situation, a second opinion could be helpful by "offering some sort of sense that the patient is getting the right kind of treatment. A second opinion may say that you're on the right track but that you've got to keep going ... although it's reasonable to expect some improvement in six months or so, something to let you know that you're on the right track."

It's a bald-faced fact, Tashjian said, that a lot of "heads are bent out of shape by pejorative psychotherapy. You're in a situation and feel tyrannized by the therapist—and it can happen in individual therapy, couple, and family therapy. One person becomes a scapegoat ... but this does not constitute good treatment."

Is it possible, as the woman suggested, that the psychologist disliked her because she reminded him of his former wife?

Things like this happen "more than people think," said Tashjian, and this is why it's so essential that the therapist "have his head screwed on straight so he doesn't act out his own conflicts with his patients."

"I had friends who had been in a stormy marriage for 25 years, but they had stayed together in the storm. Then they saw a therapist who had separated and divorced, and he counseled them to separate and divorce—and they did. This is not to say that it wasn't better this way, but he seemed almost transparent" in his motives.

It's not only all right but also downright vital for a patient to ask questions about treatment and its implications, Tashjian said. "If you don't, ultimately you're willing to sacrifice yourself because you don't want to upset the doctor by asking questions ...

"If your leg hurts after the doctor has set the bone, you have a right to ask why. If the doctor responds as if you're an idiot for asking, you still have a right to know why your leg hurts. It's the same with the woman you're talking about. She could have asked 'Why do you seem to be attacking me?'—and she could have kept asking until she got an adequate answer."

How do therapists—or anybody else, for that matter—respond when a patient announces that he is going to seek a second opinion?

"Usually it's the shaky practitioner who doesn't like a second opinion. He'll say something like: 'What's the matter? Don't you trust me? Do you think I'd do something that wasn't in your best interests?' Stable and competent people tend to welcome second opinions. If they're right, it validates their judgment. If they're wrong, it's nice for them to learn from it. Being stable doesn't mean that you're never wrong."

The positive side of guilt
June 7, 1982

All right now, here's today's quickie quiz:

It's bad to feel guilty. Do you agree or disagree with that statement?

If you're one of those who agrees—and there are many—hang on because you're about to get a jolt. A Philadelphia psychologist is going to tell you that guilt has received a lot of bad press, that to feel guilty for appropriate reasons is ... well, appropriate.

Why? Because this kind of guilt can help get you into a frame of mind in which you're less likely to repeat the actions that caused you to feel guilty. In other words, says Edward B. Fish, guilt can act as a deterrent—just like a judge's sentence or a parent's disapproval.

In recent times "guilt has sort of become synonymous with 'hang-up,'" says Fish. "A lot of people think that the goal of therapy is to help you not feel any guilt. But that is an erroneous concept.... I feel at times guilt is appropriate—but it's important to make the distinction between appropriate and inappropriate guilt."

OK, doctor, what is appropriate guilt?

Hurting somebody, deliberately or by accident, is a legitimate reason to feel guilty, says Fish. Other reasons include "responding out of prejudice, not keeping commitments, breaking promises," but the amount of guilt should be in proportion to what triggered it. "There should be a connection between cause and effect, between stimulus and response. If something merits five units of reaction, you shouldn't give it 100 units."

How about some examples of hurting people?

"You go into a luncheonette, and the little old lady at the cash register who can't see very well takes your dollar and gives you change back for a $10 bill. You do nothing about it—although you know that the money probably will be taken out of her paycheck. If you do that, you ought to feel guilty—because you're hurting her, not giving due respect to her.... Appropriate guilt is a way of enabling us to live in social situations," a kind of bridle that keeps us from going hog wild.

What about inappropriate guilt?

In therapy, Fish says, he sometimes sees clients who "feel much guilt but who have done very little, perhaps nothing, to merit it. Some people always seem to feel guilty. They blame themselves for everything. You say, 'Gee, it's snowing' and they say, 'I'm sorry,' as if it's their fault."

People who are burdened by inappropriate guilt "walk around with a dark cloud over their heads. They always think they did something wrong; they always need to say they're sorry, even if they haven't done anything. Or, if they have done some little something, the amount of self-punishment is out of proportion.... Some people feel guilt even from their thoughts. I once saw a married woman who was very depressed because she had found another man attractive. Her thought was, 'What kind of woman am I to think this?' and her reaction was to become depressed."

What this all adds up to, Fish says, is that guilt, like punishment, should fit the crime, and if there's been no crime, there should be no guilt.

It's important to remember, Fish says, that even appropriate guilt must be tailored in severity and duration to fit the cause.

"You shouldn't feel guilty forever—no matter what. Let's say you kill somebody in a car accident. You're dismayed. It's a chance thing that you regret. But to what extent did you do it deliberately? You do what you can to make amends, but then you let it go. You have to be able to let it go."

What about somebody who causes a fatal accident because he's driving while intoxicated? Isn't it more difficult to turn loose of that guilt?

Yes, says Fish, "and you should learn something from what you're feeling. If you drink at a party and then drive and kill somebody, it should be a lesson to you either to stop drinking or never to drive when you've been drinking. Your guilt can help you never to permit it to happen again—but you shouldn't go through life thinking that you're an awful person ... although there always will be a regret that it happened."

Perhaps surprisingly, Fish says that in his practice he now sees an increase not in those who are excessively wrapped in guilt but in those who don't feel guilt even when guilt is appropriate. Some people, he says, can "lie, cheat, and do others in" without batting an eye because they are narcissistic beyond belief. Narcissism, "which is the opposite of guilt," is undeniably on the upswing, and much of it can be attributed to permissive parenting, Fish says. If nobody tells you that others have rights, too, then you're likely to grow up thinking that you and only you have standing in the world.

Conscience is at the root of feeling guilt or no guilt, Fish says, because conscience "is like an internalized judge. If you do something wrong, the conscience passes a sentence. It can be light or it can be punishing and out of proportion. Conscience can be so strict that it produces guilt that ties somebody in knots."

Conscience comes in two varieties, authoritarian and humanistic, and, Fish says, if we're fortunate, we're able to achieve a blend of the two. Somebody who is totally one or the other can make life miserable for himself or for everybody else.

The authoritarian conscience, he says, is "determined by demands from others. It's not your value system. You're simply following orders. You have to follow the leader, and you find security by identifying with authority. The big sin is disobedience. You're given an order and you must carry it out. To be a good military man, it helps to buy into authoritarian conscience.... It's frightening what you can do without guilt when you don't think on your own."

On the other hand, the humanistic conscience is "concerned about values ... and what happens to others. You still listen to what people say, but you don't obey blindly.... You're able to make independent judgments."

That all sounds mighty fine, Fish says, but the hooker is that if "you're too humanistic, you probably won't get too far in the corporate game ... because you'll always be putting others first" and you'll be hesitant to look out for your own best interests.

Is it always obvious to us when we're feeling guilt—or can guilt feelings sometimes be disguised?

That's an interesting question, Fish says, and the answer is that sometimes guilt produces symptoms that can mask what's really going on.

"This is an unconscious kind of guilt. You take a Catholic woman who takes birth-control pills ... or has an abortion. What she feels at a conscious level may not be guilt but fatigue. It's not uncommon for guilt to be translated into fatigue."

Coping with the I.C.U.
July 27, 1982

It's a good bet that many of us, if we were exposed almost daily in our jobs to stress, frustration, death, and dying, would burn out in a hurry and go shopping for another way to earn a living.

Yet at Methodist Hospital in South Philadelphia, there is Clara Simpson, who for many of the 20 years since she left nursing school has worked under the gun and who still is going full speed ahead.

How does she do it—and why?

Simpson, who is patient-care coordinator in Methodist's 14-bed intensive-care unit, responds with an answer that you'd get if you asked a mountain climber the same question. She does it because it's there.

"People see me at my best and worst. It was particularly frustrating in the first few years of critical-care nursing. I was a new graduate, and I had a new job. I thought I could save the world and be all things to all people. But it doesn't work that way, and I found that I had to compromise. I learned what was possible, and it was a hard adjustment for me to make," to let loose some of her idealism.

Tempered by her duels with reality, she today recites this philosophy: "You do the best you can every day, and you try not to take it home with you. Every day is a new day. You can't let yesterday hang over so that you're still depressed the next morning."

She is unmarried, and in her job this is a plus, she said, because she needs time after work to unwind.

"If something very traumatic has happened, it follows me when I leave the hospital. I have to spend some time by myself after work. I can't leave the job and be with people immediately or try to socialize. I need some time between here and there to get myself together. I have a half-hour drive home, and usually I'm calmed down by then, even if it's been an especially rough day."

Most of her friends, she said, are "outside work. My social circles and work circles are separate. I don't discuss work outside the job ... unless some really big problem is pressing at me. My roommate is a nurse, too, and I can talk with her about it, if I need to. But I have a life here and a life out there, and somehow they get together.

"If I were married, I'd probably have to leave here and fix supper and deal with kids or a husband, and that wouldn't work too well. I have to have my time to get it together."

To "get it together" from what?

"In intensive care, you tend to get very involved with patients ... and in intensive care, we get a good share of deaths. When a patient dies, especially if you've really been involved, you feel it. The care has taken time and energy and no matter what you did, the patient still died. It's a loss to the family, but it's a loss to you, too. You did your best, but the patient died. It's not an easy feeling to get over ... and it still bothers me after all these years. You've got to know that you did the best you could. Then, eventually, you can live with that."

Patients typically stay in intensive care for only three or four days, but it's possible for nurses to form emotional attachments to them in that short time. "It's possible to form emotional attachments in a few hours. The family always is here, and it's hard not to get involved with the family. The families rely on the nurses because the doctors always are in and out. But we're always here."

The threat of death often is present, Simpson said, but most patients don't want to acknowledge it or talk about it. Few patients are ready for death, "no matter what they say," and few families are willing to let their loved ones die, she said.

"Part of the blame for this is the state of the art. Intensive care is viewed as a savior. Families think that once the patient gets here, everything will be OK. But patients come to the unit and die, too."

If a patient brings up the subject of death, nurses talk about it, she said, but they must walk a tightrope. "Sometimes it's difficult to answer directly without turning off a patient. If he asks, 'Am I doing to die?' you can't just say, 'Yes, you're going to die.' You might ask, 'Why do you say that?' But mostly patients either are too critical to ask or else they're in denial."

She has known a couple of patients, she said, who "seemed as if they were prepared. They were awake and alert, and they told you that they were going to die. As a nurse, that's hard to accept because you're taught to save patients. But you say, 'OK, you're going to die, and we're going to help you.' It's a total reversal of roles.... We help by being there. Nobody should die alone. We're there if there is no family ... or no friends."

Most families respond to death with "quiet grieving ... but occasionally we have somebody who is hysterical, who screams and lies down on the floor and kicks. Mostly families are able to be philosophical about it: 'Yes, I know father is better off now; he was suffering so before.'"

Most people who die are comatose, but those who are alert tend not to want to be sedated, she said. "They want to be awake to the end, and they have a right to be in control ... if that's what they want."

Most people, as death starts to knock on the door, "want to talk to somebody. We have a large Catholic population in this area, and I can't think of any Catholic who would die without seeing a priest.... I've never heard any deathbed expressions of unusual faith. I've never heard anybody say, 'I know I'm dying, and God is waiting for me.' I've never seen any miraculous conversions at the gates of death."

Simpson's way of coping with stress is knowing herself well enough so that she quickly is aware when she's acting out of character.

"I know when I reach the limits of what I can tolerate. That's when I start saying and doing things that are not normal for me. When I'm at the point that I don't care what I say or do, I know it's time for me to get out for a while, to take a long weekend or a week's vacation."

It's necessary for her to escape every three months or so, she said, and she squirrels away parts of her annual four weeks of vacation for emergency use.

"We have a great group here. They understand when somebody is near the end of the rope. Many times when somebody explodes, you hear others say, 'Oh, she needs a day off.' Or they'll say, 'Don't aggravate her for a couple of days, and she'll be OK.'"

Because everybody is "attuned to what's involved emotionally," people are not shy about asking for time off, and the hospital always tries to accommodate them. The four-day work week was a step toward minimizing burnout, she said. "The five days were just killing people. Now we have three or four days off to recuperate."

She does not intend to continue in intensive-care work forever, Simpson said. "I couldn't continue forever without taking away from myself" something that would be impossible to replace, regardless of how much vacation she took.

She didn't explain what that was ... but she didn't have to.

Being "just friends"
November 16, 1982

Even though it's not a new question, it remains an unresolved question, and it is this:

Is it possible for a man and a woman to build what amounts to a good-old-boy friendship, the kind of friendship that two men—or two women—might have, the kind of friendship that is based entirely on enjoying each other's companionship and savoring time spent together?

In other words, is it possible for a man and a woman to be close friends without romantic involvement or without sexual intimacy?

Over the years, during which I've presented the question to lay people and to mental-health professionals, I've found that something akin to a consensus answer has emerged:

Yes, of course, it's possible for a man and a woman to be friends and nothing more, but it's not too likely. The reason: Whether we want to dwell on it or not, the reality remains that men are men and women are women and that, if they are thrown together often enough under favorable circumstances, something usually begins to stir in somebody's stomach. After that, friendship never is quite the same again.

The sexual issue, almost everybody seems to agree, has to be dealt with, not necessarily by acting it out, although that's what often happens, but surely by discussing it to help define the nature of the relationship. Only after the sexual issue has been resolved, to the extent that it's been clarified, can a man and a woman have a reasonable opportunity for genuine, long-lasting friendship. That's what people seem to think, anyway.

The question of man-woman friendship arose anew for me the other day when a woman telephoned to discuss her tottering relationship with a man of whom she is fond, in a good-old-boy sort of way, she said.

She finds no difficulty, she said, in going out to dinner with him, spending quiet time with him, sharing herself emotionally with him. It's as if she's with a woman who's a best friend. The problem, she said, is that the man isn't comfortable with what's going on, not because he wants anything physical from her but because he's sensitive to what other people seem to think about it.

There has been a lot of talk, she said, among his friends, many of whom are convinced that a torrid—or maybe lurid—romance is being conducted under the guise of innocent friendship. That doesn't whittle away at her insides, but it's giving the man the hives—to the extent that he's considering calling off the whole arrangement. After all, he said, life is tough enough without your friends gossiping behind your back. What did I think about it, she asked. Had I ever written anything about man-woman friendships? Would I consider writing something else—something that might help the man understand that what she wanted from him really was possible?

I told her that, yes, though I had interviewed people about it before, I would take it up again sometime because it was a subject that personally interested me and apparently many others, too, because I frequently hear it discussed when folks get together to try to pinpoint what's wrong with the world and what to do about it.

And so that's how the question came up the other morning at breakfast when I met with sociologist Lynn Atwater, former department head at Seton Hall University, who now is editor-at-large for *Forum*, which bills itself as "the international journal of human relations."

Yes, said Atwater, although we've come a long way, baby, we still have a long way to go before male-female friendships are commonplace and not suspect. But we're making progress, she said.

"We used to think that the only thing between men and women was sexual, but we're moving away from that stereotype ... as part of the changes that are taking place between the sexes. There are no rules yet for this kind of friendship, but, slowly, rules are developing."

One reason for the development of rules, Atwater said, is that men and women, as never before, are being "thrown together at work in positions of equality. It's not like the old boss-secretary relationship, where she was infatuated with his power and he saw in her what he was lacking at home."

No, said Atwater, the equality of the 1980s demands redefinition of male-female relationships, and part of the redefinition that eventually will emerge will extend legitimacy to honest-to-goodness friendships.

In the work world, we "meet so many potential sexual partners ... and it's not possible for all of them to become sexual partners," Atwater said. "Some choices have to be made," and presumably friendships increasingly will be among the favored choices.

She personally knows of a number of men-women friendships, she said, and they seem to be working even though tongues may be wagging. "I know one man whose best friend is a woman. It's difficult for him to be [emotionally] intimate in talking with another man, but he can be intimate with her."

Is it impossible, as some have suggested, for friendship to flower without the sexual issue being dealt with in some way? Yes, said Atwater, it probably is impossible. "They have to define the friendship ... and communicate what each wants from it. It may be more difficult for the man voluntarily to take himself out of the sexual running, but the woman could say: 'I don't want sex in this relationship, but I would like to have you as a friend.' This must be handled considerately, because the ego is very important, but it can be done."

What about married people who develop opposite-sex friendships? How does that tend to work out?

Not badly at all, Atwater said, if the people have close, open relationships with their spouses. "Couples need to learn to discuss this. We all see people we consider attractive, and we need to talk about it. Talking helps build up confidence so that the partner can deal with it."

With development of confidence, the partner is able to support the friendship rather than be threatened by it, Atwater said. That's a real plus, too, because it enables everybody to get a little breathing room and to function better within the marriage.

"Some couples are too emotionally dependent on each other. They expect to get everything from each other, and this isn't possible since nobody can be everything to somebody else." OK, there it is. What do you think?

Discipline: More than punishment

December 14, 1982

The teenager was white-faced with rage.

"Look, Daddy!" she screamed. "I want to go on this date. It's really important to me."

"No, not this time," the father responded in a calm, even voice. "Lately, you've been out more than enough."

"Oh, I hate you! I hate you!"

"Gee, that's funny. I love you."

"Yes, I do," the girl persisted. "I hate you."

The father seemed to remain unruffled. "Look, I'm not playing the game. You want me to say that I hate you, too, so you can feel justified in doing what you want to do."

The girl opened her mouth, but nothing came out. Finally, she cracked a smile and answered: "You're right ... I'm sorry."

Psychologist Irwin Hyman told that story to illustrate a point that he believes is essential for parents to remember in providing discipline for their children: Offer feedback to the children on how they are feeling and behaving. Listen to them and let them know that you understand what they're saying. "Accept their feelings but don't necessarily approve of their feelings."

In the story of the angry girl, Hyman said, the father gave her feedback: "Hey, I'm not going to get into your thing; I don't hate you." But at the same time, the father didn't deny his daughter the right to hate him—if that's what she felt at the moment.

"It's OK to hate your parents sometimes," said Hyman. "I don't think that you're a sinner because of that."

Hyman, who has two daughters, 17 and 19, talks about disciplining children with the fervor of a football fan talking about football. To him, discipline is the mold that casts children into solid, responsible adults—but he goes to great lengths to distinguish discipline from punishment. The two, he said, are poles apart but, unfortunately, tend to be fuzzed into the same thing by many parents and educators.

Hyman is director of the National Center for the Study of Corporal Punishment and Alternatives in the Schools, which is based at Temple University and is part of Temple's College of Education.

"Most Americans equate discipline with punishment," he said. "I like to see punishment used as a last resort, and I'd like to see physical punishment abolished. I'm 100 percent against hitting children."

Hyman acknowledged that he was swimming upstream in his battle against physical punishment because "we're living in a society that seems to believe that the way to change a kid's behavior is to hit him.... We're in a society where we're taught to hit kids. Our religion says it's OK—spare the rod and spoil the child.... But research shows that positive methods are needed to change behavior. The overwhelming thrust of literature shows that [physical] punishment doesn't work. Reinforcement causes people to do better—not punishment."

What parents should try to do, he said, is "catch" their children being good and reward them—rather than catch them being bad and punish them.

The goal of discipline, said Hyman, is to shape children so that they "want to learn to behave appropriately because it's a good thing to do—not out of fear of punishment. We want to try to help children develop internalized controls—so they'll behave in certain ways because it's right."

Is this pie-in-the-sky stuff?

No, said Hyman, whose center recently established what is called "the discipline help line," to which parents and teachers can turn for advice on handling children when they feel that their backs are to the wall. But it's going to take a lot of education before the message trickles down to everybody that parents and teachers who whack children are doing potentially enormous harm and no good at all.

"There's been a lot of research on discipline ... and the key concept is that discipline is complex. There are no simple answers. But too many programs seem to offer simple solutions.... You look at assertiveness training, Tough Love, the programs of Fitzhugh Dodson, and they all try to apply certain simple principles" that are supposed to work in all instances. Anybody who believes that really is engaging in wishful thinking, said Hyman.

"The truth is that we live in a society in which parents can't control the conditions of their children's lives. Both parents often work, and they're not home when the children get home. We have single parents, TV that gives a message of violence and tells children that the way to handle problems is through aggression instead of rational persuasion.... We have schools with large bureaucracies that parents can't get through to find out what's happening to their children, schools in which children are treated like idiots by teachers who are idiots....

"You take all of this and then you conclude that discipline can be solved easily ... and it's crazy."

There was a time, said Hyman, when the national movement was to blame parents for everything that went wrong with their children. Now this has flip-flopped, and the trend is to absolve parents of any and all guilt. "This is just as bad as the other.... Most parents have done something, consciously or unconsciously, to cause their children to behave as they do."

To think otherwise, said Hyman, is for parents to engage in a classic head-in-the-sand ritual.

What are Hyman's suggested guidelines for parents to follow?

"The old axiom of firm but fair discipline still applies. Consistency still is important.... Kids who feel good about themselves generally don't misbehave. Kids who are raised with love learn to love; kids who are raised with fairness grow up to be fair...."

But what about when a child messes up, and punishment is appropriate?

"If a child is beyond the bounds of accepted behavior, first offer restitution instead of punishment. If a child breaks his little brother's toy, have him buy his brother a new toy or give up one of his toys."

Withdrawal of privileges is another solid form of discipline, said Hyman, yet he so often is faced by parents who tell him that nothing they take away from their children has any effect on behavior.

If that's true, he said, then the parents are in big trouble. "When parents can't take away something and get results, it means that the child is controlling them, that they're in a power struggle with the child and that the child is winning."

Hitting children is a dead-end road, said Hyman. "It only temporarily suppresses behavior, and it doesn't teach new behaviors. What it teaches is that might makes right, that violence is the way to solve prob-

lems. It causes anxiety and humiliation ... and this is contrary to learning new behaviors."

Verbal abuse of children "is just about as bad. Anything that demeans
is counterproductive" to creating the desired result, which is a change
of behavior.

If parents are fair, firm, and consistent, their children know it and the
children's behavior reflects it. "If children know that the remedy for X
act is Y ... and if the parents always follow through, things tend to be in
fairly good shape."

Friend's divorce: Choosing sides

December 16, 1982

A while back, Ed Fish and his wife planned a party, and as they went
over the list of people to be invited, they sensed a potential problem.

Here's how Fish described it: "We wanted to invite this separated
couple.... We didn't want to offend either of them, but both said that
they wouldn't come if the other was going to be there. We like them
both, but we didn't want it to appear as if we were choosing sides."

So what did they do?

Well, we'll get to that in a little while, but first let's join Philadelphia
psychologist Fish as he explores a dilemma with which more and more
of us are being confronted these days: How do we react when good
friends break up their marriage?

While it's wise never to choose sides, we're often forced into it, Fish
said, and this can mean alienating one or both of them. "Many times this
is what happens.... Separation has a ripple effect; it affects many."

The way friends respond to a couple's separation hinges to a great
extent on their perception of the nature of what's happening, Fish said.
The separation can be quiet and subtle, or it can be "done in stages and
talked about so extensively that it's almost like they send out a daily
press release."

In a quiet separation, almost nobody knows for sure. "It's often
underground, with the secretiveness of an affair. They tell nobody, and
often people find out about it through the gossip mill. They're invited to
a party, and they decline, explaining that they don't feel well or that they
have other places to go. They make excuses, and it's a closet-type separation." Because of this, friends often have no overt reaction—because

they don't want to appear to be butting into something that they're not supposed to know about.

In a much-talked-about separation, friends tend to keep their distance after a while because they get tired of hearing about it. "People who discuss their separation so much have a high degree of narcissism and feel that everybody is interested. But it can be a tremendous bore. They talk about it, but after a while nobody is interested. People don't really care, but it's a way to get attention." How friends react also can be influenced by these factors, Fish said:

• How long were they married? "If people have been married only one to five years, their social network, as a couple, is not as solidified. Both still have single friends to fall back on and, if they have no children, they can return to the single lifestyle rather easily" without causing their friends much discomfort. On the other hand, marriages of longer duration involve more relationships with couples, and a breakup often dents active friendships.

• Did the separation come as a complete surprise? Fish recalled that he once was in a group in which a couple's separation was greeted with what amounted to, "Oh, it's about time." Aware of what was going on, friends already had begun to invest either in the husband or the wife—not in them as a couple—and the actual separation didn't change anything. A separation that comes out of the blue often causes stunned friends to try to act as peacemakers—usually with disastrous results for everybody.

• Was the separation friendly or bitter? If it's amicable, friends are prone to maintain their relationships with both because they often see the separation "as a temporary storm that may blow over." But if it's viewed as all-out war, friends "go for their foxholes. They expect you to take sides and, if you try to be neutral, it means that you're fraternizing with the enemy."

As Fish said, it's a smart friend who avoids taking sides, but it's often difficult not to be drawn into it, especially if it's an angry separation.

"The wife calls her friends and makes the husband out to be a number-one [creep]. The husband does the same thing with his friends ... and friends begin to see one as the hero and the other as the villain. Friends probably will stay away from the villain because they don't want to be contaminated."

What is an appropriate response when half of a separating couple tries to recruit you as an ally?

"Let's say that one spills his guts to you. You could say, 'Look, I know it's rough, but I don't think that you should be telling this to me. Maybe you should seek professional help.' It's best to stay clear. If the person is a really good friend, it's OK to listen, but don't give advice."

Despite the red flags, most friends can't resist the temptation to get involved, Fish said. "You often take on a mediator role. You tell people to do things that you might want to do ... and sometimes it means encouraging others to act out your fantasies." The end result: "You give bad advice, and then you're angry if they don't follow it."

The friendships that tend to continue despite separation are those that existed before marriage and that are not based on a couple-to-couple relationship. "If somebody is really your friend, he continues to be your friend"—no matter what—because of the emotional stake that both of you have invested in the friendship.

What about if a separated person wants to bring a date to a party to which you invite him? Is that courting trouble?

Yes, often it is, Fish said. "It depends on the length of the separation and the nature of the event. If you sense that they might get back together, I might be cautious about it. I might go to dinner with the guy and his girlfriend, but not invite them to an important event with others there.

"Is the guy doing this to spite his wife? Is he trying to use me to get back at her? I would not allow anybody to play games at my expense. But I might react differently if he said: 'I'm going with this lady; the relationship is important to me, and I'd like her to meet my friends.' Then I'd probably say OK."

What happened with the separated couple at the Fish party? "We invited them both. One came, and the other heard about it and was not happy. I think we lost a friend. I regret it very much because I like that person."

But that, Fish said, is the way the ball so often bounces.

Easing pain for the dying
January 3, 1983

Phyllis Taylor met them years ago, but the memory remains fresh and ever-lasting:

He was 67 and suffering from lung cancer; his wife was 44 and a victim of leukemia. Both were dying.

"The hospital had the man on one floor, the woman on another floor," said Taylor, a registered nurse who has specialized in death and dying for more than a decade. "It seemed insane to me, splitting them apart ... and I talked to physicians and other nurses about it. No, they said, the problem was that somebody had to die first, and this would be too terrible for the other to endure. It was better, they said, to keep them apart."

But Taylor pounded away. "Let's ask them what they want." Well, OK, everybody said, if that would make Taylor happy.

"I went to them and said: 'You've got to help the staff. What do you want to do?'—and it was clear that they wanted to be together ... I looked at the hospital room, and there was no reason why it had to be arranged with a bed, a night table, a bed and a night table. Why not have the two beds together in the center? That way, if they were too debilitated to get into bed with each other, at least they could hold hands."

The transfer of husband and wife was made to the room with the two beds that had been pushed together, and they spent two weeks there. "He died in her arms," and in all ways it was a quiet, peaceful, beautiful death.

The wife wanted desperately to go to the funeral, but she was terribly sick—with a low, low white blood count because of the leukemia therapy. There was no question about it, said Taylor: "From a physical standpoint she shouldn't go to the funeral. But from the standpoint of the spiritual pain that she would have suffered otherwise, she had to go. I went with her for support. The next day she relapsed, and I asked her: 'Was it worth it?' She smiled and said: 'Yes, yes, to hear the prayers and the hymns, to see the flowers, yes, yes, it was worth it.'"

For the last three years, Phyllis Taylor, 41, has been an enterostomal therapist at the Osteopathic Medical Center of Philadelphia. Before that she was a counselor in the death and dying program at Albert Einstein Medical Center's Northern Division. Through her writing and speechmaking, she has become one of the most widely known people in her field on the East Coast.

She can give you flesh-and-blood examples to expand on any point that she makes. For instance: A form of spiritual pain that the dying experience comes from their struggling to make meaning out of what is happening to them.

"He was 26 and dying of leukemia. He'd been sick for 11 years, but he'd married and had a child—which was a real affirmation of living. At eight months, the child died of leukemia ... a horrendous coincidence since it's not contagious or transmitted genetically.

"When the baby died, the man said that it brought him closer to Christ. When he died, he felt, it would bring his family closer to Christ. And he was anxious to die. This was the meaning he found."

Then there was the minister who was dying from Lou Gehrig's disease. "He had reached the point that he was unable to do anything for himself. Not even wipe his nose. Others had to do everything for him. This was a man who'd spent all of his life doing for others, but now he only could receive. Where did he find his meaning? Out of the knowledge of how good it had felt for him to give to others. By receiving, he said, he could bring good feelings to those who gave to him."

In her counseling with families of the dying, Taylor explains what "the physical process of dying looks like ... and I encourage them to touch the person, to talk the person through death. This preparation is invaluable to a family. It's a privilege to talk somebody through death. The facial expression changes, and something happens ... It's important for their healing later on. It's important for them to be there at death."

How does she talk somebody through dying? She and her mother did it when her father died. "We're here with you, Dad ... We love you ... You're doing fine. You don't have to struggle any more ... You can let go." It was a quiet kind of farewell. "I named the people who were in the room, and I told him again how much we all loved him. His facial expression changed, then his breathing."

What does the physical process of dying look like?

For many it is marked by changes in the breathing pattern, Taylor said. "There's a breath, then no breath, a breath, then no breath. Inevitably I find myself holding in my breath so that I'm in time with them. Then the breathing becomes more and more shallow.

"For others the breathing simply moves up ... from the lower abdomen, to the stomach, the chest and neck ... and finally it stops."

For most people, "the death part" is peaceful, but without doubt the dying process is bittersweet. "The bitterness comes from the loss of strength and the ability to communicate. The sweetness can be from being surrounded by loving people who are honest and who don't play games."

She often will ask a dying person: "What is the enemy for you? If it's no longer death, what is it?" For many people who have made peace with death's footsteps, the enemy is "suffering"—which usually means some kind of pain—and all energy should be channeled into helping the person cope with that pain, whether it's physical, spiritual, social, sexual, or financial.

It has been her experience that religion—or the lack of it—can be a major factor in how death is approached.

"It depends on how people believe in God. The book by the rabbi about why bad things happen to good people [*When Bad Things Happen to Good People* by Harold S. Kushner] answers a lot of questions for a lot of people ... with the sense that God hasn't caused the bad things to happen. But a lot feel that God did cause it and that they've got to trust in God.

"There was a boy, 8 years old, who was hit by a car and killed. His father's position was 'God knows best.' But 14 months later, his wife died of toxic shock syndrome. I was preparing him for her death, and I asked if there was anybody I could call, any clergy. He exploded: 'Don't talk to me about God!' The first death had strengthened his faith, but the second had destroyed it."

Despite what we've all heard about how nobody dies an atheist, it's a fact that many people do die as atheists—without any deathbed conversions. "These are the people who say 'To hell with it.... Life has no meaning anyway.' These deaths tend to be harsh."

The best thing that can be done for anybody who is dying is to keep him pain-free, and this is medically possible in almost all cases today, said Taylor. The reason that physical pain elimination is so vital is that pain and anxiety go together. "When we're anxious, we can't sleep, and this leads to insomnia. Without sleep, we become irritable—so irritable that friends and family begin to avoid us, or bring somebody with them to talk to when they visit. This produces real isolation ... and real depression, which in turn produces more anxiety. It's a vicious cycle ... that can be broken only through management of physical pain."

No, said Taylor, she never has assisted a patient in the acceleration of death—although some patients have pleaded for her help. "Sometimes I tell them: 'I can't do it, but I will sit with you if you choose to do it. I'll not hide the pills, and I'll not call the rescue squad for the stomach pump.'"

Her experience, she said, is that "once somebody knows that he has the option to kill himself, he no longer needs to do it. But he wants to know that this option is open."

Are tears in the death room appropriate?

"Some people leave when they begin to cry, but I think this is a mistake. To cry with somebody is important. It's important for the staff, too. I don't let myself sob, I don't lose control, but I do cry with them. Yes, I do cry."

Behind a suicide attempt

February 7, 1983

In more than a few instances, psychiatrist Marvin Kanefield said, he has been convinced that suicide attempts were based not on a desire to die but on anger—on getting even with somebody for real or imagined grievances.

Kanefield, who is president of the medical staff at Friends Hospital in Philadelphia, said he had recently seen in the hospital a girl who slashed her wrist because, she told him, "My mother said something I didn't like." A teenage boy said that he had tried to kill himself, because his parents "wouldn't give me what I wanted."

There is, he said, a classic fantasy that is held by some enraged, suicidal people:

"They'll tell me that they did it—tried to kill themselves—to get even with others. They see themselves at the funeral, in the casket, and the others are standing around and crying. They say, 'You see, you never treated me right, and now I've gotten back at you.' People actually have told me that story, and for them, suicide is the classic act of revenge and destruction."

Often, Kanefield said, he will ask those who have attempted suicide why they wanted to kill themselves. "Sometimes their answer will be, 'They'll all be better off without me.' My answer to that is, 'Well, the problem is over for you, but what about the others? What about the children? Do you want them to say someday that Mommy showed them the way out?' "

Without doubt, Kanefield said, there is a "selfish element in suicide. It's over for them, but they don't realize that the world goes on, that people still carry the burden.

"One woman told me, 'If I'm gone, nobody would miss me.' But she had three children, and I asked her, 'Do you really think that three children can grow up without a mother?' Her answer was that she wasn't a very good mother, but I told her that even a half-good mother is better than no mother at all."

Not infrequently, Kanefield said, his head-on approach is "a jolting kind of thing" that shocks suicidal people back into reality and causes them to reconsider the wisdom of killing themselves. Often, they had failed to weigh the consequences of their death on others—and when they take it into consideration, they are dissuaded from trying suicide again.

Does he find a pattern in suicides? Yes. In suicide attempts, he said, men tend to use guns and women tend to use pills, but for men, at least, death by auto accident ranks a close second.

"There's a fantasy that some of them talk about—driving a car off the road at full speed."

Does this suggest that some "accidents" really are based on suicidal intentions?

"I can't answer that question, but it makes you wonder, doesn't it? Sometimes, I think, it's a disguised suicide so that the family will get the insurance money. Any time somebody doesn't go out by traditional means, doesn't leave a note, I wonder. I wonder about people who drive into the river, who fall out of buildings....

"I can't prove it, but my belief is that it happens more times than not, especially in fatal car crashes."

Can suicide come as a total surprise to a spouse—if the relationship has been reasonably good?

"My impression is that most people who are suicidal are not in control of their senses when they do it," Kanefield said. "They're severely depressed or psychotic, and their reality testing is so distorted" that they don't know what they're doing. "In a good relationship, the spouse should see that the other person is really depressed" and seek professional help.

But it's necessary to take into account the impulsive people who act first and think later. "These are the people who don't like what you say and hit you in the mouth and then ask what you meant by that.... Often they can kill themselves on impulse, and it can be a complete shock and surprise" to the spouse, even though the relationship has been close.

But it's unlikely that an active, planned suicide would come as a shock, Kanefield said.

The shock tends to be greater in accidental deaths that resemble suicide, he said, and it is amazing how often these deaths happen. "Somebody takes a sleeping pill, but he wakes up at 1 A.M., can't go back to sleep and takes another pill. Then at 2:30 he's awake again, and he's confused and doesn't realize that the drug is working. So he pours out a handful of pills and instead of taking just one, he takes them all" because he's in a grog. The shock is so great, Kanefield said, because death occurs without any warning whatever.

Does Kanefield ever think that suicide is justified?

Well, he said, a lot has been written about suicide as an alternative to a painful, stretched-out death, and in Europe, for example, a suicide manual has been published to show people how to depart without agony.

Intellectually and philosophically, he said, "I believe there's a place for this kind of death, but in reality I've never seen anybody who reached that point. You read about the husband who shoots his wife to stop her suffering. You read about the old couple in the nursing home that dies in a suicide pact because they can't bear the pain of living, but personally I've never encountered this.

"If it happened to me—if I were dying by degrees—I'm not sure I'd know when to give up hope" and commit suicide. "My feeling is that I'd think that there might be one more thing that the doctors could try," and he'd shy away from suicide.

Kanefield's impression, he said, is that most people "who kill themselves to escape their pain exit quietly, without fanfare," and we never really hear about it.

Becoming a confident lover
February 20, 1983

When romance goes haywire, it's wrong to point the finger of blame at love, said Alan Loy McGinnis, a Presbyterian minister turned psychotherapist.

No, said McGinnis, "love does not fail. Instead, it is people who fail. And perhaps one reason we fail so frequently is that we enter the wild, dangerous world of male-female relationships unaware and unprepared, urged on by a society that encourages everyone to pair off but that offers almost no instruction in the art of bonding.

"Yet at no point in life does our ignorance and lack of preparation get us into so much trouble. The heartbreak, ruptured lives, and suicide with which I deal are frequently due to ignorant handling of conflict and to a neglect of rules that lovers have known for centuries.

"So important are these rules that they should be taught in every classroom in the country. You can live without knowing the principles of calculus, but you cannot live without learning how to relate to the opposite sex. Your general happiness and even the success of your career will depend in great part on your ability to create a happy home."

This view of the importance of establishing and maintaining a significant opposite-sex relationship comes from McGinnis' new book, *The Romance Factor,* in which he takes the position that great lovers are not born but rather they are created—created out of their own desire to love and be loved in return.

In an interview, McGinnis, who is co-director of the Valley Counseling Center in Glendale, Calif., and author of the 1979 book *The Friendship Factor,* which sold more than 300,000 copies, said that it's possible for every one of us to copy and use for ourselves the "techniques employed by confident lovers"—techniques that not only can help us ignite romance but that also can keep alive the flames forever and ever.

What are these techniques? McGinnis, who has been remarried for eight years after divorce ended his first marriage of 18 years, listed these four:

• Confident lovers use their eyes to attract. You can see this technique in almost any restaurant, McGinnis said, "when a guy begins to put a move on a woman." Much of the move comes from what he's saying with his eyes. "All our talk about erogenous zones and sex organs neglects one of the most powerful organs of all—the eyes." Studies, said McGinnis, have established that if you hold somebody's gaze for two seconds longer than normal, you clearly have given a sign of interest.

• Confident lovers turn up their energy levels. "This is difficult to describe, but I think everybody understands what I mean. Maybe it's best summed up by a woman who told me how she attracts men: 'I'm not brazen about it, but if I want to get a man interested in me, I don't try to parade in front of him or do any of the preening rituals that some people try. I just turn up the energy level. And I focus on him.... I stop thinking about myself altogether, and I concentrate all my attention on him. Maybe it shows in the way I'm looking at him or the way I'm talking. I don't know. All I know is that it works.'"

• Confident lovers touch freely. Yes, said McGinnis, there's no doubt that "wonderful amounts of sexuality" can be communicated with a light caress or a brush against somebody's hair. "The tactile organs can, if used correctly, build an emotional crescendo.... Here, as in the use of the eyes, the whole secret is in the intensity of the exchange."

• Confident lovers seduce with talk. A lot of people, McGinnis said, have the notion that "a witty line is the answer. But I think that's a turnoff. I know a guy who's not good looking—in fact he's quite ugly—but he's always surrounded by beautiful women. He told me that if he can get a woman to talk to him for five minutes, he has a good chance of connecting with her." Rather than mouthing a cliché like, "Haven't I seen you someplace before?" it's better at a party to ask something as sensible as "Hi, are you having a good time?" If you meet somebody on an elevator, you can ask: "Do you work in this building?"

Every one of these techniques spills over to marriage, McGinnis repeated—especially seductive conversation. "Everybody in my line of work, as a therapist, has heard the same line from so many clients: 'We just don't talk anymore.'"

In his second marriage, McGinnis said, "there is one thing I do almost religiously: I insist on time at least once a day for us to talk. It may be over a second cup of coffee, in front of the fireplace in winter, or in a lounge chair on the patio in the summer. We sit and just talk. It's not necessarily romantic talk; it's talk about what's going on with Loy and with Diane."

The children—Mrs. McGinnis has two from a previous marriage—know that they're out of bounds when they worm their way in during these talks, but they do it anyway. "They come to check us out. They wander in and make small talk with us. It pleases them, I think, that we value our private time together."

At least once a week, he and his wife make it a point to have lunch together. "We're not necessarily on our way to anywhere. We just make a date to talk. After work ... we may go shopping or go to a movie. It's nothing exciting necessarily, but we're together."

The implication clearly was that couples can drift apart—without really being aware of it until it's perilously late—unless they consciously make and execute decisions to spend time together.

In the fire of a new relationship, how is it possible for participants to determine if what they feel is romance or physical attraction?

Well, said McGinnis, it's a mistake to put the bite on physical attraction as something that's wicked or immoral. "You can have physical attraction without romance, but you can't have romance without physical attraction." Sometimes, in the beginning, the two can be difficult to separate, but often, if only physical attraction is involved, the flame can flicker after a short while or one person can be afflicted with the nagging concern that exploitation is rearing its nasty head.

It's fashionable nowadays, said McGinnis, for some to roar that "all romance is pure lust, animalism. But I don't believe it. Love has inspired too much great sculpture, too many great songs. It's so much more than sexual animalism."

Even while he beats the drums for love, McGinnis warns that love can be a two-edged sword if it carries unrealistic expectations. "Putting too much weight on love—as if love can solve all problems—can be a disaster. Some emphasize love in a way that it appears as holy as religion—and the result of that can be that love collapses under the weight. But if you accept it as it is, love can bring wonderful things."

In this whole love business, there is a catch, McGinnis said, and it is this: "You have to be a romanticist to believe in romantic love after you've been married for 10 or 15 years. But what if you then tumble for another person? Sometimes that happens, you know, if you're a romanticist."

The reality of the dream
March 7, 1983

Once in the mellowness of after-dinner brandy, a psychiatrist friend told me that perhaps two or three times in a lifetime we have dreams that, if unraveled, literally could yield the meaning of life for us—dreams that gouge straight to the core of our very existence.

Not too many nights ago, I had a dream that caused me to bolt upright and, even in my sleepy-eyed grog, to think: "This is it—a dream that is trying to provide the answers."

The problem was ... how do you find answers if they are so grotesquely disguised and so horrifying that they baffle your intellect and seem to mock your every attempt to come to grips with them?

I tried to use the dream-analysis system that San Francisco "dream psychologist" Gayle Delaney explained in her 1979 book, *Living Your Dreams*—a system that calls for endless questioning of every aspect of the dream. But I wasn't even scratching the surface. With a normal dream I'd probably have called it quits at this point, but this was not a normal dream, I felt, and I couldn't turn it loose.

So I did something that I've never done before—I telephoned Delaney, whom I have interviewed and with whom, over the years, I have built a casual friendship, and I asked if she'd try to shed some light on the meaning of my dream. In a way, what I did was the equivalent of calling Michael DeBakey and requesting a long-distance heart consultation, and I felt guilty about it. But the possibility of ultimately understanding the dream muted my guilt.

Delaney, who is married to a psychiatrist, talked with me for an hour and 20 minutes—and, by golly, her skills in questioning and piecing together seemingly unrelated bits of information are awesome. When we finished, I felt that I had a handle on the dream—and a clear indication of the direction in which I needed to move. Ironically, it was a direction that already had occurred to me, and just a few nights before the dream, I had remarked to my wife, Marilyn: "This is going to be the toughest year of my life—because of the commitments I've taken on. But I've learned from it; and after this year, you're never going to see me in this fix again."

My dream:

•

Scene One: I was in the Air Force, and Marilyn and I were living in a military-type barracks. One day I was standing in a field, alongside a friend, and watching another friend, a well-known Philadelphia psychiatrist, perform stunts in an airplane that had no wings. He started a loop too close to the ground, and his plane crashed, exploded, and burned. I said to my friend: "How on earth could an experienced pilot do that?" And my friend answered: "Didn't you know? He was a homosexual, and he didn't want to live anymore."

Scene Two: I had accepted an Air Force assignment that surely would result in my death. I didn't want to die. It was as if I had no choice; this was something so vital that I had to do it. I stopped at my mother's house, where my toddler sons, Jay and Grant, were staying, and I told them that I loved them, but that I wouldn't ever see them again. I started crying, and this frightened them, and they cried, too.

Scene Three: I returned to the barracks to say goodbye to Marilyn. But strangely, she shed no tears. In fact, she didn't seem overly concerned. Later, as I entered a friend's quarters in the barracks, I saw some of Marilyn's clothing there. I was out of my mind with rage, and I confronted her and screamed: "Couldn't you even wait until I was dead?"

Scene Four: The death mission began. I entered a green, gauze-like tunnel that started in the heavens and ended ... well, I didn't know where. I was on a sled that scooted down the tunnel at blinding speed. Then I stopped at an airplane-like vehicle, climbed into it and took off. What I thought as I unflinchingly approached death was this: "This is the first time in my life that I've had no hope, no plans for tomorrow. It's an awful feeling. If I were going to live, I'd write a story about this, about how terrible it feels to have no hope."

Scene Five: I woke up, in bed with Marilyn, on a beautiful, sunshine-filled, warm day. Birds were chirping, and I was overcome with love and joy as I realized that I wasn't dead. I was absolutely overwhelmed that life could be so magnificent.

●

Well, what would you make of that?

In a nutshell, here's what Delaney helped me arrive at through her patient and perceptive questioning:

Scene One: Since all characters in dreams tend to be ourselves, the pilot who died was me—or rather a part of me, a part that I don't like but that I know still lurks there. The part: My overworking. Despite the progress that I've made over the years in bridling my tendency to work too much, the reality is that I still work too much. The pilot's death somehow was calling my attention to the necessity for me to kill off completely my crazy need to work.

Scene Two: In real life, when Jay and Grant were little, I'd never really known them, because I always was working. This was a re-creation of that—my accepting another responsibility that would result in our not being able to be together. The clear message: Knock it off—and straighten out priorities.

Scene Three: On some level I must fear that the marriage to Marilyn won't make it, because I continue to pile up obligations that cut into our time together. The fact that I'm so furious in the dream perhaps represents the energy that I put into denying that I'm piling up obligations.

Scene Four: The sense of hopelessness and desolation offers insight into what I may be doing to myself and those I love. The speeding sled may suggest an out-of-control life that is so filled with columns, books, speeches, teaching, and a condominium newspaper that it directs me, rather than my directing it.

Scene Five: Clearly this is a preview of what life could be like—if I cut back on my outside-the-office commitments and regained control of my schedule.

The dream, said Delaney, was "a very special letter to you" with the bottom-line mandate to make sure that first things are put first—frequent quality time with the people I love most, my wife, my sons, my mother.

When she asked the question, "If you had 10 years left to live, would you continue to do things the way you are now?" the answer was obvious. No, I said, with just 10 years left, I'd limit myself to doing things that I really wanted to do, things that intrinsically had value to me. With just 10 years left, I'd make time for the leisurely vacations that I've so often put off, for the visits that time or credit-card balances didn't seem to permit.

Our conversation ended this way:

Delaney: "How old are you?"

Sifford: "Fifty-one."

Delaney: "You know, you may not have more than 10 years."

I'm sure I'll recall that conversation in a few weeks when Marilyn and I are lying on the beach in Ixtapa, Mexico.

Yes, that's right.

When to leave a job
March 24, 1983

It's an elementary reality that knowing how to get the best job available is the first step in career-path planning. But what isn't so widely grasped, said consultant Ned Klumph, is the second step: knowing when to leave.

Yes, in Klumph's words, "there was a time when people joined companies just as they married—for life. In the 1950s, a typical interview question from a company such as Philco Corp. was, 'How long would you plan to stay here if we offered you a position?' Any answer that indicated a period of less than the rest of your life was met with less than enthusiasm—and no job offer."

But, continued Klumph, "Today's career planning demands not only how to get a good job but also when and how to make a change." But job change, like any other major decision, should be approached with great caution and introspection. "All too frequently today, people let a need for a change stimulate them into an impetuous move that proves in the long run to be less rewarding than anticipated and in far too many cases less challenging than their previous position."

Klumph, a former executive for a number of large corporations, including Philco, is president of Ned Klumph Associates in Cherry Hill, N.J., and he devoted half of a recent issue of his company's newsletter to identifying the right times to leave a job.

While a lot of people don't quit when they should, even more quit when they should not, Klumph said in an interview.

"In the 1950s, we assumed that three out of four bosses during our career would be bad. If we got a really good one, we felt lucky. But we were prepared to work long years for a corporation and put up with many bad bosses...." The wisdom of this philosophy is open to question, but the reality today is that young people tend not to seriously consider putting up with a bad boss.

The result is that they tend to move too early and too often. "They don't want to sweat out a tough boss.... Instead of trying to sell the boss on their attributes, they expect the boss to see their attributes. But they should realize that they have to keep showing the boss how good they are. It's an exceptional boss who says, 'Hey, you're doing a helluva job, and we're promoting you.' People rarely get enough praise" no matter where they work—and that is a fact of business life that needs to be understood and accepted.

In other words, somebody who leaves job A because he feels unappreciated isn't necessarily going to be made to feel more appreciated in job B. It just doesn't work this way, Klumph said, because so many bosses take the position that money is a substitute for praise and that "I'm paying you well to do your job—so don't expect a pat on the back, too."

When is a proper time to leave a job and what is a proper reason?

Probably the number-one reason is being hopelessly at odds with the boss. It's one thing, said Klumph, to quit too quickly if friction develops, but it's something else to ignore a reality as plain as "I hate my boss, and he hates me." When this happens, when all avenues of compromise for mutual satisfaction are blocked, then "it's time to go. I rather expect to see a lot of movement when the economy turns around. A lot of people are just hanging in there now. They'd rather be part of the 89 percent employed than part of the 11 percent unemployed."

Here are some other guideposts for leaving, said Klumph, who suggested that "before you quit a job, stop, look, and listen—regardless of the economic times. If you've had three or four jobs and you're under 30, that's OK. But by 30, you can't jump around too much. People get the impression that you don't know how to face bad times, and management is looking for people who can solve problems, not run from them." The guideposts:

• You feel that the honeymoon is over. "This feeling is more than the basic 'getting grooved' or settling-in that always occurs" as a person gets familiar with the job. "If you're unable to create new situations and challenges or make little headway for a more satisfying atmosphere, now is the time to re-evaluate your situation, your boss, and to project the length of time it will continue before corrective action is taken. What does your boss think? Have the two of you discussed it?"

• You want more money. If your pay increases are tied to a percentage that is uniformly structured throughout the organization, you'd better accept the fact that you'll lose ground—because inflation will gallop while your salary merely plods along. Often you can change jobs and enter a new organization at a higher salary than people already in that organization at the same level. This is because they, like you in your job before, have been held down by standardized percentage increases over the years.

• You feel that you're about to be fired or caught in a cutback. "You've been ignored at meetings; the boss doesn't seem to like your ideas. These are danger signals, and they shouldn't be ignored. Don't wait for your annual review to find out what's going on. It's a mistake not to walk in, close the door and ask: 'Boss, what's wrong? How can you help me?' It may be that he'll say there's nothing he can do, but at least you won't have to wait for the annual review and then be surprised."

• You've learned all there is to learn on your job. This feeling that you're stuck on a plateau is experienced by every achiever, and it presents a critical moment in career planning. It's a time to consider a new job, a whole new career or geographical relocation. If you really feel stuck, you need to do something—but it doesn't necessarily have to involve job change. If you're able to make peace with staying put and comfortable, that can be your solution.

But whatever you do, said Klumph, don't do it in haste. It's true that haste makes waste—and in no other place is the price of waste greater than in the work place. So remember: Better safe than sorry.

Hospitals and power
April 5, 1983

At 10 o'clock on a Wednesday morning, I was in the office—listening to a lawyer lecture on libel laws and journalistic responsibility.

At 3 o'clock that afternoon, I was admitted to a hospital as an emergency patient, with what they first said could be either acute pneumonia or tuberculosis, but with what they later diagnosed, after a biopsy, as a gross inflammation of the air ducts in my upper right lung.

The cause? Nobody really knows, but somehow it apparently was tied to my crazy 20-year history of allergic reactions to nonspecific causes.

At any rate, the hospitalization, which lasted eight days, was my first in more than a decade, and it reacquainted me with what it's like to be a patient—something that I'd almost forgotten.

Yes, I was treated well. I can't imagine that any patient ever got more unqualified attention—not only from medical people, but also from dietitians, administrators, and clergymen. Yet as I lay there in my feverish state and stared at the ceiling, it occurred to me that something other than how rotten I felt was bothering me. What was it? Simply, it was the realization that I had surrendered control of myself to a great extent, and that I pretty much had to do whatever I was told, by whomever I was told, in whatever way I was told.

If after a duty shift a different nurse came in at 2 A.M., woke me, and asked 'Are you a heavy smoker?' I felt an obligation to respond—even though a dozen other people had asked the same question on the same day, even though surely somebody must have written down the answer somewhere: No, I've never smoked in my life.

It was just that I felt that I didn't have a right not to answer, that I couldn't or shouldn't refuse to cooperate—no matter what.

I was so intrigued by my reaction—normally I'm not so helpful if something rubs against my grain—that I presented the question of what it means to be hospitalized to Philadelphia psychologist Edward B. Fish. In a nutshell, he confirmed what I had suspected: The worst thing about hospitalization for many people is the sense of giving up control—not symbolically but literally.

"You're going along your merry way, and all of a sudden you're in the hospital. It's like hitting a stone wall at 60 miles an hour.... You sign in, not knowing when you'll come out—or even if you'll come out.

"Psychologically, what it does to you can be devastating.... You give up control of your life, and there is a total loss of power and rights. You sign something and don't know what it is because you don't bother to ask. You don't even have the option, in many cases, of not signing."

Once in the hospital, he continued, "they disrobe you. Why? Who knows? A lot of the routines go back to the Middle Ages, and nobody ever questions them. You come in on Friday, and they put you in a gown even though maybe nobody will see you until Monday. Everything you do seems to be for the hospital's convenience. You go with the hospital's procedures. Why? Because you're afraid to question them—afraid that they'll withdraw treatment from you."

It's a goofy, irrational fear, Fish said, but most patients share it at one time or another. "The fear in asserting yourself is that, if you do, they'll punish you by not taking the best care of you—or even by giving you a more dire diagnosis. The fantasy is that you want them to like you because, if they don't, they may find out that you're going to die."

The people who tend to have the toughest time adjusting to hospitalization are those with the "most power on the outside," said Fish. "Once you're hospitalized, your economic standing doesn't matter—except that you may have a better room. A cardiac attack to a Rockefeller can be just as terminal as a cardiac attack to a guy who sleeps on the street."

In other words, said Fish, when you remove your gray flannel suit, you also remove your outside identity, and you have no clout.

"You're used to giving orders, but you have to ask a young girl for a bedpan or for permission to go to the toilet. You can be the president of the United States, but a nurse's aide at that moment has more power.... Your life is controlled by somebody who doesn't make a fraction of what you make," and this drives up the wall people who tend to measure everything by money.

The people who best handle hospitalization, said Fish, are those "with the capacity to adapt. These are the people we call mature. They have flexibility, and their well-being doesn't hinge on one variable, like their business. They have a solid philosophy of life that enables them to roll with the punches.... But even they can get scared."

What should you do when you're scared?

It's important to verbalize your anxieties, said Fish, if it's possible to do it reasonably without driving everybody up the wall. The distinction needs to be made between verbalizing anxieties and endlessly whimpering about what's happening to you. Compassionate people will understand the former, but even they will tire of the latter—and start shying away from you.

It's important to be able to assert yourself in healthy ways, said Fish, and sometimes it's a matter of simply insisting on your rights. "If you push a button and the nurse doesn't come in a reasonable time, it's OK to raise hell.... If they do something that doesn't make sense to you, it's OK to question it."

But it's also important to remember that people who work in hospitals are just like people who work anywhere else, and that how they respond to you likely will be dictated by their personalities, not by their jobs.

"Sadistic people have a field day in the hospital. They may appear downcast when they look at you. You're wondering 'Hey, am I really sick?' You're trying to read clues, and they're giving you clues—not because there's necessarily anything wrong, but because they're sadistic.

"People who work in hospitals use power in ways that are the same as they use power in other places. If they are arrogant, they use power arrogantly; if they are concerned, they use power in ways that show concern."

Ideally, what patients need, said Fish, are doctors, nurses, and caretakers "who are aware of the human aspect of what's going on in terms of what you need. These are the people I want to go to ... because a good part of recovery has to do with morale."

Marriages without sex
April 21, 1983

When the couple came to psychiatrist Harold I. Lief for help, they angrily pointed fingers of accusation at each other.

The husband complained that the wife was not feminine enough. She didn't wear perfume, and in many ways she was a tomboy. As Lief looked at the woman, he said, he had to acknowledge that there seemed to be "some accuracy" to what the man was saying.

The wife's complaint was that the husband was too fat, that he'd put on so much weight in their five years of marriage that he now was shaped like a triangle. As Lief looked at the man, he said, he had to acknowledge that the wife was more than a little on target.

Their problem, distilled to basics, was that sex activity had gone down the tube rather quickly. He had been an ardent lover in the early courtship, but as soon as their engagement was announced, he had seemed to click off the thermostat that regulated his passion. In their five years as husband and wife, they had engaged in intercourse two or three times, they told Lief.

As he "got down to it ... and began digging into their backgrounds," Lief discovered that both had been programmed for sexual disaster from their early days.

When he was a boy, the man found out that his older brother had impregnated their sister. It was a closely guarded family secret, something that nobody ever talked about—but it had left its mark.

When she was in her early teens, the woman had fought off her father's attempt to have an incestuous relationship with her. It, too, was a deep, deep secret—and it, too, had left its mark.

For both of them, Lief said, "sex was loaded with all kinds of negatives. It was incredible that they found each other."

Harold Lief is medical director of the Philadelphia-based Institute for Marital and Sexual Health Inc., and he was saying in an interview that sexless marriages—or marriages with very little sex—are far more common than people might think.

He has counseled a couple with "five years of unconsummated marriage.... There are some with 20 years of unconsummated marriage, some who have sex only one or two times a year. This is no problem if both agree to it," but the rub comes when one partner wants more. And typically this is when Lief enters the picture.

Although he sees a good many people with traumatic childhood sexual experiences that sabotage their capacities and appetites, he more often sees those who suffer from what he calls "a prevalent sexual dysfunction."

And what do you suppose that is?

In Lief's words it's "low sexual desire"—which simply means that one partner has no hankering to go to bed with the other. It doesn't necessarily mean that the one doesn't love the other. It's just that the desire for sex has flickered and died for all practical purposes.

Low desire, said Lief, is in males second only to impotence as a major sexual problem. In impotent men, Lief often finds "a secondary inhibition of sexual desire ... as a protective measure" against their having to perform.

In women, Lief said, low desire is the number-one sexual problem. Altogether, he said, it's estimated that 20 percent of the population suffers from inhibited sexual desires.

As a therapist, how does he approach this problem?

"First you have to determine if this lack of desire is generalized or situational. If it's generalized, if he has no desire for anybody, that can be the result of depression or organic factors. If it's situational, if he can't function only with his wife, then you know that it's the relationship. And this is the more typical—situational dysfunction, in which the man hungers for other women even as he turns his back on his wife.

For the most part, this is a red flag that signals a snag in the relationship, and "the primary choice of therapy would not be sex therapy but marital therapy" to get the relationship back on track. When that happens, the sexual dysfunction tends to evaporate.

What tends to be the underlying cause of low desire?

Boredom ranks high on any list of causes, Lief said. "There is a certain amount of boredom associated with sameness, but if people really love each other, they can find variety to overcome the sameness. That's my feeling."

Anger also is a major contributor to situational inhibition, and "we try to get at the causes of anger" and deal with them.

The much-talked-about Madonna-whore complex is yet another common reason for lack of sexual interest in the wife, Lief said. "Sometimes we find this at the time of marriage or even when the engagement is announced. We generally don't find that it comes on later in the relationship ... although pregnancy can touch it off later. We frequently see men desert their wives during pregnancy or after they have children," and one reason is that some men can't bear the thought of having sex with the mother of their children.

And that, of course, is what the Madonna-whore complex is all about—men who think that sex is permissible only with "bad" women.

Surprisingly, Lief said, there is a "female version of this—when a woman is not interested in her husband because he's like a father to her. She can have sex with strangers but not with her husband. This is much less common than with men, but we see many examples of it."

The Madonna-whore complex is treated by "making men aware of the extent to which they can modify their behavior. We try to trace the attitude back to its origin ... so there will be some intellectual understanding of why they're this way. It always stems from childhood, to the family of origin, to the attitudes toward Mother.

"What we're talking about, really, is changing perceptions ... so that the man sees his wife as sexy. But there can be a problem with this because the wife may not be sexy, and then we have to work with her to change her behavior. It's quite possible that she's been acting like the Madonna.... We try to emphasize the positive aspects of the man's relationship with his wife. Often a man tends to pick out the negatives to enhance his feelings" about not wanting to have sex with her.

By any therapist's yardstick, Lief said, "these are tough cases"— those that center on low desire. "We fail on probably 30 or 40 percent.... In a relationship, it's much easier to take away the passion than to put back the passion."

The right connection to adult children

May 1, 1983

Over the years, I've done a number of interviews about the awful things that can happen when parents don't turn loose their adult children and, instead, continue to treat them as they did when the children were little, needy, and dependent.

What tends to happen when parents don't form more appropriate relationships is that the parents often feel neglected and rejected by grown children who are merely asserting normal independence and leading their own lives. The grown children, on the other hand, tend to feel resentful toward parents who want to control them—and they expend a lot of time and energy trying to keep at arm's length from their parents.

In the end everybody loses—and because it seems that so many lose so often, it's an area that I think needs to be written and rewritten about.

As a rule, it seems to me, therapists agree that the best parenting is the parenting that gets children ready to fly from the nest and make it on their own. The worst parenting is the kind that forever ties children to the parents, makes them feel an unhealthy dependence on parents or, at the other extreme, makes them feel guilty if they lack unhealthy dependence.

But as I've written these stories, I've frequently been asked by parents a question that amounts to this: "Hey, you have a lot of stuff about what parents shouldn't expect from their children, but why don't you have more about what is reasonable for parents to expect?"

A primary concern of reasonable parents seems to me to focus on the nature of what constitutes an appropriate relationship with adult children. As a father of two boys—actually two men, because they're now 24 and 23—I have trouble sometimes in sorting it out for myself.

My difficulty is in walking what I think is a proper line between encouraging them to take all the rope they need to be free to commit and learn from their mistakes, which puts me at risk of appearing not to be interested in what happens to them, and trying to be too close to them, which puts me at risk of appearing to want to influence them excessively.

To put it another way: If I write or telephone "too often," do they perceive that I am blowing down their shirt collars and do they, in one way or another, respond by backing off? Conversely, if I don't write or telephone "often enough," do they perceive me as unloving and cold?

How much contact and what kind of contact is appropriate—when your children are grown and living hundreds or thousands of miles away? How much do you say when they don't respond to your letters as often as you would like—or even respond at all? How far do you go, how far can you prudently go, in letting your grown children know that you're disappointed in not hearing from them more often?

I didn't get Christmas presents this time from my sons, Jay, who lives in Tulsa, Okla., and Grant, who lives in Asheville, N.C. I didn't even get Christmas cards from them. What I did get from both were letters thanking me for the Christmas checks that I had mailed them. Grant, whose letters are so infrequent that I feel like breaking out champagne when one of them arrives, once did write and, in effect, told me: "I really appreciate all your letters, and I don't want you to think otherwise. It's just that I'm not much of a letter writer."

Yet it was Grant, who, when I was hospitalized early this spring, told my wife when she telephoned him: "I really love him, and I want you to tell him that." And then a day or so later, he, himself, called and told me. And so did Jay, whose contacts with me always have been more frequent than Grant's since he and I bridged the valley that was created by my divorce from his mother.

As a father, do I expect too much? What is realistic to expect? How do I handle the genuine disappointment that I sometimes feel?

I brought up those questions during an interview with Philadelphia psychologist Matti Gershenfeld, who is the mother of four grown children and who this spring directed, as president of the Couples Learning

Center, a series of seminars on parenting the adult child.

Here is some of what she said: An appropriate parent-adult child relationship is one in which everybody has plenty of breathing room but in which enough contact is maintained to keep a reasonable sense of family. "If you write regularly, the child will tend to do the same ... because writing basically tends to be viewed as a reciprocal process. But the trouble is that parents frequently feel that only the child has an obligation to write."

What if the child—like Grant—doesn't reciprocate?

"You keep doing it.... Moms and dads are supposed to love their kids all their lives. I assume that parents are more mature than the kids" and thus are able to keep writing even though few letters are answered. "Kids need to know, no matter what, that their parents love them," and it's only through contact—letters, telephone calls, and visits—that this love is manifested.

But what about feelings of disappointment that can result from not hearing from the children?

"I think that parents are allowed to express disappointment—but not to try to lay a guilt trip on the kids. It's OK to say 'Yesterday was Father's Day, and I'd hoped to hear from you.' It's not OK to say 'After how I sacrificed for you, you didn't even remember me on Father's Day.... After all I did for you, you're really an ungrateful slob.' This is to be avoided."

It's important to create "special days" when parents and children are together, said Gershenfeld, days on which they can celebrate events that took place when they were apart. "You can celebrate a birthday on another date if that's when the two of you are together. You create an auxiliary day" and make it special.

What if the child never responds—no matter what?

"If the relationship truly is ruptured, there's a piece of you, as a parent, that never can be whole. You don't want to go the rest of your life not talking to your kid, so it becomes a matter of doing the best you can. Given that it's an imperfect world, how do you create some kind of relationship? Maybe it means your dropping in for 10 minutes some Sunday afternoon and saying that you just happened to be in the neighborhood"—even though that's not really true.

If that's the best you can salvage, then that's what you go for—because, for almost any parent, a little bit of a relationship is far better than nothing at all.

Does Gershenfeld agree that the best parenting is parenting that prepares the child to leave home as an independent adult?

Yes and no, she said.

"I think the best parenting is that which in a warm, respectful environment raises children to be independent but also to need relationships, to need spouse, children, family. It's not to raise children with the idea that parents should be cast aside when the children grow up. I think the ultimate is for children not to leave their parents in the sense that they outgrow their parents.

"They should be independent, but my hope is that parents would create the model that the family is an important connection that should be preserved. Parents, I think, can help their children to be independent but to be close, too. After all, who wants to make it alone?"

What do you think?

Healthy and unhealthy religion
May 3, 1983

From psychologist H. Bruce Ewart: "I find in so many patients some confusion or bitterness over religion. I think it got there because they tried to reject some distortion that they were taught as children. Finally they decide that God must be displeased with them ... because they're in conflict with parental attitudes," and that's when real problems can begin. "Often they throw off religion and get lost in the process."

I hadn't expected Ewart, 39, a Lutheran who converted to Catholicism, to discuss religion during our interview, which was pegged to his belief that the "wrong" person—the victim—often comes into therapy while the "right" person—the one who is causing the pain—goes on his merry way. But it was apparent, as Ewart discussed case after case, that religion was heavily on his mind.

Almost routinely, he said, he encounters in his private practice "distressed people who have problems with religion—either a misunderstanding ... or a type of 'supernatural guilt' that must be dealt with."

Ewart's line of thought triggered for me flashbacks to the many religion-based interviews that I've done over the years—interviews that not infrequently have focused as much on the negative as the positive aspects of religion. Once, a year or two ago, I retrieved some of these interviews and used them as resource material for a speech that I had been invited to give at a Unitarian church in South Jersey. The topic: Does rock-hard, black-white religion enhance or inhibit emotional development in a healthy, functioning adult? Or: How the good news of the Gospel can become bad news.

Some of the interviews had been with theologians, some with academicians, therapists, pulpit clergy, former clergy. Here is some of what the interviews added up to in my mind:

"Healthy" religion helps a person accept the light and dark sides of himself, accept himself in spite of the rotten things he sometimes does. Therapists seem to believe rather strongly that a healthy person in a religious sense is fairly rare.

"Unhealthy" religion tends to offer one of two extremes—either the person views himself as a dastardly sinner without hope of absolution, or he views himself as a saintly person who is surrounded by hopeless sinners. Religion perpetuates these extremes, one clergyman told me, "if religion forgets that the Gospel good news is that God loves us as we are."

A good test of whether we have healthy or unhealthy religion is this: Can we say that we're sorry when we've goofed up—and then turn it loose and not forever be hounded by the memory of it?

Clergy who act as counselors, as many now do, not infrequently deal in repression, rather than try to flush out the problem and meet it head-on. A minister who trains clergy in the counseling skills said that many will "try to give you the feeling that Christians are not supposed to have problems, and all you need to do is read more Scripture and pray more." The price of buying into that, he said, is that you may spend your life pretending that you're happy—with the predictable result that "the problems come out in other ways ... through physical sickness, emotional breakdown, troubled children."

A red flag to be considered when dealing with a clergy counselor is this: Is the Bible quoted as law to be followed, or is the Bible used to generate dialogue and raise thought-provoking questions? If it's quoted as law, be prepared to run—because the clergyman may be trying to repress the problem. Another thing to consider, the clergy/counselor trainer said, is this: Does the clergyman have all the answers? Or does he try to help you find the answers? "Only you have your answers," he said.

But the rock-hard, black-white religions believe they do have your answers, a number of sources agreed in the interviews. The great attraction of these religions, a theologian told me, is that they are in some ways like est: "They pound at you and move you toward total despair. Then they hold out an option, and you embrace it. The relief you feel is fantastic. You're not a nobody anymore."

With this kind of religion, he said, "the more wretched you believe you are, the more relief you feel at surrendering your life to God. It's been described as relief not unlike orgasm ... and people get enlightened time after time in one spectacular zap. It's not unlike strong drink: Once you get accustomed to the burning in the throat and nose, there's nothing else in the world you want more than to repeat the experience. This is what keeps people coming back."

But this, the theologian said, also is what causes resentment and drives away many people.

"The resentment comes from toeing the mark but being told again next week that you're still a hopeless sinner.... The answer is to move out of this 'adolescent religion' in which the Bible is the only source of light."

People move toward adult religion, he said, when they "get older and realize that life operates on a wider range than only what's in the Bible. They learn life's realities and that maybe they shouldn't take the Bible so simplistically, that maybe there are numbers of other things to consider."

To the person in rock-hard, black-white religion, he said, "to use your head is to dethrone Jesus Christ from your life. It's an adolescent way to think—on/off, either/or. The mature person out of adolescence believes that he can learn not only from the Bible, but also from what elders can teach him. He's open to accumulated wisdom of the ages.... We graduate from adolescent religion by opening ourselves up to other people."

Psychologist Ewart, it seemed to me, was talking about problems that were rooted in adolescent religion. The cure, he seemed to say, was somehow to graduate into adult religion.

"I once had as a patient a 26-year-old man, really a kid in a lot of ways. He said at our very first meeting: 'I'm not going to see you unless you promise me that you won't talk about religion.' He'd come in with the fear of religion" hanging around his neck like a millstone, and he "pictured God as a hawk that flew around and pounced on him."

The point, said Ewart, was not to discover who influenced him this way. The point was "not to find a culprit but to find the fears, distortions, and unmet needs of his parents" and deal with them now, on a rational level. "The goal was for him to forgive his parents, not to blame them."

Religion-based problems from childhood are time-consuming to fix in adulthood, Ewart said. "It amounts to a process of relearning. You have to start almost from scratch ... and throw out almost all of the concepts" that you've accepted without question for much of life.

That is difficult, isn't it?

Taming sibling rivalry
May 23, 1983

The woman was 25, and she had been happily married for four years to a man who treated her better than good. Then one day the husband announced that he was bringing somebody home to live with them—somebody he described as "slightly younger, slightly more attractive than you."

Because the woman will be "my second wife [and] will be new to the home, I'll have to pay more attention to her," the husband said, but he urged his wife to "get used to her, to love her, to consider her our second wife."

Then, as if to commemorate the event, the husband gave his wife a box of candy.

Psychologist Burton L. White often tells that make-believe story to young parents who are wondering when or whether they should have a second child. It's an appropriate parallel, White said, because it's normal for a child who's 18 months or 2 years old to react to a new brother or sister with about the same level of hostility with which a wife would react to a new woman who entered the household.

White, who is director of the Center for Parenting Education in Newton, Mass., outside Boston, is the author of the landmark book *The First Three Years of Life*, which appeared in hardcover in 1975 and in paperback in 1978 and which has been distributed internationally—"even in Russia," said White.

White was speaking to me a few days before he was to be the guest speaker at a seminar sponsored jointly by the Childbirth Education Association of Greater Philadelphia and the Osteopathic Medical Center of Philadelphia. One of the subjects he would discuss was sibling rivalry, and in an interview that is what I asked him to talk about—because I think it's a subject that is misunderstood or not even considered by many parents and parents-to-be.

White said that he virtually stumbled into his interest in sibling rivalry as a byproduct of his research into how children could be helped to get off to the best possible start in life.

"As part of the project, 17 of us, one at a time, went into hundreds of homes of families ranging from poor to well-to-do. We made our observations for periods of up to two years, and it's something that never had been done before and maybe never will be done again.... In doing it, we learned a lot of useful things—which toys babies actually played with, how children a year of age are much more interested in steady staring at things and people than virtually anything else they do.

"... One thing that was most striking to us was how tough a job it is for a stay-at-home parent who has two kids under 3, when the older one is at least a crawler. It struck us much to our surprise, because this parenting is much more difficult and far less rewarding than we had dreamed."

What White and his researchers also found was that the difficulty was reduced and the rewards were enhanced when there was only one child or when there was wider age spacing than three years between the first and second child.

"If there was more than three years' difference, especially six or seven years, the older child seemed to like the baby nearly all the time," he said. "There was a nice tone to the whole thing ... and everybody seemed to have a good time. But if you had a 2-year-old and a 1-year-old, the tone was very different ... because the older child didn't seem to like the younger child."

The trouble typically doesn't begin when the new baby comes home from the hospital, said White, who this summer will conduct on cable television a series of programs dealing with the first three years of life.

In the beginning, the baby sleeps most of the time and is "kept in a box in another room," White said. "The problem begins when the new baby is 7 months old or so and mobile for the first time. The mobility leads into a dangerous time in life because the baby is subjected possibly to poisonous substances"—and surely to the older child.

Because of his potential for getting into trouble, the baby gets a lion's share of attention from the parents, White said, and this tends to burn to a crisp the older child, who "doesn't like to handle second place, who really can't do it.

"... The reality is that it's tough as heck to have two kids who are after each other all day long on a day-to-day basis. It's the norm, and the pattern we see is simple: The older child shows displeasure and jealousy. This may involve yanking a toy back when the younger child innocently tries to play with it, but it can get more and more intense. The younger child can't figure out what's going on, because he's not used to hostility in his young life.... Sooner or later, the younger child gets hurt and cries. The parent hears it, sizes up the situation, and can't believe her eyes: 'How can my angel do something mean to my other angel?'"

After this goes on for a few weeks, White said, the younger child begins to "cry in anticipation of being abused, and the older child ceases doing it, because he's learned that the cries are followed by a parent's catching him and punishing him. So it becomes a standoff situation from the time the younger one is 11 or 12 months until about 15 months.... Then the fat goes into the fire when the younger one is 16 or 17 months ... and becomes aware of his personal power. He tests it out, tends to dominate the older child, and initiate the trouble, often by biting or pulling hair."

At this time, White said, the parent "reaches a low point and doesn't even know which child has started the trouble. This typically persists until the younger is 2½ or 3 ... but we don't know how long it may continue into later years, because there has been no continuous research. Some say it lasts for decades; others say they become good friends. I don't know who is right ... but what I'm talking about is not horsefeathers; it's based on a lot of work."

The best way to minimize the rivalry, which White called "natural, normal, and not sick," is for parents "not to have kids every year. When children are three or four years apart, everybody is much better off."

When children are closer together in age, parents need to be aware of the inevitability of the sibling rivalry that will result, White said. "Parents need to know a helluva lot more about kids. They should think of the older child like they'd think of a jealous 14-year-old lover. Don't rub his nose in it by allowing people to laud the baby in front of him. Let him know that he's loved by giving him totally private time—at least half an hour—every day. Be aware of the serious damage that an older child can inflict on a baby."

The intrusion of a new baby means less to an older child if "he has private time with parents and if he knows he is loved.... At 4½, a child is not so cramped [by the arrival of a new baby] because he is oriented less toward his parents. He's in nursery school, and he has other fish to fry.... The parents' job is easier."

Despair where optimism should reign

May 26, 1983

There they were, the winning short stories in the annual "excellence in writing" competition sponsored for high school students by the Lansdale, Pa., branch of the American Association of University Women.

There was one titled "The Reunion," about an old man who felt terribly alone and left out when the family gathered and everybody ignored him: "Nobody so much as looked at him. He wondered if any of these people would come to his funeral. Maybe they would, just to pass the time and to have a gossiping session. But would they care if he died? He doubted it."

There was one titled "The Loser and His Tribe," about a Green Beret who, although he has been mortally wounded by the enemy, manages to fire a makeshift arrow into the barracks that houses the other Green Berets to warn them that they are about to be attacked: "The gliding arrow landed on a barracks door. But the only eyes to see it were the blank and sightless eyes of the Green Berets, already slaughtered."

There was one titled "Men Make Matches to Burn Themselves," about a computer operator whose brain is stolen from him by the computer: "While you slept, Mr. Chauncy, I simply transferred your brain from your body to my 'body.' You see, although I have the ability to reason, I still needed the ability to feel. I needed a soul."

There was one titled "The Free Throw," about a high school basketball player who in the final second misses two free throws that would have won the game: "The ball was shot a shade too hard. It hit the back of the iron, bounced high ... and came down on the left side of the rim.... The dreary sounding horn rang out through the old arena. The game was over."

Because I was speaking at the awards presentation, I had access to the entries in advance, and, as I read them, I wondered why every short story was constructed around despair, death, anger, disaster, defeat. The writers are 16, 17, 18 years old, and if you can't find reasons for optimism at that age, what's it going to be like to bite the bullet as an adult, when you finally realize that not every dark cloud has a silver lining?

I thought back across the decades to the short stories that I had written. I even read, as part of my speech, one story from a notebook of many that I had written when I was 10 and that my mother miraculously had preserved and presented to me a few years ago. The story that I read, like the others, contained a thread of Charles Bronson-like hope and justice in which the good guys won and the bad guys got what was coming to them.

If you don't have that kind of expectation as a child—that some sense of justice prevails some of the time—what's it going to be like as an adult when the walls of injustice seem to surround you?

If, as a child, you haven't built into your system some kind of idealism, what's it going to be like, as an adult, when you're buffeted by all the forces that society hurls at you to stamp out any trace of idealism?

I was appalled—yes, appalled, that's the right word—that these bright young people, presumably the cream of the crop, were so immersed in sadness that they seemed to me to be in danger of drowning in it.

What's responsible for it?

I discussed my feelings with some of their teachers, and yes, the teachers said, the stories do tend to be sad and tragic, and that's the mindset with which the youths have been writing for several years now—not just those who write prize-winning stories but everybody else, too.

Said one teacher: "I think that it reflects the kids' basic sadness, their fears about whether they'll even have a world in which to grow up—because of the possibility of a nuclear holocaust."

Another teacher said that there was more sadness today because there are more one-parent families today, and "unquestionably there's more stress in one-parent families."

Another teacher said that teenagers were more aware of world problems today than when she and I were children, that television had brought the ugliness right into our living rooms and that teenagers, because they felt that they couldn't escape it, tended to internalize it.

Still another teacher said that the tragic theme might represent not feelings of impending personal tragedy but the undeniable reality that many of the great works to which students were exposed contained tragic themes and students came to equate tragedy with good writing.

After my speech, during dialogue with the audience, I turned the tables and instead of answering questions I asked one of my own: Why did the students write with such sadness, despair, and hopelessness?

Some of their answers:

• "When I was 10, I wrote happy stories, too ... but when you're 17, you realize that there's another side to life, an unhappy side, a grim side, and you have to confront that."

• "A lot of us pick up the sadness from our parents. Personally, I don't think that my parents are sad, but many of my friends feel that their parents basically are very unhappy people."

• "As a teenager, you're beginning to realize that things don't always go the way you want them to go. This is disillusioning, and the writing reflects it."

• "We're just realizing that the world is full of disappointment and unfairness" and that mothers and fathers can't shield their children, even if the children wanted to be shielded, which they don't.

• "A lot of us basically are happy, but I don't think there's much market for the elation that we feel when it comes to writing. So we often write about the other side of life, the tragic side."

In an interview the day after that speech, I put the question about the tragic side to Leo Madow, who retired last year as professor and chairman of the department of psychiatry and neurology at the Medical College of Pennsylvania and who now has a private psychiatric practice and is a consultant at the Institute of Pennsylvania Hospital.

Here is part of what Madow said:

"Perhaps it's the recognition that times are tougher, that fewer of them will go on to college, that fewer dreams will come true.... The world is grimmer now.... The tuition for medical school is almost $20,000, and who can afford that"—no matter how desperately somebody wants to become a physician?

Perhaps, said Madow, some of the despair is a spinoff from normal adolescent turmoil, since adolescence is a time of great conflict between feelings of wanting to be independent and wanting to remain a dependent member of the family.

"Kids used to try to deal with their anger and frustration," he said, "by using drugs and participating in cults. It seems to me as if there's less of this now, and I'm wondering if they're not turning their anger inside. And, of course, anger turned inside becomes depression."

What do you think?

Where's the ounce of prevention?

May 31, 1983

A long time ago, somebody uttered what would become an immortal line: "An ounce of prevention is worth a pound of cure."

Nowhere is belief in the wisdom of this more evident than in physical medicine today, where major emphasis unquestionably is swinging toward preventing illness rather than focusing solely on curing us after it has grabbed hold of us.

If you ask your doctor for advice on reducing the chances that you'll develop heart disease, he can preach a sermon on the necessity of not smoking, of getting reasonable exercise, of reducing your dietary intake of fat, of.... And the list goes on and on.

But what about somebody who wants to guard against mental illness? Is there preventive medicine for that? For mental health, has anybody come up with an equivalent of monitoring cholesterol levels?

I put these questions to John A. Talbott, president-elect of the American Psychiatric Association, who was a guest speaker at the spring meeting of the Pennsylvania Psychiatric Society. Talbott, 47, is professor of psychiatry at Cornell University Medical College and associate medical director of Payne Whitney Psychiatric Clinic in New York. He shook his head and said that, no, before prevention can be more than a gleam in somebody's eye, researchers must uncover the root causes of mental illnesses like schizophrenia and manic depression.

"Major work has been going on in both areas for years," said Talbott, but so far nobody can say with conviction that the causes have been isolated—although, he said, there are some in the field who believe that "mental illness will be the next to be cracked. With cancer under such assault, some think that the next major breakthrough" will be on diseases such as schizophrenia and manic-depressive illness, and "then maybe something can be done" about prevention.

Was that all Talbott had to say about prevention?

No, not by a long shot, but he stressed that his advice was based more on common sense than on medical research. Here, from Talbott, are some things that all of us can do to try to stay healthy emotionally:

• Get married. Even though we're living at a time when the divorce rate is 40 percent or higher, it's a fact that marriage "protects us against a lot of things" by providing a support system and a buffer against the harshness of confronting life alone. "When we're divorced, single, or widowed, we have mental illness to a greater extent"—so great that it can't reasonably be considered happenstance. There obviously is a cause-and-effect relationship.

• Pick good parents. This is tongue in cheek, of course, but Talbott's point is that healthy parents tend to have healthy children. "I'm talking about parents with no genetic loading, who are not alcoholic, who don't abuse children."

• Build a broad range of coping skills. This is something that is within our power to do, and it's definitely to our advantage to develop more than one way of looking at the world and ourselves. "If you have just one way, and if that way doesn't work, then you're stuck."

• Realize that you can't do very much about preventing mental illness and don't spend a lot of time fretting, which, in itself, could make you more vulnerable to mental illness.

There's no doubt, Talbott said, that stress is a factor in triggering mental illness; but it's important to understand that stress is a part of life and, if you try to avoid all stress, "you cease to live. You could enter a monastery, I suppose, and maybe you'd be subjected less to the bombardments of pressure, but this obviously is not for everybody." So the best thing for most of us is to realize the damage that stress potentially can inflict and try not to overreact to inherently stressful situations.

It seems obvious, said Talbott, that some of us have biological predispositions for various diseases, both psychological and physical, and that "it takes some stress to bring them out."

There was, he said, a well-documented study that involved men who were drafted into the Army—men whose stomachs were normal as opposed to men whose stomachs were high in acidity that predisposed them to develop ulcers. "During basic training, the men with high acidity got ulcers" while the others did not, and it seems reasonable to assume that if the ulcer-prone men had avoided the stress of basic training, they wouldn't have come down with ulcers.

"It's the same thing with schizophrenia or manic-depressive illness.... If you can avoid the stress" that triggers it, you likely won't get it, even though you might be genetically predisposed to it.

"Usually, some role is played by a stressful environment. But it's not a one-to-one correlation, and people differ in their reactions to stress. Some can lose a penny and get depressed. Others can lose their homes, and for them it's not so stressful.... You find some people who were on the fringes of a fire and they have a much stronger stress reaction than those who were at the center of the fire. Some have a bigger vulnerability to stress, but it can't be judged beforehand."

How is it possible for us to broaden our range of coping skills as a means of defending against mental illness?

What this amounts to, Talbott said, is "figuring out a number of ways to solve problems. Most of us have only one rote method, and it doesn't always work....

"It doesn't hurt to have a wide variety of experiences, to read the great works, to have friends, family, and teachers with a wide variety of styles of life and different ways of looking at life.... We often see families as conflicted and judge this to be bad if parents think so differently," but the truth is that this can be a bonus for the children.

"If both parents see the world as bad, then it's likely that the children will grow up feeling that there is no other way to deal with the world except by thinking that everybody is out to get them and that they always must protect themselves.

"But if you have one parent who feels that way and another parent who thinks that people are kind and gentle, well, at least the children have multiple models to think about."

And that, Talbott said, can't be anything but good.

The lose-lose decision
August 1, 1983

Years ago, when he started a practice that became heavily involved in domestic law, attorney Emanuel A. "Manny" Bertin found that he turned to putty in many cases that involved children.

"A child whose parents were divorcing would say, 'I want to live with my dad.' If I sensed emotionality, attachment, warmth, a pleading look in his eyes, well, that did it. I didn't care about facts, smacks. I took the case, assuming that I liked the parent. During the trial, if things got rough, I'd remember the kid in my office with the pleading look in his eyes, and I had to come through for that kid. I was immersed in that."

But, said Bertin, who practices out of offices in Philadelphia and nearby Norristown, as his reputation ballooned in child-custody matters, he began to get what he called a different type of case.

"This woman had a daughter, 10, whom she had raised by herself. Now the kid wanted to live with her father. The mother had gone to all the teacher conferences; she'd done everything for the child. She was a good mother. The kid comes into my office, hugs and kisses her mother but says she wants to live with her father.

"I was thinking, 'Hey, Manny, remember your philosophy that kids should have a say in their destiny.' But this mother had done everything right. Do I not take the case? We hired a child psychiatrist, who examined the child and said that she was going through a stage. He explained beautifully why it was so natural and healthy for her to want to live with her father. What I found out from that was that a real expert can explain what's happening so logically that you forget about the teary-eyed kid in your office.

"I took the case. We won, and the mother retained custody of this child who loved her mother but wanted to live with her father.... In another case, a kid who lived with her father said that she hated him and wanted to live with her mother. She wouldn't touch him; she screamed and cried in my office. I had a psychologist examine her, and he explained it: She was going through a stage, and it would be the worst thing in the world to pull her out now ... because six months later she'd have another stage and want to come back. We couldn't play musical chairs with custody and with schools."

It was the beginning, said Bertin, of a new philosophy that caused him, as a lawyer, to put less-than-absolute stock in what a child might want in terms of custody. "If I have a performing parent who has given of himself and done a wonderful job and a nice kid who's doing well in school, that's one thing"—in determining what to do about the child's request to live with the other parent. "If I have a parent who's not so good and a troubled kid, that's a different situation."

Whatever he decides, Bertin said, at least two things are certain: The custody battle is going to be "a bloodbath," and he will "get no kick out of it ... because these are unpleasant cases, the worst cases."

Bertin, who was chairman of the Pennsylvania Bar Association custody committee, which helped guide through the legislature the joint-custody bill that went into effect in 1982, is the author of a new book, *Pennsylvania Child Custody: Law, Practice, Procedure.*

It's a 475-page book that retails for a whopping $40, and it was originally intended for law libraries, judges, and lawyers who needed a refresher course before they went into battle. But as it turned out, Bertin said in an interview, it's a book that appeals to custody-battling parents because it tells them what to expect and why when they get to court.

Considering that child-custody laws are remarkably similar from state to state, the book is relevant just about everywhere, Bertin said. "I've drawn on all my experiences over the years ... and shared every trick in the trade, different methods that have been proven successful."

Bertin said he sees a trend these days—a trend in which the father divorces the mother and leaves the only child at home with the mother.

"The mother raises the child all by herself. She's a working mother.... and when the child is from age 10 to 13, a number of things seem to happen....

"The absent father remarries, often to a woman who has a couple of kids about the same age as this kid. It's a seductive situation. The father's new life looks exciting. The kid feels that his life is boring because his mother works and he's alone so much of the time. He likes his father's new wife and he likes her kids. He decides that he misses his father greatly, and one day he walks in and tells his mother that he wants to live with his father.... It's a most tragic thing."

Why is it so tragic?

Because the judge is "supposed to look at the situation through the child's eyes—but the child's eyes have to see things clearly. I feel sorry for this mommy. She's given 10 years of her life to produce this terrific kid.... and now the kid dumps on her"—and the child's reasons have nothing at all to do with what she has done or not done.

If this case comes to court, it's not possible to determine how the judge will rule, Bertin said, because some judges have some strange biases.

"If a kid is 10, one judge won't listen to the kid's preference because he thinks that 10 is too young. But if the kid is 13, what the kid wants is absolute."

Another complicating factor, Bertin said, is the responsibility that is placed upon the child to state a preference.

"Picture a 10-year-old kid who is marched into a marbled courthouse, where he sees all big people. He's whisked into chambers, and there sit a judge in a robe, two lawyers, and a court reporter with hands poised to take down every word the kid says. It's scary, but the kid is supposed to be relaxed.

"The judge asks, 'Why do you want to live with your father?' If the judge spent three days with the kid, went fishing with him, talked with him morning, noon, and night, then maybe he could understand what the kid is like. But not in 10 minutes. But in 10 minutes, the kid is supposed to verbalize feelings, and he knows that he must choose his words carefully because his parents will find out what he says. I couldn't do that—and I'm 38.

"We're asking a kid to give an adult-type response. He doesn't want to hurt one parent, but he wants to be honest with the judge. He may say: 'I like my dad's house.' But the words may be more meaningful than they sound. Maybe the kid really means that there's a lot of warmth there, that he's comfortable there. But the judge says: 'I'm not going to give custody to the father because he has a house and the mother has an apartment.' You almost need a psychiatrist to figure out what the child really is saying."

What is virtually assured in these cases, Bertin said, is that there will be no real winners.

Can a marriage survive an affair?

August 4, 1983

The letter from the woman touched on a theme that I hear so often from so many women. Here is some of what she wrote:

"My problem is not unique, but I do need some answers.... Earlier this year, my husband left me for another woman. He stayed with her for a month and a half, until she asked him to leave. After that, his whereabouts are something of a mystery to me.... But then he came back to me after three months.

"What I would like to know is this: How have other women handled this problem? Does love ever come back—or has it never gone away and does it just take a while before it can be said? Does the relationship get stronger? When does trust come back?

"I'm sure that you've written about this problem before, but I would appreciate it if you could write about it again. I'm sure that there are many other women out there who are going through the same thing."

I mailed a copy of the letter to clinical psychologist Carol Gantman, 34, and a while later I went to her office near Philadelphia and asked what she would say if the woman came to her for help.

Right off the bat, Gantman said that she didn't think that this would be likely to happen—and that, indeed, was one of the woman's problems.

"She doesn't seem to me like a person who would come for therapy, like a person who is able to do things for herself, to reach out and seek help in active ways. She can write a letter, maybe ask friends for advice, but I doubt that she would go for help," and this perhaps indicates the drastic degree to which her passivity has knotted her into a one-sided relationship.

Gantman said that, though the letter contained no information on the marriage, it appeared as if her husband's leaving had taken the woman by surprise. "This leaves me uncomfortable—that something could be that awry in the relationship and only one person is privy to it.... Yet her expectation seems to be that they should be able to pick up where they left off, and she wonders why she can't trust him again."

It appears, said Gantman, that the woman is coming from a "traditional marriage—a male-centered, closed system . . . in which the relationship is built on rules rather than on trust, primarily the man's rules. It's chauvinistic in the sense that he's the active one, she's the passive one.

"A reaction that I might see her having is similar to the reaction of an infant when the mother leaves. It's the old separation theory. The infant protests, despairs, then detaches. It sounds to me as if her reaction is part of the detachment, which comes toward the end of abandonment.... In this phase of the sequence, it's tough to recommit [to the relationship] ... and I see the way she feels as a reasonable and natural reaction.... She sees herself as having no options, and this is typical of this kind of relationship."

Also typical of a male-dominated relationship, said Gantman, is that the woman "seems to have no option about expressing feelings.... She must swallow her feelings."

What would have to happen to turn around things?

"If she wants love and trust, she must confront the issue of forgiveness ... by making a rational decision to give up, let go, stop haranguing. This is very much related to trust, which comes from a sense of security about the individual, the relationship, and the future. To forgive, she has to have something on which to build and support trust. It's not clear to me from the letter if this trust is warranted. Her expectation seems to be that she should produce willy-nilly her feelings again as in the past, and it's not clear to me if it's reasonable for her to do that. She needs information on what happened and how he feels before trust and forgiveness are reasonable."

In short, said Gantman, the woman "needs to ventilate. The closed system should be opened up."

Gantman responded this way to the woman's question about how other women have handled this problem:

A "continuum of reactions" would include these three:

• Take back the husband without any questions and without getting any of the root issues resolved. This seems to be the position of the letter writer.

• Refuse to take back the husband. In some women, the strong feeling exists that "disloyalty disrupts the contract."

• Take back the husband, but only if certain conditions are met.

Said Gantman: "I wonder what she would do with these other two positions" because she seems to have such a need to hang on to the relationship—at any cost.

What is likely to happen to the woman?

"If she holds it all in, tries to accommodate by denying her feelings, she may end up very depressed and need hospitalization. She seems to be the kind of woman who often ends up in a psychiatric hospital in her 30s or 40s—a woman with no psychiatric history but who lives" in an environment that fertilizes the prospects for depression. "Something happens to trigger depression—the death of parents, the husband's leaving—and it's the straw that breaks her back."

But a more optimistic prospect, said Gantman, could be that "through some input, some insight, she recognizes that she has some rights to challenge the system and request some things from her husband—things like, 'Where the hell were you?' and 'What things aren't working in the marriage that we might change?' She needs to get him to cooperate with her in getting the stuff out. Sometimes men are willing to do that, and it can be a neat, fulfilling venture for both."

Is it likely that a husband who's had things his way for so long would be willing to change?

"He might be reluctant to give up something and get nothing back. She must communicate that she'll not do anything too threatening to him." If she's able to do this, then, yes, it's entirely possible that the husband could change and that the marriage could be rebuilt along more equitable lines.

How much do children owe?
August 7, 1983

It was obvious from the handwriting and from the tone of the letter that the woman was elderly. Here is some of what she wrote:

"Three years ago, I wanted to write to you, but I didn't. This was after you'd written about your widowed mother and how you offered her your help when she needed it.... I have read almost every story you've written and I also attended a speech in which you talked about the problems you'd had with your two sons after your divorce. I hope you don't feel too guilty about the kind of father you were when they were little....

"The reason I'm writing to you now is to tell you that I'd like to talk to you. I would like to talk to you about what responsibility children have to their parents—children who are about 35 or 40 years old and whose parents are between 70 and 80. Mostly, it seems to me, the sons with their doctoral degrees have forgotten the sacrifices their parents made to give them their opportunities....

"Do you ever give interviews? I would like very much to tell you my story."

I get a lot of letters in which people ask to be interviewed—and I've found out the hard way that many of these people don't have as much to say as their letters suggest. As a result, I seldom grab my briefcase and head out to somebody's house with no more to entice me than an invitation. Yet, there was something about this woman's letter that seemed out of the ordinary, and that's why, at 9 o'clock on a sunny morning, I knocked on her door.

How did the interview go? That's what this column is about—a column that I decided to write only after considerable mental wrestling with myself. As you read it, you'll understand why.

She is 77, and she grew up as one of eight children in a European family in which closeness "never really was possible" because sheer numbers worked against it. In her mind, she created a fantasy of an ideal family relationship—one in which people "would not just be nice but be genuine and loving."

It was a fantasy that she brought with her when she and her husband came to America so many years ago—a fantasy that was fanned into reality when their two children were born, a son who today is 38, a daughter who is 41.

It was glorious in those early years, she said—and especially was it glorious with the son, who was "my prince ... who from the very first day taught me to love. To my son, Mom was beautiful," but all of that began to change as he grew into adolescence.

"At 11, he began to criticize me, and at 16 he began to get away from us. My husband and I thought it was normal—and maybe it is. Unfortunately, maybe it is."

The son became a man, received his doctoral degree and became a faculty member at a Midwestern college. The mother, by now a widow, discovered she had cancer three years ago and underwent surgery, which seems to have been successful.

At the time, she said, she was terrified—as anybody would be—and she cried out to her son for help. "I called him and said 'Joe, I need you,' but the line was silent. I said 'Joe, I want you to come here for a few days and be with me.' But he said nothing. The next day, I called again, and I got the same no answer. I said 'Joe, one day you'll feel guilty about this.' That's when it hit me—about my fantasy of the perfect family relationship. If I dropped dead, nobody would know it.... I was blown out by the rejection.

"He would call me, but there was a certain detachment. He was not with me. He was nice like a nephew but not loving like a son. This always was between us, this detachment. I went to therapy because I was crying all night, and I'm not the crying type. They told me that I should forget about my son, that our children are ours only until they don't need us any more. I blew up at that, but I'm afraid the therapists were right....

"When my son calls, he tells me to 'go to your friends.' But my friends are old, too. When they play bridge, they want to have fun—not hear about somebody's problems.... My son doesn't have to love me, but there should be compassion. I can't demand love, but I should be able to demand compassion."

It was a sad story, no doubt about that, until she began to talk about her daughter, a daughter who had fulfilled her obligation as an adult child, the woman said, by staying close to home and caring for her. After all, she said, children have an obligation to their parents, an obligation that is best discharged by the children's being geographically close to their parents, even if it means changing jobs.

How often did she see her son? Well, he and his wife come to visit two or three times a year. She visits them in the Midwest, too. And there are phone calls.

Doesn't that suggest that the son has loving feelings toward her? Yes, maybe, she said, but she needs more. She needs open expressions of love because "older people need the security of feeling that they belong, that they are loved. I don't have that" from the son.

Has she ever told the son that she's not satisfied with their relation-ship? No, she said, but "he knows it." How can she be sure? Because a mother knows these things.

I told her that if I wrote anything about our conversation, I would expect to get letters from angry parents who would like to trade places with her, angry parents who seldom even get letters from their grown children, let alone several visits each year. Had she ever considered that she was better off in the relationship with her son than she thought? Had she ever considered the possibility that her expectations were not realistic, that a grown son can't reasonably be expected to keep mother on the center stage of his life?

Well, she said, she knew that many other mothers might be thrilled to get a birthday card from a son, but that wasn't enough for her. "Once, when he was little, I had the whole cake. Now I have only crumbs, and I'm not satisfied with crumbs."

As a mother, she had "given, given, and given to him, but now I'm supposed to be satisfied with what I get back," and it's not fair.

Strangely, I found myself siding with the son—even if he had not responded to his mother's cry for help. Perhaps I identified with him because his mother is only a year older than my mother, who lives 1,500 miles away and who tells me that she regards the two letters I send her each week, and my annual visit, not as crumbs but as essential parts of her life. The most important thing I can do for her, she has told me repeatedly, is to carve out a happy, satisfying life for myself—and to share with her and love her.

When I told the woman about that, she didn't seem impressed. Her son "used to say so easily 'I love you' to me. But now he can't seem to say that any more."

I suggested that she give him time. At 38, I had great difficulty telling my parents that I loved them. At 51, I have no difficulty at all.

She wasn't sure that she had much time, she said. What she was sure of was that life hadn't treated her fairly.

I started to repeat a story from my mother about elderly people who complain, but who don't do anything to try to fix what's wrong. But I didn't—because my perception was that the woman wouldn't want to hear it.

When I left, I wasn't sure that it had been wise for me to come. I'm pretty sure that she felt the same way.

Parents who want too much

September 4, 1983

I had gone to the 77-year-old woman's home after she had written a letter in which she said that she wanted to talk to me about "what responsibility children have to their parents—children who are about 35 or 40 years old and whose parents are between 70 and 80. Mostly, it seems to me, the sons with their doctoral degrees have forgotten the sacrifices their parents made to give them their opportunities."

But, as I interviewed the woman, it seemed apparent to me that she expected too much from her son, who is a faculty member at a Midwestern college. He and his wife visit her two or three times a year, and she visits them, too—and there are telephone calls. This wasn't enough for the mother, who said that she'd had "the whole cake"—her son's total devotion in his early childhood—and she wasn't about to settle for "crumbs."

As a mother, she had "given, given, and given to him, but now I'm supposed to be satisfied with what I get back," and it isn't fair. A child had an obligation to be geographically close to aging parents, even if it meant the child's changing jobs, the woman felt. Her daughter, the woman said, had remained close to her—but even that wasn't sufficient to soften the sting she felt from what she interpreted as her son's detached attitude toward her.

When I wrote the story, I expected that I would hear from many angry parents—angry because they'd gladly settle for the kind of relationship that the woman described as crumblike. But I wasn't prepared for the response that came—not only from parents but also from adult children who found in the woman's attitudes a resurrection of their own unresolved furies with their mothers and fathers. Here are some of the comments:

"The mother obviously has let her son know that she expects him to give love, attention, devotion, and respect—and that's why she doesn't get love, attention, devotion, and respect. I receive all of this and more from my six children ... because I don't expect it.... It is human nature to rebel against handing out affection on demand. My mother expected me always to react the way she wanted me to, not the way I felt. Consequently, we were both very frustrated in our relationship. I was 40 before I could tell her how I felt. She listened. When she stopped looking for love, I was able to give it."

"I wish you could have interviewed the woman's son. I'll bet that you'd have gotten a very different story. Perhaps one day, you could interview a discontented parent and then interview the offspring. Many older parents, I think, would fear hearing they are possessive, demanding, overdependent, and manipulative.... Wasn't it Robert Burns who said, 'If we could only see ourselves as others see us?'"

"For almost 60 years I lived with the kind of mother that you described in the story. Nothing I ever did for her was enough, and for so long I was hounded by guilt. When I finally overcame my guilt, I found that it was replaced by rage—rage that a mother could do this to a son she said she loved. It helped me to read your story, to realize that it happens to other people, too, that I'm not alone. But it fanned my rage, which I hope to heaven I'll be able to put to rest some day."

"The question that your column asked was: What do children owe their parents? The answer is that they owe nothing. They didn't ask to be born. I had them because I wanted them.... I am now a 65-year-old widow, and I live alone. I know where my children are, and they know where I am. I don't bother them, and they don't bother me. We are all individuals, with lives of our own. We are the best of friends. We all love one another, but we do not smother. We give room to breathe, but at the first sign of trouble or need, we all flock to the side of the troubled one. This is not because we 'owe' anything but because we have a bond, a love that is free and unrestricted, with no strings attached."

"My husband gave his mother much love and affection—and he still does, with twice-weekly visits and nightly calls. And he keeps her home in good repair, too. And guess what. It's not enough for his mother. She actually wants us to live with her. Nothing ever can be enough for this kind of person."

"Manipulative parents often find that they have manipulated their kids into moving clear across the country to get out of their reach. Love and obligation are two different things. It's a pity that more parents don't understand the distinction."

"It's 5 A.M., and I got out of bed to reread your column, which rekindled my anger toward my own father. Why doesn't this woman you wrote about take the initiative and contact her son—instead of complaining about what he doesn't do? Why doesn't my father call me? He, like the woman, seems to feel the total responsibility for maintaining the relationship rests with the child. My father slammed the door in my face last week because he hasn't heard from me in three weeks.... He willingly admits that he made no attempt to call me, but yet he feels justified in his anger that I don't keep in touch....

"My husband is disabled, and I work two part-time jobs. I also take care of the house, the lawn, our children. But if I say 'Dad, I've been busy,' I'm told that I'm a crybaby.... I never miss your column, but I wish to God I'd missed this one—because it just refreshed all the hurt that my father has dished out for so long."

"I'd like to give parents like the woman you wrote about a good shake and tell them it's time they gave their lives new purpose, because their children are not their children anymore, and they should stop seeing them as children. Their parenting days are over, and it's time that they stop making their children feel guilty for not being able to be with them as much as they'd like. It's a grossly unfair demand to expect one's children to continue to need you as a child when they are adults...."

"My mother-in-law lost her husband when he was only 42. She had three children, and she felt so guilty about not being able to give them the best of everything that she would not eat to buy them a party dress. And now she expects the world in return. That's very unfair to her kids, and because she's so demanding, you never can do enough for her—and those things she's done for you as a child are always thrown up in your face.... Giving should come from children and parents with joy and love as the motive, not repayments or guilt."

"I am a senior citizen now, and long ago I decided that I would love my children so much that I would never pressure them in any way to spend time with me. I asked nothing—and I got nothing. Yes, maybe some crumbs, but the crumbs were all. When I'm invited, I feel that it's a duty invitation, and when I'm called, I feel it's a duty call.... For eight months, I have not had a visit from a son who lives half an hour away—not even when I was hospitalized."

"In this day and age, it astonishes me how so many mothers cannot cut the apron strings, especially from their sons. Why are so many women so possessive? I am 68 years old, a widow, and I have two sons, 35 and 32.... If they don't remember my birthday or Mother's Day, who cares? Am I so shallow and empty that I have to have a card to get me through the day? No, indeed, I had the joy of holding them in my arms, experiencing the ups and downs of child-rearing—the fun we had, the places we visited, the things we did. We are friends."

"I loved my mother, but she was domineering. I was 58 when she died, and I was still her little girl. If I stood up for myself, I was sassy. Sometimes I really hated her.... My sister could never shed a tear for my mother's death. To this day, 10 years later, I can still see my sister looking at mother in the casket and saying quietly: 'There was a bitter woman.' How true.

"My children do not owe me anything. They enriched my life. All they have to do is to be good parents themselves and help others when they can."

"My husband and I know that the tighter you try to hold a child, the more the child will fight to be free.... There are two things a parent can give a child—roots and wings. Parents who put unreasonable demands on grown children only create their own destiny and could lose them completely.... Our greatest legacy is knowing that our children are well, living useful and fulfilling lives, and are good human beings, whether they be around the corner or 3,000 miles away from us."

"Your story about the woman made me realize how fortunate I am to have parents who turned me loose, with love and encouragement. I hope that I will be able to do as well with my own children. I really believe that the best parenting is the parenting that gets children ready to leave—and that shapes them to be independent."

"I saw myself, as a mother, in that story you wrote about the bitter woman. I didn't like what I saw, and I hope it's not too late for me to change. I'm 74, and change isn't easy at this age—or at any age, I suppose. But I'm trying. I called my son, and when he asked why, I told him it was because I wanted to tell him I loved him ... not because I wanted anything from him. That's a start, don't you think?"

A close look at depression

December 11, 1983

The icy facts look like this:

In their lifetimes, 25 percent of all females and 12½ percent of all males in North America will experience a "significant depression." Fewer than one-fourth will be treated, according to psychiatrist Layton McCurdy.

At any one time, 6 percent of the population is in the grip of a major depression, the cost of which, in human terms, is "incalculable when we consider the misery and pain, the impaired family life, divorce, and child abuse that frequently are associated with depression."

Up to 15 percent of those whose depression goes untreated ultimately will commit suicide.

Sixty percent of all Americans see depression as a weakness rather than an illness. It's because of public opinion "and the many faces of depression that most cases go undiagnosed and untreated," McCurdy said.

Finding out more about the causes of depression and what can be done to combat it is the goal of the Dave Garroway Laboratory for the Study of Depression, which is targeted to open in the spring of 1985 at The Institute of Pennsylvania Hospital in Philadelphia.

McCurdy said the laboratory would carry the name of Garroway because of the television personality's "concern with mental health and depression ... which added much to public awareness of this illness." Garroway, who had to cope with depression himself, lived in the Philadelphia area before his death in 1982.

"Work will emphasize discovery of new knowledge of the biologic and psychosocial factors believed to be linked to depression," McCurdy said. "The outcome of this research will be shared with physicians and their patients across the United States, giving the laboratory promise of an important national mental-health mission."

McCurdy, who holds a faculty appointment as clinical professor of psychiatry at the University of Pennsylvania, is director of the psychiatry department at Pennsylvania Hospital and psychiatrist-in-chief at The Institute, which is the hospital's psychiatric branch.

In an interview, McCurdy said one facet of depression on which the laboratory hopes to shed light is this: Why do females, who in adolescence suffer from depression at the same rate as males, have in adulthood depression twice as frequently as males?

Well, what are some possible answers, doctor?

One answer might be that women are more inclined than men to seek professional help. Thus their numbers appear with greater frequency in the statistics because their cases are reported—while men suffer in silence. If this is true, then it's possible that women don't have more depression than men.

But a more realistic approach, said McCurdy, might be to examine "psychological and cultural factors that perhaps weigh more heavily on women ... and that might put women at higher vulnerability" for depression.

What kinds of factors?

"Women [historically] have been cast more as dependent persons, put in a role of [relative] helplessness.... And we know that feelings of helplessness foster depression.... It's possible to conclude that women's greater vulnerability to depression comes from the social and psychological roles that women are assigned.... The laboratory will be an opportunity for us to start with depressed people and look backward" to try to find some of the answers.

McCurdy said three "environments" must be considered in trying to isolate the causes of depression:

• The internal-biological environment. "This is what we get from our genes," and it's a fact that people inherit a predisposition for depression.

• The internal-psychological environment. "This comes from our life experiences." Whether or not we become depressed hinges to some extent on how we perceive these experiences and react to them.

• The external environment. This is what goes on in the world around us, and it needs to be studied carefully—especially where loss is involved. Why? Because loss seems to be a major contributor to depression.

McCurdy said these three factors "begin to interplay" to create depression, and part of the research will be to determine, in individual cases, "how much water each of them has put behind the dam."

For a long time, it has been known that depression could be caused by environmental factors and by chemical imbalances in the brain, but it's apparent now that it's not an either-or situation. Usually, both are involved because one influences the other, McCurdy said.

What this means is that a traumatic environmental experience, such as the death of a child, can trigger chemical changes that relate to depression. On the other hand, he said, chemical changes can alter the way a person perceives the environment so that events that once wouldn't have been traumatic are now seen as shattering and debilitating.

On top of that, he said, depressed people often have to deal with a society that responds not with understanding but with well-meaning but ill-chosen suggestions like: "Come on, buck up; pull yourself out of this." It's as if society thinks that the lifting of depression can be willed. But it doesn't work this way.

In explaining that the social environment can lead to biological changes, McCurdy said he had participated in what he called "a short, dumb experiment" when he was at the University of North Carolina in the early 1960s.

"We had some lovebirds, and we found that if you put one in a cage, it will live happily.... If you put two in a cage, they'll pair up and live happily, and it doesn't matter if they're both males, both females, or one of each. If you put three in a cage, two will pair up and the third will die. Why? Nobody knows, except that there's an impact on the biology" of the third lovebird, presumably because it's left out and lonesome.

A longer experiment that was by no means dumb took place about the same time, McCurdy said, when grieving, depressed parents of leukemia-stricken children were studied. "Blood was drawn from each parent up to and through the death of the child ... and for a time afterward. Constantly the researchers found changes in the endocrine system of all parents. In those who recovered from depression, their biology went back to normal. But in those who stayed depressed, their biology stayed the [altered] way it was."

It amounted to proof positive, McCurdy said, that trauma can profoundly influence the body's chemistry and create deep depression.

It's normal for everybody to feel depressed at times, McCurdy said, but feeling depressed is vastly different from being depressed. It's a matter of severity and duration. For clinical depression (that is, depression that requires treatment) to be diagnosed, at least four of these symptoms must be present for weeks:

- Poor appetite or significant weight loss—or increased appetite or weight gain.
- Sleep difficulty or sleeping too much.
- Loss of energy; fatigability or tiredness.
- Objective evidence of psychomotor agitation or retardation.
- Loss of interest or pleasure in usual activities—or decrease in sexual desire.
- Feelings of self-reproach or excessive or inappropriate guilt.
- Complaints or evidence of diminished ability to think or concen-

trate—such as slowed thinking or indecisiveness.

• Recurrent thoughts of death or suicide—or thoughts of wishing to be dead or any suicidal behavior.

It's important to stress, McCurdy said, that in clinical depression some of these feelings must "be sustained for weeks.... In serious depression, there usually is no relief from these feelings, although some people can get away from them for brief periods. Some drink to escape the feelings, to create temporary periods of euphoria." This, he said, is why depressed people sometimes become alcoholics.

Matching the depressed person and the treatment
December 12, 1983

Let's play make-believe. It's 1993, and psychiatrist Layton McCurdy is looking back on almost a decade of work at the Dave Garroway Laboratory for the Study of Depression. What accomplishment does he feel best about?

"It's a dream come true—our finding a more accurate, faster way to determine the right combination of treatment for each patient."

You can be sure, said McCurdy in an interview, that this really is make-believe stuff today, in 1983, because, even though medicine knows a lot about what causes depression, much of the treatment is trial and error, because there presently is no way to be certain which patient will respond most favorably to which treatment.

Finding a reliable way to match patient with treatment indeed would be a dream come true, said McCurdy, because it positively could influence the lives of millions of Americans, up to 25 percent of whom will suffer from a significant depression at some time in their lives.

McCurdy is director of the psychiatry department at Pennsylvania Hospital. It is expected, McCurdy said, that the laboratory will be involved in "an important national mental-health mission," since research results will be shared with physicians and their patients across the United States.

Depression, said McCurdy, is "like a fever" in the sense that depression can be caused by any number of underlying problems, from genetic predisposition to environmental loss to chemical imbalance. Somebody who is predisposed can be knocked into a major depression by forces that might cause another person to suffer no more than a bad day or two.

Taking a complete family history is a first step toward diagnosis, McCurdy said, because family history sometimes can reveal genetic predisposition for depression.

A family-history interview might go like this:

"Has anybody in your family ever suffered from depression?"

"No."

"What about alcoholism?"

"Well, I had an uncle with an alcohol problem."

This, said McCurdy, will cause the interviewer's ears to perk up because there is a high correlation between alcoholism and depression. Why? One reason is because some depressed people drink heavily and frequently to achieve the euphoria that can temporarily alleviate their depression.

"OK, so much for that. Any suicides in your family?"

"Well, yes. My grandfather committed suicide."

This, said McCurdy, is another strong indicator of possible depression because studies suggest that 15 percent of people whose depression goes untreated ultimately kill themselves.

The interviewer also would look for "some sort of loss" in the life of the depressed person as a way to explain the depression. "Loss often is a precipitating factor ... the death of somebody who is important to you.... Loss is a powerful thing to cope with, not necessarily a death but the loss of a job, the loss of preferred self-image, the loss of a part of the body."

For a long time, said McCurdy, medical people have been aware of the numbers of women who became depressed after undergoing mastectomies. "But somebody can lose a finger and become profoundly depressed, too.... The doctor may say: 'Look, you only lost a finger; you're lucky because you could have lost your life.' But it doesn't matter to the person who has lost the finger. There can be profound depression," and understanding this is a crucial step in deciding how to treat the depression.

Basically, there are three methods of treating depression:

• Psychotherapy. This is talking therapy, and it definitely can influence, in some people, the chemical imbalance that is at least partially responsible for the depression. It also helps some people cope with the environmental trauma that has triggered the depression.

• Pharmacology. This involves the use of drugs to balance the chemistry. Insight into the effect of drugs on depression is at least 30 years old. One breakthrough came when doctors who treated patients with tuberculosis noticed that those patients who had not only tuberculosis but also depression became less depressed. Another breakthrough came when doctors who used a certain medication to reduce high blood pressure found that in 15 percent of the cases the patients became depressed. What was happening, McCurdy said, was that the tuberculosis medicine was increasing a critical substance in the brain, but the high blood pressure medicine was depleting that substance.

• Electric shock. This treatment has gotten plenty of bad press, and it definitely has been overused in the past. But, said McCurdy, it's a "viable and effective treatment ... for the appropriate person." Electric shock corrects chemical imbalance—but nobody knows exactly why or how.

Who is the appropriate person for electric shock treatment?

"Those who are profoundly depressed, those who are older, those whose cardiac status might make some of the [chemical] treatments too risky, those who have been unsuccessful in trials with two kinds of antidepressant medication, those who clearly are suicidal and there's no time to wait for two weeks while you find out if the drug works."

How does the attending physician decide which treatment to use?

Right now, said McCurdy, it usually comes down to one of these approaches:

• Trial and error. The physician begins with the treatment that is least likely to cause problems and "works from there until something useful occurs."

• Reliance on intuition. It's incredible, he said, how some physicians have a knack of sensing the approach to use, "and often it's right."

• The fitting of the patient to the treatment of the physician. This is something that makes people like McCurdy bite their fingernails, but it's true that some doctors do what they're best at doing—rather than try something else that might be more beneficial to the patient. Thus an analyst will analyze the depressed patient, a pharmacologist will try drugs, the advocate of electric shock will get out the little black box.

Is it any wonder, asked McCurdy, that finding a way to match patient and appropriate treatment is one of the laboratory's primary goals?

Programmed for failure
December 13, 1983

It is, the psychiatrist was saying, a contemporary Catch-22—a no-win situation that snares some people in a revolving-door jailhouse from which escape seems not only impossible but also undesirable.

What classically causes these people to cry out for help is this: They are miserable because they have not achieved the goals that they have set for themselves. It's an unusual situation for them to be in, because they are bright, aggressive people who tend to know what they want and how to go about getting it.

So what's the problem? Have they programmed themselves for failure with impossible goals?

No, the psychiatrist said, the goals aren't impossible. The problem is that the people won't allow themselves to reach the very goals for which they claim to be striving. Why? Well, that's the Catch-22.

"They fear that if they ever reach their goals, they'll lose their overdrive," their ambition, their frenzied race to climb over the bodies of their competitors and plant their flag at the summit. So they sabotage themselves—either by doing things that make it impossible by an eyelash for them to succeed or by redefining the goal so that it's always just outside their grasp.

The result: They're miserable about their "failures" but presumably secure, on some level, in the knowledge that they have not diluted their ambition by achieving their goals.

Crazy?

In a way, yes, it surely is. They've painted themselves into a corner with no way out—except with the eventual understanding, through therapy or bursts of insight, of what they're doing to themselves and why.

But in another way, is what they fear really so crazy? Isn't their fear of success and resulting loss of "overdrive" somewhat understandable? Can't many of us identify with it—at least a little bit? Don't many people who achieve their goals tend to get fat, lazy, and dull?

There's no question, the psychiatrist said, that for the most part, we try harder when we're hungry than when we're well satisfied. That's why so many of us were committed to running always in the fast lane early in our careers—but why some of us now put the gearshift in neutral from time to time, idle our engines, and enjoy the scenery. This doesn't mean that we're any less serious about our work; it means that we've reached the point at which we know that career achievement isn't everything and that there's another side to life, the side away from the grindstone.

Happy, well-adjusted people set realistic goals, pursue them with appropriate vigor and rejoice when the goals are met. Then they arrange new goals—and the process of achievement begins again. They do not fear that success will diminish unreasonably their appetite for more success.

Like everything else, it comes down to self-acceptance, somebody's knowing that he is more than the sum of his successes, that he is worthwhile because of who he is, rather than because of what he has done.

If that's not a definition of maturity, what would you call it?

•

And speaking of happiness, do you know many happy people?

Do you know many people who are genuinely satisfied in their marriages?

Well, it occurs to me that how you answer those questions may tell you more about yourself than about other people.

In my previous life, when I was struggling to make it without knowing what "it" was, I was not happy and, strangely enough, I seemed almost never to meet happy people. In fact, most appeared to me to be just about where I was—hanging on by the fingernails.

In my previous life, when I was struggling with a marriage that wasn't working, I seldom met people who seemed to be in solid marriages. In fact, most appeared to be in marriages that were mired down every bit as deeply as mine.

But then a strange thing happened: As I got my ducks in a row, I discovered that other people seemed to be making progress, too. Now, it appears to me, I am in contact everywhere and every day with people whose baseline of happiness seems reasonably high and reasonably stable. They're not always dancing with glee, but generally they're satisfied. If you ask how things are going, even on a rotten day, you'll likely hear something that amounts to this: "Life is good."

I also find so many people who are thoroughly happy in their marriages, people who aren't nagged by chronic discontent, who cherish their good fortune in being in a relationship of equality, who don't have to or want to play games or tell lies.

What I'm seeing, of course, is a reflection of myself and where I am today—just as what I saw back then was a reflection, too.

Yes, the psychiatrist said, when you're unhappy, when you're in a failing marriage, you tend to be unable to perceive in others little except unhappiness and marital distress. To view anything else would be too threatening—because it would impress upon you in spades the desperate nature of your own situation.

It's really true, he said, that misery loves company—but the flip side of that is just as true: joy begets joy. So if you want a reality check on how you're doing in life, you might take a look around at how you perceive others are doing.

Does the psychiatrist see many happy people?

Yes, he said, there are a lot of happy people out there—and don't ever let anybody tell you otherwise.

What do happy people tend to have in common?

Two things, he said:

• They have a sense that what they're doing—occupationally or personally—has meaning, that it affects others in positive ways and that the world is a little bit better because they're here, that they matter.

• They are in relationships that they treasure, relationships in which what they put in and take out are essentially equal. "I can't imagine a

happy adult without a good relationship. I'm not talking just about somebody to sleep with; I'm talking about somebody to share with—on an
intimate level."

The fear of public speaking
December 19, 1983

Because I average about 50 speeches a year, I long ago desensitized
myself to the discomfort, sweaty palms, and fright that once engulfed me
for days—and sometimes for weeks—before a scheduled appearance.

But I still remember vividly how horrible it was and, in talking with
other people about public speaking, I am reminded constantly of how
widespread the fear is. Somebody, it's said, once took a poll that showed
public speaking to be the number-one fear of most people—far greater
than crashing in an airplane or developing cancer.

What can be done to help people who don't speak often enough to
overcome their fears through confronting them regularly, people who
get invitations—or orders—to speak two or three times a year?

I put that question to Arnold Zenker, who is among the forerunners
in an emerging field that is known as "image making." Zenker, whose
firm, Arnold Zenker Associates Inc., is in Boston, has made a name for
himself by working mostly with corporate clients who pay him big
bucks to come in and teach their executives how to do their very best
when they give speeches or appear in television interviews.

But in his just-published book, *Mastering the Public Spotlight*, Zenker,
who is a graduate of the University of Pennsylvania's law school, aims
not only at executives but also at the man and woman in the street, those
among us who may never appear on TV but who, at one time or another,
may have to face the Rotary Club, the men's club, or the sisterhood.

Zenker's advice to "amateur" speakers: Get selfish—like the pros—
even if it means that you may appear to be something less than the nice
person you consider yourself to be.

"If you're selfish, you get to the room early. You find out where
you're expected to stand," and if you don't like it, you demand that the
position be changed. "Sometimes they'll set up the lectern in a place so
that the only path to the bathroom is right in front of you. Be fussy, selfish about the room setup. Demand what you're comfortable with....
You hear always that Barbra Streisand is a real — about her appearances. But if things don't go well, she's the one who pays the price.

Nobody blames the director or somebody else. So she demands what works for her, and she gets the reputation for being difficult. But she's simply looking out for her own interests. You should, too. The difference between professionals and amateurs is that professionals look out for their own interests."

Some other tips from Zenker:

Don't speak too long. About 18 to 20 minutes is the most that any speaker can hold an audience's attention—"unless you're Don Rickles. I've never heard anybody say that a speaker sat down too soon." So say what you have to say in 18 or 20 minutes and then quit—even if you've been asked to talk for 30 or 45 minutes.

Talk only about things that you're qualified to talk about. "They may ask you to talk about television in the 21st century. What do you know about that? Probably nothing. So say one line about it and then swing into what you want to talk about. No audience ever slavishly followed your assigned speech topic" and was disappointed when it wasn't adhered to.

Don't try to write a new speech each time. Instead, rework previous speeches, taking blocks of material from several to get the "new" speech you want. "This is what causes the amateur a lot of grief. It's hard for anybody to shape new material." It's far easier and quicker to alter what you already have or to borrow from the speeches of others.

Find out where you are to appear on the program and, if you don't like the position, demand that it be changed. "A problem for the amateur is that he doesn't even find out who else is on the program. You want always to go on before a blockbuster speaker—not after. No matter how good you are, you'll look bad by comparison if you follow. Don't go on the program at 4 P.M. At 4 P.M., the audience is on the way to the airport or to the bar. Don't go on the program right after lunch. We don't have a formal siesta time in this country, but people in audiences, after lunch, sleep with their eyes open—during your speech. It's better to speak at 10 A.M. than at 9 A.M. Why? Because at 9, they're straggling in with their coffee. By 10, they have their eyes open."

Don't give in if you're following other speakers who have run long and the program chairman asks you to cut your speech short. "Smile and then go ahead and say what you intended to say. It's not your fault that the others talked beyond their time. The question is: Were you a hit or not? If you're a hit, everything is forgiven for a program that ran late. If you're a flop, it doesn't matter if the program ended on time or not because you were worth nothing. You need to learn to be a star; it's important."

A primary step in learning to be a star, Zenker repeated, is demanding to have things your way. "The amateur wants to be polite, and he's surprised when the performance is lousy. The pro wants the performance to be good, and he's not so interested in being polite."

Zenker is a great advocate of tape-recording each speech and then playing it back "while you listen with a glass of wine or something. You can hear if it's good or not. Nobody has to tell you," although good speakers tend to solicit feedback because their feeling, which Zenker shares, is that "nobody is good enough to make it without outside input. To the extent that you can, you need a 'producer,' somebody who'll tell you if it's too long, too serious, too slow, too fast. You need opinions."

What about conquering stage fright?

One way is to "have your material cold. Know what you're going to say and how you're going to say it. Practice, practice, and then practice some more. Say the speech out loud, say it into a tape recorder. Have it videotaped, if you can. If that's not possible, practice in front of a mirror. Make certain that your facial expression matches what you're saying. If you're telling the audience how glad you are to be there, don't have a frown that makes it look as if you're headed to a funeral."

Another way to combat stage fright is to have control of the audience, Zenker said. "The amateur thinks the audience is in control, but the pro knows that he's in control." A tried-and-true way to gain visible control, he said, is to "say to somebody in the audience: 'Will you come up here, please?' After that everybody else is cowering and thinking: 'OK, God, not me; I'll be nice.' After that you've got complete control. But really you're in control anyway—because you know everything that's going to happen and the audience doesn't."

What if the audience isn't responsive?

A speaker needs to examine his material and presentation, Zenker said, to determine whether anything is wrong. "Sometimes you just bomb," and you have to figure out why. But sometimes it's an audience that nobody could turn on—not even Don Rickles. When that happens, it's a good idea "to take your money and run. You do the best you can, and if that's not good enough, you smile, cut the speech short, and leave."

1984–1986

Reaching out from isolation
April 1, 1984

After she had yet another argument with her boyfriend, Maggie felt that she was engulfed by more emotional pain than she could endure.

"I didn't want to take it anymore.... I was very upset, but I was very rational, too. I knew exactly what I was doing."

Maggie checked into a Philadelphia hotel, went straight to her fifth-floor room, and slit her left wrist with a razor blade that she carried in her handbag. She would have bled to death—no doubt about it—because the wound was savage. But miraculously, someone found her in time, because there had been some kind of mix-up in registration at the front desk and they needed to get in touch with her.

•

The loneliness crushed Ralph because it never left him—even when he was surrounded by people, as he often was.

"I felt isolated ... because people tended to leave me. To me that meant only one thing: They didn't care anything about me. This created unbelievable depression and loneliness. I almost jumped out the window. There was nobody in the whole world I thought I could count on."

•

For John, the episodes of depression lasted far longer and were much more debilitating than the times when he was manic.

"When I felt severely depressed, I wouldn't shave, wouldn't eat with anybody, wouldn't get out of the house. This was the most gut-wrenching time for me ... because I felt totally without hope. What was the use ... of living?

"But in the manic phase, which often brought on destructive behaviors for which I might be jailed, I felt in control.... I'd get pushy, overly loud, and have delusions of grandeur. But I did get control of my life. All pieces of the puzzle fit. Maybe the Mafia or Christ was protecting me—that's how delusional I was—but all of the uncertainties were taken care of."

•

In the dark times of her life, June lost job after job because she couldn't get along with anybody. Her response typically was to pull the blinds, unplug the telephone, go to bed—and pretty much stay there ... for days, even weeks.

"Occasionally, a neighbor would knock and ask, 'Are you all right?' but sometimes I wouldn't even answer. I just about gave up on outside contact. I'd get up at 1 in the afternoon, watch the TV soaps, take my Valium, and go back to sleep. I'd never see a soul."

What was the payoff for June?

"I wanted to get very sick ... so I could take my husband to court to prove that I was disabled. It was mismanaged thinking—very mismanaged."

•

Twice before, Bob had "attempted" suicide, but the efforts, he admitted, were feeble. "I didn't really want to die; I wanted somebody to pay attention to me."

But this time he was serious about it, and he wolfed down enough pills to stagger an elephant. He sat there in his tiny apartment, waiting to die, and then he noticed his cat, watching him intently.

"Who will take care of my cat if I die?"

Frantically, Bob dialed the number of the Suicide Prevention Center but, he would say later, nobody there took him seriously. "I couldn't convince them that I was for real, that I'd really tried to kill myself. It almost was comical. I was saying, 'Yes, I did,' and they were saying 'Oh, come on now.' We talked, and finally I convinced them. They sent a van to my place and took me to the hospital, where they pumped out my stomach.

"God, I love my cat."

•

Twice a week, sometimes three or four times, Maggie, Ralph, John, June, Bob (not their real names), and others like them ride the elevator to the fourth floor of what is called the "main building"—that's a polite way of saying that it's very old—at Thomas Jefferson University Hospital.

For at least six hours every week, they are among friends, and in the process of nurturing these friendships, they often discover that which has escaped them for a lifetime—how to receive love and how to be lovable.

"If you've never known what it's like to be loved, it's hard to receive love," said psychologist Frances Grabosky. "It's hard to know what love looks like. But with the support that comes from here, they begin to understand what it's like ... and then they're able to look for relationships in which they can get more of it. What we do here—when we're effective—is get very involved. Our involvement is a form of love, and it's perceived that way."

Grabosky is director of the Jefferson Evening Program, which is attached to the university's department of psychiatry and human behavior and which is described as a "comprehensive group-oriented psychotherapy program for adults." What makes the program different from other therapy groups, she said, is that "people can get a lot of support, enough so they effectively can use therapy."

She's aware of nothing else like it in the nation, she said, and routinely, when professionals hear about it, she is contacted and asked: "Hey, what are you guys doing?"

What Grabosky and staff are doing, she said, is trying to help people mend their lives of quiet desperation—lives that for the most part are marked by unbending isolation.

"Yes, isolation is a common factor. They experience life as not being cooperative. They tend to have no existing supports in life to get them through the times when the rug is pulled out from under them," Grabosky said.

She is not talking necessarily about building social skills. "A lot of these people—almost all of them work during the day or go to school—have better social skills than I have. They've been in and out of relationships. But they create problems while they're involved with others, and this is why they're alone.... They tend to be less able to form intimate relationships. This program provides something stable. They see the same people every week.... They have the same problems with relationships here as on the outside, and they begin to understand why."

Average stay in the program is two years for people "from difficult family backgrounds," Grabosky said. For less troubled people with "uncooperative lives," the average stay is from six to nine months. Most are in their 20s and 30s, she said, and while "they come with serious problems, they also come with great strengths, too. At times, a lot are high functioning ... and in responsible jobs. But they experience intermittent crises.... They may lapse into depression, and their lives start to fall apart. After that they struggle to re-enter, to re-establish relationships, and to be seen as capable."

As part of the program, Grabosky said, participants become therapists to each other in group therapy, in which feelings of isolation often come out. "People are able to get a sense of what they do to cause the isolation. They only get feedback [from group members] when they ask for it, and we teach them how to give feedback. The rule is that feedback is appropriate only when it comes from love and concern."

The long and short of therapy
June 10, 1984

Back in the early 1950s, Peter E. Sifneos underwent psychoanalysis—not because ghosts from the past were rattling excessively in his closets but because experiencing analysis would be an important part of his training as a psychiatrist.

It was, Sifneos would say, "a learning experience for me, a marvelous educational tool. I learned a lot about myself.... but I didn't need analysis. I functioned well without it."

It occurred to Sifneos that a good many people with emotional problems probably didn't need psychoanalysis either to get back into the groove of life—but the fact was that many of them were getting it anyway.

Why?

Because it was what the doctor wanted. "With many psychiatrists there is a kind of perfectionism.... If they help solve one problem, then there's sometimes the feeling, 'Oh, the patient needs me to solve other problems,' and that's what leads to longer treatment."

Longer treatment tends to be vigorous treatment—"it means coming in four or five times a week [for years] and saying what's on your mind. It's difficult [physically and emotionally], and not everybody is able to do it." But unfortunately, said Sifneos, some who are "incapable of facing it" are led into psychoanalysis—and the results not infrequently are disappointing to everybody.

There had to be a better way.

•

A better way for many people, said Sifneos, is short-term psychotherapy, which he has studied since 1956. It sometimes can be completed in six or seven weeks, and the longest time that he ever has treated a "short-term" patient was six months. The results of short-term therapy can be uncommonly good, he said—and of 78 patients in one research group "only five, we felt, had not been helped. They didn't get worse; they essentially were unchanged."

Obviously, the key to making short-term therapy work is in the selection of the right patients, and it was the evaluation process that Sifneos focused on most heavily in an interview while he was in Philadelphia to speak at a meeting of the Pennsylvania Society for Clinical Social Work.

He is professor of psychiatry at Harvard Medical School and associate director of psychiatric services at Boston's Beth Israel Hospital. He is the author of two books—*Short-Term Psychotherapy and Emotional*

Crisis (1972) and *Short-Term Dynamic Psychotherapy: Evaluation and Technique* (1979).

"One thing that is most important is to understand that short-term therapy is not viewed as a kind of quick, magical answer to psychological problems. It has a place with a selected group of people.... It doesn't apply to everybody," but Sifneos estimated that at least 65 percent of patients might benefit.

Sifneos said the ability "to select people and to know the situations when it's appropriate to use short-term therapy" is critically important in determining the success or failure of the therapy. In other words, he said, treating the "wrong" person would result in the same outcome as appendix removal for somebody who has not appendicitis but pneumonia.

Who is a candidate for short-term psychotherapy?

Sifneos listed these two guidelines:

• Somebody who has "the ability to choose one area of difficulty even if he has several, assign top priority to it, and resolve it with the help of a therapist."

• Somebody who understands that the outcome of the therapy won't necessarily bring about any improvement in any of the other areas of difficulty. But the good news on this point, said Sifneos, is that "we find that many patients who are able to resolve problems in one area then are able to utilize what they have learned from the therapist and solve the other problems" on their own.

One key to making short-term psychotherapy work is the patient's ability to "learn certain ways of associating emotional problems with the source," said Sifneos. What that means is that the patient is able to understand that how he reacts today may be influenced greatly by experiences from long ago.

Another key is the therapist's ability to focus in quickly on the right stuff as the heart of the problem. The first interview, said Sifneos, is "a diagnostic interview ... and often a pattern can be seen clearly." This interview normally takes 45 minutes, and with a highly skilled therapist the appropriate diagnosis is made 75 percent of the time, he said. "In more complicated cases, where some things are not so clear" a second diagnostic interview must be scheduled.

People who tend not to be candidates for short-term psychotherapy are those whose problems seem more pervasive, those with "severe difficulties in interpersonal relationships over and over—with their parents, siblings, schoolmates, those who are fearful, withdrawn, isolated, who have difficulty in assessing reality."

Listen as Sifneos offers a sample case that is tailor-made for short-term psychotherapy:

"The man comes in with anxiety and mild depression.... But as he talks, it's obvious to me that it has something to do with his relationships with people. He talks some more ... but gives no evidence of anxiety with women, with his mother or sisters.... But when his father comes home, his stomach sours and he's not hungry.... I see the anxiety as a symptom, the tip of the iceberg. My job is to find out what's under the water."

As the diagnostic interview progresses, Sifneos homes in on the man's relationship with his father. Yes, that's the key that unlocks the riddle of why the man has difficulty with male authority figures. He has lost several jobs because of this—and it becomes apparent that today's problem stems from yesteryear's struggles with his father. So let's go back to those struggles....

As therapy continues, Sifneos watches for "tangible evidence of change" to indicate progress. He finds it rather quickly, when the man tells him: "Well, for the first time I confronted my boss over a new office. I told him that I deserved a new office, and do you know what? I got it. I couldn't have confronted him before—because I was scared of him."

This, said Sifneos, amounts to major change. "His old fears of dealing with authority have loosened. If he has other problems, well, now he knows how to track his difficulties. He knows the techniques" for helping himself, and Sifneos would terminate treatment, confident that the man could make it the rest of the way on his own.

How do traditional analysts react to the short-term concept? Do they consider it a bandage rather than a cure?

Yes, some do minimize it, said Sifneos, who is trained as a traditional analyst and who describes himself as a "card-carrying member" of the profession. But the criticism doesn't bother him. "They can't say to me, 'Oh, if you only knew ...' because I do know."

Physical health and mental health

July 1, 1984

Murray Klein, in the passion of a touch football game when he was 8 years old, got into a slugging match with the boy who lived next door.

Horrified neighbors rushed in to break up the fight, but they were stunned when Klein's mother charged out of her house and shouted: "Leave them alone! He's got to learn to fight his own battles!"

The neighbors backed off, and the two boys continued to punch away. Klein can't remember if he won or lost the fight. What he does remember is that in the long run he won—won the game of life—and for that he eternally is grateful to his mother.

•

Murray Klein was born 34 years ago with cerebral palsy, which left him with partial paralysis on his left side. Nobody knows for sure why it happened, but speculation is that it was caused by a ruptured artery that deprived his brain of enough oxygen during his mother's 30-hour labor, which was ended by a physician's decision to deliver by Caesarean section.

He was introduced early to the confusion of the real world, he would say. When he was 6, his mother sought to enroll him in a school for handicapped children. They went before the review board, which rejected the application. The reason: Murray Klein "wasn't handicapped enough."

But as he went through school, it became apparent to him that he, indeed, was handicapped enough. In fact, he would say, it was more than enough.

"I started to realize that I had no peer group, that I wasn't accepted by anybody, that I was the target of some ridicule" because he walked with a limp and had limited use of one arm.

His parents were exact opposites in their treatment of him, he would say. "Dad was overprotective. But Mom insisted that I stand on my own two feet. 'You'll have to do it some day because I won't always be around.' That's what she always told me."

She also told him not to pay attention, not to give other kids the satisfaction of provoking his anger when they taunted him with cries of "Hey, gimp! You're a retard!" But it was difficult not to react. Sometimes it was impossible.

For Murray Klein, high school became a time to forget.

In college "it really hit me like a brick wall—that I had no peers, nobody to talk to. There's something for kids and adults who are handicapped, but nothing for adolescents, nobody for them to listen to, to find out what a normal adolescence is like. I felt, by the time I got to college, that I was five years socially retarded.... I was pretty much of a loner. I felt rejected. Was I really rejected? I don't know, but that's what I felt. I don't know what's going on in other people's minds. What I do know is that I felt I never had any teen years. I had to go from high school to adulthood....'"

At Delaware Valley College, where he transferred from nearby Philadelphia Community College, an unusual thing happened: Murray Klein found some friends—in a most unusual way.

"It was in January, and icy, and I was walking to class, and I slipped and fell. I hit my head and my glasses flew off. These two guys came up and picked me up. I found that they lived two doors from me at the dormitory."

In a way that was the beginning of the beginning for Klein, who learned that there can be nice people, even in what sometimes can be a cruel, cruel world.

He zipped through college and during those years came in contact with an orthopedic physician who got him interested in medicine. Klein was accepted for admission to Philadelphia College of Osteopathic Medicine, where, at first, he struggled—not just to make his grades, but to maintain his dignity.

There was the day when another student confronted him after a pathology class and snarled: "What are you doing here? You're taking the place of a 'normal' student."

Klein, enraged and bitter, "almost hit him. But I didn't, and I'm glad. Later, I heard this same student say that he'd never care for charity patients because there wasn't any money in it for him. He was that kind of person," and anything he said had to be considered in that context.

In 1977, Klein was graduated. He completed his internship at Westchester General Hospital in Miami, and then he served a three-year residency in physical medicine and rehabilitation at Thomas Jefferson University Hospital in Philadelphia. Murray Klein was on his way to becoming—well, in 1982 he was appointed assistant professor of physical medicine and rehabilitation at the college.

He was back home, in a sense, and he was working hard to make life a little less difficult for handicapped children and their parents.

Their parents?

Yes, said Klein, parents tend to feel guilty because their child is handicapped—and sometimes the guilt can be so severe that it blots the joy from their lives. They feel that it's their fault, that they somehow are responsible for the handicap. Even his own mother, for all her strength, had to wrestle with the guilt, said Klein.

"Last year was the first time Mom admitted that she felt guilty for what happened. She'd spent years in parents' groups, but this never came out. Then I asked her straight out, 'Did you feel guilty?'—and she said 'Yeah, really guilty, for ever so many years.'

"Now when I get a cerebral palsy child here [as a patient], I send the child out of the room and talk to the parents: 'It's not your fault. Did anybody ever tell you that.' And the answer almost always is, 'No, nobody ever told us that.' Parents can work through the guilt issues, but doctors have the responsibility for telling them early that they're not responsible—and for guiding them to proper places to get help."

Some other points made by Klein:

In the last year he knows of five handicapped students who dropped out of college as seniors. Why? "Fear of the outside world. In a way they're protected in college and, if they graduated, they wouldn't be protected any more. So they quit school to postpone their confrontation with the cruel world.... It's a fact, you know, that we, as handicapped people, perceive the world as extra cruel."

While parents of handicapped children often feel guilty, healthy sib-

lings also tend to be burdened with guilt—"because they're healthy. What happens to the handicapped kid when the parents are gone? They [the parents] often try to make the healthy sibling feel that he's ultimately responsible. This stifles more relationships [between siblings] than you can imagine."

He recently was married, but dating always was a "big stumbling block for me. I felt rejected, bitter. But I wouldn't let that stop me. I felt that I couldn't take the blame for somebody else's decision. My advice to others is to keep trying until they finally succeed. Most go for it. But a few don't, unfortunately. A few carry the bitterness for a lifetime."

He sees extremes in parenting of handicapped children. "Some are overprotective; some don't give a damn. They drop the kids off at camp and they're gone. They never visit. When camp's over, they have to be called and told that it's time to pick up their kids."

His 26-year connection with the Philadelphia Variety Club's summer camp for handicapped children has been a love affair from the very beginning. He was a camper for eight years—"It's a chance for kids to be peers with everybody else"—and later he served as a counselor, administrator, and camp physician. It's not possible to put a price tag on the value that comes from the camp, which remains one of the primary causes for which Klein crusades.

Health and denial
July 12, 1984

It may be hard to believe, but it's a fact, said psychiatrist Daniel Lieberman: Studies over the years have documented that at least 50 percent of patients don't comply with their doctors' suggestions, orders, and prescriptions.

Why? What's the point of seeing a doctor if you're not going to pay attention?

There are lots of reasons, said Lieberman, and one of them is poor communication. "You don't understand what the doctor wants, so you can't do it.... Another reason is fear. You get a prescription, and somebody says: 'Didn't you read about what happens if you take that medicine?' So you don't take it."

But a major reason for noncompliance—and perhaps it's the major reason—is denial, said Lieberman, who is acting chairman of the department of psychiatry and human behavior at Philadelphia's Jefferson Medical College. "If you don't do the things that you're asked to do, then this means that you don't have the illness. Of course, the ultimate denial is not coming to see the doctor at all when you're sick. This means that you're not sick."

I was about ready to tell Lieberman that nobody in the ballpark would exercise the "ultimate denial"—but I didn't say anything because it would have amounted to flailing myself. You see, I am a true-blue denier—or at least I used to be—and the last time, about a year ago, I almost needed a mortician more than a physician by the time I checked into a hospital. Why did I deny that I was sick? What was the payoff? It sounds crazy, since I was running a high fever, but daily I persuaded myself that I'd be better tomorrow, and this continued, even though tomorrow never arrived.

What about that, doctor? Isn't that silly?

Yes, it's silly, said Lieberman, but he, himself, has been guilty of it, too. "You convince yourself that it's just a passing thing that will go away.... People are able to do this because people tend to consider themselves immortal. This changes when you see your friends and relatives dying, when you see changes in yourself—the wrinkles, the balding, the paunchiness.... But earlier in life feelings of immortality are very prevalent. They're not expressed this way—'Hey, I'm immortal'— but it's always the other person to whom bad things happen."

Strangely enough, said Lieberman, there are times when denial can be beneficial to health. "There were studies a few years back at Massachusetts General Hospital on people who were hospitalized from heart attacks.... What they found was that the people who were depressed after their heart attacks had a death rate that was more than twice as great as those who denied the severity of their heart attacks....

"Those in denial, those who said, 'It's no big deal; it's really nothing,' well, they had a much greater chance of survival. But there was a turnaround later, if their denial persisted to the point of their not modifying some of their behaviors, if they didn't stop smoking, get reasonable exercise, follow a sensible diet. They died later at a greater rate than those who had acknowledged the severity of their illness" and revamped their lifestyles.

But there is no question, said Lieberman, that in the beginning denial was helpful in getting people through a critical phase.

Why?

"I don't know, but my guess is that with depression, certain biochemical changes take place and predispose somebody to another heart attack. You can see the same thing in cases in which the body's immune system is affected by depression. In a program here, we found that men who were widowed and who responded with depression were more apt to die of something than men who weren't depressed. It has to do with the immune system."

The healthiest way to face illness is not with denial but with conviction, said Lieberman—the conviction that "this is severe, but I have the resources to overcome it. I have my faith, and otherwise I'm in good health." This has all of the benefits of denial and none of the liabilities. However, he said, conviction tends to be in shorter supply than denial, which is a strong defense mechanism and which many of us clutch in hard times—even if we aren't consciously aware of what we're doing.

"The theory is that when we're faced with something we can't deal with, we deny it. In that sense it's an unconscious mental mechanism.... We also can faint if we can't deal with something, and we can project: 'This didn't happen to me; it happened to somebody else.' But denial is very common, and sometimes it's a saving mental mechanism."

What all of this shouts at full volume is that without question our mental state can influence the course of disease, said Lieberman. "How and under what circumstances we can't be sure ... but any mechanism or technique that allays anxiety or reverses depression has to be helpful" in strengthening the body's fight against illness.

For years, this has been a cornerstone of Texas radiologist Carl Simonton's treatment of cancer patients—the philosophy that meditation, relaxation, and mental imagery can play vital roles in battling disease. Sometimes cure results, but even when this doesn't happen, quality of life tends to be elevated and often life is lengthened.

Lieberman said that he has "seen miraculous things—like the disappearance of cancer. I can't explain it, but I've never pooh-poohed it, because I've seen it. What happens? Nobody knows, but probably it's the same mechanism at work. Through prayer, faith, meditation, mind control, whatever, the immune system is affected, and the disease process can be reversed."

It doesn't always work this way, but when it does, it truly is a miracle.

Reaching for something extra
August 7, 1984

It was a few springtimes ago, and I was talking with psychologist Philip Bobrove about how to handle the crunch times of our lives, when adversity stalks us like a shadow and breathes ice into our souls.

"Something bad happens, and you're forced to get back inside yourself ... and gain greater self-appreciation," Bobrove said. "You become deeper and more thoughtful. It's a popular myth, but it's often true.

"You have to face [adversity] because it's there.... An artist loses his arms and he goes on to paint with his teeth. In the depths of depression, he cries out: 'What the hell? What am I going to do—lie here and die?' Yes, some do die, but others find a way to paint."

Coming to terms with the reality of hard times and battling to survive seems to be "a quality of a basic sense of OK-ness. How else can I put it? It's a base to tap into.... You have to come to it yourself—as others have. Literature is replete with people who in despair searched their insides for something meaningful to live for.

"When I was younger, I thought it could be done by group support. Now I'm older and I think that you need a place in a group, but they can't do it for you. You want them to, but they can't," and it's up to you, alone, to search for your core.

Most people have that basic core of strength—their OK-ness—from which they can summon support when necessity demands it. "Sometimes the only way to tap into it is when bad things suddenly happen to you.... This core of OK-ness seems to transcend religion and ethnic background ... and there may be no sense that it's even there until you have to have it."

This is "when it dawns on people that the only one who can say that you're OK is you, that the rest [of the people] don't matter.... As you get older ... you don't care so much about how others judge you. You can say: 'I am who I am, and that's it.'"

•

I thought about Philip Bobrove and the core of strength when I interviewed retired Army Col. Charles W. Scott, whose book, *Pieces of the Game*, recounts his 444 days as a hostage after Iranian terrorists overran the American embassy in 1979. In reading the torture scenes described in the book, it seemed obvious to me that Scott had been able to tap into his core not just to survive but to survive, in his words, "with style."

What advice did Scott have for people who were hearing the count of nine and struggling on wobbly legs to rise again?

"I'm not a psychologist, but I know that some people won't ever turn on the afterburner ... and maybe it's because they don't realize clearly the extent of the crisis," he said. "I knew that my test in Iran was the toughest test that I'd ever have to pass. If I signed a 'confession,' it would not be a simple little thing. It would be magnified in the media all over the world."

He recognized the terrible scope of his crisis, Scott said, and perhaps this recognition is the first step for anybody in igniting the afterburner.

"You take somebody who's lost his job, somebody who feels that he's 'only' part of the mass of unemployed. Well, maybe he won't feel the same flow of adrenalin that I felt in Iran. Maybe it's harder for that person to muster strength than it was for me." Maybe it's easier for that person to accept the bad news as the luck of the draw—rather than to fight back.

"The way to turn on the afterburner is to understand self-esteem and integrity and what they mean to you: 'I have no job today, but I have skills. This is a temporary setback. It may take time, but I'll find a job, and these hard times now will give me strength later on.'"

Scott said he believed that willpower could become "a floating line" in hard times—and this is why some people, under the gun, will do things that they normally wouldn't do. In anticipation of torture, Scott sought to nail down his willpower by contracting with himself to live up to some goals from which he would never deviate—among them not writing any "confession" or revealing anything that would embarrass the United States or put his fellow hostages at higher risk.

It worked, Scott said, even though in pain and torment, his willpower cried out to be set free from the contract. It's a plan that he advocates for anybody in a crunch—to establish areas of no compromise: "I will not take just any job; I will not be panicked into settling for less than is reasonable to expect."

If there is a bright side to all of this—and there is, said Scott—it's that without doubt adversity builds strength, and people who are able to look at it this way are people who have the inside track on winning the long battle. Hard times and good times, he said, offer the "contrasts that make life worth living" because each, in combination with the other, promotes its own kind of growth. But without the contrasts, neither is worth anything—not even the good times.

"We love oysters in our family. When I came back from Panama not long ago, I brought 80 pounds of oysters. But after a while, we'd had enough," and not only did they not want any more oysters but they also didn't much appreciate the ones they'd just consumed. That's how it is with much of life, said Scott.

"If you've always had tremendous affluence, it doesn't mean much of anything" because there's nothing with which to contrast it. "I've had C-rations in the field and strip steaks at the club, and I love them both. I love the diversity....

"When I was an attaché in Iran, I dined with ambassadors and generals. The next year I was in the field in Vietnam and worrying about saving my life. People ask, 'Which did you like better?' and my answer is that I liked them both because they're both part of life. From both, I gained strength ... much more than if I'd spent my whole life in fat city, living high on the hog."

Scott said that some of his views had been "telescoped because of my experiences.... In Vietnam, I saw so many die, yet somehow I was allowed to live, and this gave new meaning to my life.... What happened in Iran magnified this more. Some say, 'It's a lousy day,' but I say, 'Hey, you don't see it as I do; to me it's beautiful. This could be the most important day of your life.'

"I'm not a religious nut, but I do have a strong faith," and this, said Scott, helped him survive not only Iranian imprisonment but also other crunch times—his divorce a year after his release and then the death of his mother last year.

"Sunrises and sunsets have never been more beautiful, and I'm still mesmerized by the line where the trees meet the sky.... My faith in God is stronger than ever, and I look to the future with my customary romantic optimism."

What workaholics have in common

September 17, 1984

The year was 1975, and Marilyn Machlowitz was beginning her research into workaholism—its causes, costs, and cures.

The more she talked with people—workaholics and those who rubbed shoulders with workaholics—the more she became convinced that six basic characteristics set workaholics apart from everybody else.

They are intense, energetic, competitive, and driven. Their zest for life is overwhelming, Machlowitz found. A workaholic banker told her: "I have a tremendous amount of energy.... My father says Con Ed should have plugged into me during the energy crisis."

They have strong self-doubts. While workaholics "appear assured to the point of arrogance, they secretly suspect that they are inadequate," Machlowitz said, and "no matter how undeserved and/or suppressed these suspicions are, they still inspire insecurities. Working hard can be a way of concealing or compensating for" real or imagined shortcomings.

They prefer labor to leisure. What workaholics do for a living, Machlowitz said, "has evolved into an endlessly fascinating endeavor. They have no use for and little need of free time. They find inactivity intolerable and pressure preferable." Never in a coon's age would a workaholic thank God because it's Friday.

They can—and do—work anytime and anywhere. A securities analyst told Machlowitz: "I'm forever thinking about new companies and new industries and, to a degree, this puts me in my office 24 hours a day."

They make the most of their time. For workaholics, "killing time" is akin to committing suicide, Machlowitz found. "The quest to conquer time is constant. They glance at their watches continually."

They blur the distinctions between business and pleasure. Said one workaholic: "I don't think of work as any different from play. I mean, I do enjoy it—I'd rather do that than anything else. I'd rather do that than play—at anything else." As a result, Machlowitz found, the professional and personal lives of workaholics tend to become intertwined—and virtually impossible to separate.

Over the years, as she interviewed and consolidated her notes, Machlowitz concluded that she had not only material for loads of magazine stories, which she wrote, but also for a book. That book, *Workaholics: Living With Them, Working With Them*, was published in 1980 and has been called "the first formal study" of the concept of workaholism, which today has been written about by almost everybody.

In gathering her material, Machlowitz, who has a doctoral degree in psychology and who runs her own consulting business in New York, interviewed dozens and dozens of workaholics, including me—even though by that time I had figured out the price I'd paid for that craziness, had done what amounted to a 180-degree flip, and had become what I considered a nonpracticing workaholic.

As an aside, another person she interviewed for the book was Dick Vermeil, who was quoted this way: "I don't actually know what the word [workaholic] means, but I am tired of its being used in describing my personality. I do what I'm doing because I enjoy it very much and really don't consider it hard work."

This is the same Vermeil who, when he resigned in 1983 as coach of the Philadelphia Eagles, said: "I am emotionally burned out.... What leads to burnout is giving so much to try to do your job that you lose perspective in terms of how many hours you should sleep and how many days of relaxation you should include in your monthly routine.... It's a weakness in my personality."

In an interview not long ago, Machlowitz reflected on her research into workaholism and how it logically had led her into her current book, *Whiz Kids: Portraits of Success at an Early Age*, which will be published this fall. Has anything happened in the intervening years to change her attitudes about workaholism?

As a matter of fact, she said, what has happened since way back then has tended to validate her research and, from that standpoint, the book is as current today as when it was published. If anything has changed, it's that workaholism is more widespread now—and one reason may be that technology has beckoned seductively to many to become workaholics.

"Computers, portable telephones, and everything else ... well, they've made it easier to work more of the time. They all aid and abet workaholism.... In the past, the home influenced the office. But today the office is more dominant. Kitchens look like laboratories.... The living room is the office, and the bedroom houses the computer terminal."

When she first started studying workaholism, Machlowitz said, the term mostly was applied to men. But the worm has turned and now people "tend to think I mean women when I talk about workaholism."

Why?

It's the old psychological rule, she said: "If a man and a woman do the same thing, the man always will be judged less harshly. So society is more disparaging in its view of women workaholics, more critical of successful women."

Are women set up to become workaholics because of the widespread belief that they must surpass men in all areas to be considered equals?

There may be a good bit of truth to that, Machlowitz said. But women need to ask whether they have to be like men. Do they have to dress like men? Read sports? Tell jokes? Do they have to put on a masculine strait-jacket? It may be that some women feel that, yes, these things are important to their success, Machlowitz said, but they can be freed to a great extent if they realize that they "don't have to wear a typical feminine straitjacket. They don't have to be Betty Crocker. Now it's OK to say 'Hey, I don't do windows.' They don't have to feign dumbness . . . and technological phobia."

In other words, she said, even if women adopt some of men's craziness, they can shuck some of women's traditional craziness and not end up as floundering superwomen.

Many of the domestic problems that tend to be blamed on women's workaholism really should be blamed on other things, Machlowitz said.

"You have two busy career people and a small child, and so you discuss the woman's work hours. Maybe the problem is not really her work hours, but the fact that there's not enough household help or the right kind. Maybe her commute is too long and that's the problem—not her attitude about work."

What do you think?

Can women have it all?

October 18, 1984

It's a fact of life in 1984 that as more two-career couples emerge, more problems emerge, too, and this has brought about the development of a new specialty in marital therapy—treatment of conflict in dual-career marriages.

A University of Wisconsin psychiatrist, David Rice, quoted in *Success* magazine, said that the struggle for power was often the most serious problem for marriages in which both husband and wife are heavily invested in careers.

"Competition to achieve outside the marriage can be constructive," Rice said, "but competing for control within the marriage is destructive. In most families, it is still the man who earns the higher salary. That has traditionally meant that the wife defers in decisions and expects little help from her husband in ... domestic chores. But when both have careers that they consider important, decisions must be made that do not consistently favor one partner over the other, regardless of income. When this doesn't happen, the woman may feel victimized and resentful."

Rice, who wrote a dual-career clinical guide for therapists, said that men "may rationally agree that their wives should have equality in the relationship, but on an emotional level they may still feel rejected if they believe they are playing second fiddle to her career. The prevalence of high-achieving career women is new, and most men have not had working mothers. They have no role models to follow and often inwardly feel deprived of some of the supports they expected to find in a marriage."

●

While men may holler about playing second fiddle, career women may complain about the unfairness of their near-solo performance around the house.

No, said Philadelphia psychologist Suzanne F. Scott, that's not really true. It would be healthier if women did complain, but often they don't—at least not directly. What so many tend to do is go ahead and shoulder most of the load in sulking silence—or try to manipulate a better deal.

"There still is an unequal distribution of labor [at home] and it comes down to a question of how assertive the woman can be if she needs help," said Scott in an interview.

But being assertive "always has been a problem for most women. That's why you see stridency in the feminist movement. It's the natural course of non-assertive people who are learning to be assertive."

Many women who are neither assertive nor strident grit their teeth and play the Superwoman role to the hilt. "After a hard day's work, they'll come home, make dinner, clean up the kitchen while everybody else is watching TV." Then they may even do the laundry and vacuum a carpet or two.

Sometimes they try to sneak in a little something for themselves by using the back door of manipulation, said Scott. "Instead of saying, 'Hey, I'm too tired to cook; who's going to help me?' they'll say something like 'Wouldn't it be nice if we all went out to dinner?'" The problem with that is that the husband and kids may say they'd rather eat at home and watch TV. After all, it is less expensive and not really that much trouble—for them.

Even when husbands are willing to share some responsibility, said Scott, it's most often the wife who "gets stuck with cooking, most of the marketing, maintaining the inside of the house, with the child care. The husband so often says, 'She understands the children better than I do'—and it's left up to the woman," who somehow buys into the deal that it's her duty.

Is the woman's response to this overload typically to pull back on her career and conclude that she really can't succeed to the extent that she had hoped?

Sometimes this is what happens, said Scott, but a woman who doesn't succeed "can't blame it on her husband—not if she wants it badly enough. She has some options."

Options?

Yes, said Scott, and one option is for the woman to "learn to articulate what she needs. This is a common failing of women. We can ask for what we want but it often is so difficult to ask for what we need."

If the man doesn't respond positively to that, said Scott, the woman must be prepared to "tolerate the possibility of divorce. Is what the woman wants that important? If it is, and if her husband finds it unacceptable when she communicates it to him," then divorce surely becomes a down-the-road option to be considered, if counseling doesn't help them reach some middle ground.

More and more career women are finding that they've been sold a bill of goods about being able to have it all, Scott said. Many were swept into it because they had been programmed by their parents to put a priority on being wife and mother and by the feminist movement to storm the corporate towers. When they found that they couldn't have it all, many were disillusioned—and either retreated to the "safety" of the home or forged ahead madly in business, even if that meant abandoning the home.

"A woman [who is trying to be Superwoman] needs to ask why she is resentful," Scott said. "Is it because the husband won't help with the dishes? Or is it because she's tired and doesn't have enough stamina to devote to her many roles?

"A woman has a right, a responsibility to take care of herself. If she doesn't take care of herself, she resents it. She needs to communicate her feelings to her husband"—without causing polarization.

But the news is far from all bad, Scott said. Despite the inherent problems, many two-career couples are in thriving marriages. "This is a generation of pioneers who have few role models and must and can forge their own.... It is exciting that there are new ways to choose."

Saying good bye at life's end
October 28, 1984

She is fully aware of what is happening, Rosara Berman said, and "I have put my house in order. I've talked with my sons, with my daughter-in-law, with my husband. I'm not afraid to die."

There was the conversation with the older son, Mark, who is 29: "He had such profound grief. He told me that I had provided him all his life with a voice of reason, a voice that told him, 'Hey, step back and examine this in a different light; don't go off half-cocked.' His fear was that this voice would be gone. I asked 'Where is the voice coming from?' I tried to tell him that the voice was inside him, that it came from him—because he's me. He can have the reason, hear the voice always, without me."

There was the conversation with the younger son, David, who is 26: "He told me he loved me. It was a very hard thing for him to say. He told that I'd been such a good mother to him. His grief—much of it—was because the woman he eventually will meet and marry won't know me, won't have the experience of being part of this family as it is now.

"He helped me a lot, David did. With everything that's going on, he spent a night with me at the hospital, just the two of us alone. He said, 'Aren't you angry? I'm so angry, Mom—so angry that I want to scream and yell. You lie here day after day. Aren't you angry?' It allowed me to be angry, to yell and scream, to get out my anger. In his wisdom, he was able to do that for me."

With her daughter-in-law, who is due to give birth to Rosara Berman's first grandchild in January, the conversation went to how they felt about each other. "I love her so much, and she told me how much she loved me, how much she appreciated the closeness we've always had."

With her husband: "He said he'll miss me so much, that I was a voice for him, that I put reason into unreasonable situations. He said that I'll always be on his shoulder.... I hope that's not true. A time comes when you have to put things to rest and go on with life. He will; he's very strong.... He doesn't want me to suffer. I'm hooked up, out of control—all the things I don't want to be. He cried last night. I cried. We cried together.

"... I never realized how many lives I'd touched, how many people I'd helped. I'm in constant amazement—at how people come, friends and family. The support is beautiful. But even with the love and support, I feel lonely and isolated. No, not lonely, but alone and separate, different. If I didn't have this outpouring of love and support, I don't know what I'd do. I don't know how people face it without love and support.

"I've worked with families in this position, and I thought I knew something about what it was like. But it's not really possible, not until you're in it yourself."

•

At age 50, Rosara Berman got her bachelor's degree from Antioch University and at 52 her master's degree from Bryn Mawr College. She became a social worker/therapist at the Jewish Family and Children's Agency of Philadelphia. At 53, in the spring, doctors told her that she had a rare form of cancer that inevitably is fatal and that she had six months to a year to live.

"First I asked, 'Why me?' I asked what I had done, why I was being punished. But then I asked, 'Why not me?' I'm not immune. It's going on all around us.... Look at the statistics: One in four will get cancer. So why not me? When tragedy befalls you, it's what you do with it that's important. It's how you react."

•

It was so many years ago that she met Buddy Berman, while she was a student at New York University. She followed what was then a rather standard life script for women: "I got married, had children, got involved in community affairs. I always was busy ... but the idea of going back to school never left me. I didn't want to be a volunteer always; I wanted to be a professional.

"Buddy was never threatened. He always was secure in his own identity. He encouraged me. He never minded on weekends when I had to cancel our plans and go to the library.... We had such grand plans."

•

Last December she began to feel bad—because of what she assumed to be a renewal of a years-long battle with gastrointestinal problems. "The doctor checked me out but couldn't find anything.... Then I put myself on the back burner because Buddy was going in for surgery. It was strange. He was operated on in March, and I followed him by a month—in April. I'd gone to the gynecologist.... He told me that I had a tumor, a tumor that turned out to be cancerous. It was a rare, bizarre kind of cancer—Krukenberg—not even exotic. The prognosis was bad. They gave me six months to a year."

The physicians laid it on her, just like that?

"I felt it was my body. I wanted to know all the facts. I wanted to know the options, the kinds of alternative therapies that might be available. They were trying to rush me into chemotherapy, and I didn't want that.

I pushed the doctors to the wall. Under different circumstances, I think they would not have given me this information. But I need to have control; I pushed them.

"I said, 'Look, you've got to have a scenario. You must have faced this before. What happened to the other people who had it?' It wasn't difficult for me to push them because it's my nature to be confrontive. And so they told me.... They weren't able to tell me if chemotherapy even would help or not. At most, it would be palliative."

She began to work with psychologist Clorinda Margolis, who uses hypnosis and mental imagery in treating cancer patients. She examined alternative therapies, and "decided to go the nutritional route. I went to a doctor in Toronto.... Essentially it was a vegetable diet, 75 percent raw. I felt better. I did yoga, walked six miles a day, practiced hypnosis, imagery ... and I flourished."

In the mental imagery, she viewed her cancer as jellyfish, of which she always has been fearful, and the exterminator of the jellyfish as E.T., of whom she long has been fond. "That really worked for me. I went to the beach in June, and the jellyfish appeared, and I wasn't afraid. I stomped them."

But in late summer, Rosara Berman "started to get some pain. They told me I had adhesions from the earlier surgery. They tried to open the blockage without surgery, but it didn't work. So they rushed me to the hospital ... and I think now that this is what blew me away. They opened me up, and there was no sign of cancer. I was clean.... We had a victory celebration. It was marvelous."

But the joy was brief. "Two weeks later, in a checkup, they took some tissue samples and found some cells that they couldn't immediately identify." When they did identify the cells, they found them to be cancerous. Krukenberg was there, in all its ugliness.

"When the oncologist told me—the same oncologist who'd told me two weeks before that I was clean—I felt like I was on an emotional yo-yo.... From there on it was sort of downhill.

"I started chemotherapy. I never thought I'd sign the form. It was like somebody else's hand was signing the form. But it was mine, I who was so adamantly against it. I did it—because I was in pain, because I have a grandbaby coming in January. There's no guarantee I'll see the baby, but it's a goal of mine. That's why I'm doing chemotherapy.... I'm fully aware of what's happening. I have put my house in order."

●

Rosara Berman said that she can't ask for any more love and support than she is receiving from family and friends. "I just want them to be with me. If I'm down, I'm down. If I'm a little up, I'm a little up. I want them to be where I'm coming from.... There are times when I want to talk about my illness, but not all the time. I don't dwell on it.

"... There's a friend here from Arizona, a friend for 31 or 32 years. She came to visit. We've had a lot of quiet time we need together. We've talked about old times, when we pushed our baby carriages together. I need to reminisce, too."

She has "made known what I want to do in terms of my funeral. I've asked some women to be pallbearers. Is that macabre? They cried. I joked, 'Do you think you'll be able to handle it?' And they all, every one, said they'd be honored.

"... Faith helps. I guess I never really thought that much about my spiritual self. But I find more and more I have the feeling of 'Thou art with me,' that there really is somebody out there. It's comforting.... The rabbi asked the congregation to pray collectively for me, and it was beautiful. The rabbi came to the hospital during Yom Kippur and blew the shofar.... I feel very spiritual, very close to God."

Workshops for "pre-orgasmic" women

November 27, 1984

They sit in the room, the seven women, and the first thing they notice about one another, in the words of psychologist Talia Eisenstein, is that "they're all normal, just like everybody else.... There's nothing strange about them."

Some of them pack their briefcases every morning and head for their corporate offices. Others are housewives and mothers who, after everybody is off to work and school, scoot to their exercise classes or volunteer efforts. Some are in their early 20s; others are in their middle years.

In the beginning, they shift uneasily in their chairs, but Eisenstein and her associate, psychologist Patricia Fields, quickly begin to thaw the ice by acknowledging that uneasiness is a normal human response to the situation. Before too long, the women are talking comfortably, sharing without great difficulty what previously had been their deep, dark secret.

The secret: They never have achieved orgasm.

•

142

For three years, Eisenstein and Fields, both of whom trained at Hahnemann University's Van Hammett Clinic, have conducted workshops in the Philadelphia area for "pre-orgasmic" women.

Pre-orgasmic?

Yes, indeed, said Eisenstein in an interview. "They used to be called 'frigid' when they weren't sexually responsive or didn't reach orgasm. This term—pre-orgasmic—is more optimistic ... and not pejorative. It's also more accurate. All women can be orgasmic if they know how."

The aim of the workshops, which run 90 minutes a week for 10 weeks, is to teach women how to become orgasmic. What's holding them up? Isn't orgasm a natural function?

"A lot of people expect it to be natural, but it may not be," said Eisenstein. "It requires communication, an understanding of your body—and practice. If you've not learned about your own body, it's hard to communicate to your mate what you like" and what it takes for you to reach orgasm.

Sex researcher Alfred Kinsey reported more than 30 years ago that 50 percent of married women were not "consistently orgasmic" in their sexual relationships, said Eisenstein, and later studies "said about the same thing." Kinsey also reported that 10 percent of married women never reached orgasm, a figure that is believed to be accurate today.

What it means, she said, is that a lot of women need help if they are to realize their sexual potential. In increasing numbers, women seem willing to seek this help.

"A lot of women are taught to be attractive to men but not to be open sexually. Even women today in their 20s—women who supposedly are part of the liberated generation—tend to be affected by the message that while it's important to attract a man, it's also important not to go too far."

There are, said Eisenstein, lots of negative social and religious messages passed on to young girls—and a primary one is that it's sinful, evil, or undesirable to masturbate. "Not many parents anymore tell their children that it'll make them go blind, but the negative message about touching yourself" still is prevalent. Yet, she said, it is through touching themselves that children discover their bodies—which is a necessary step toward realizing their sexuality.

It's more difficult for girls than for boys to take this step, Eisenstein said. Why? "A boy grows up knowing he has a penis. A boy says to a parent 'What's this?' and the parent says, 'It's your penis.' But a little girl doesn't know that she has a clitoris ... because it's not seen and not talked about. I don't know any parent who ever said to a daughter, 'This is your vagina and this is your clitoris.' To hear parents talk, you'd think that between a girl's bellybutton and her knees is nothing."

Eisenstein said that a theme she encounters in many women who never have reached orgasm is that they come from backgrounds of "religious extremes" in which anything sexual tends to be viewed negatively.

"I'm not coming out against religion, but anytime you say that something is bad, it can be taken to an extreme. They say that 'you can't do something until ... ' But the problem is that if you're always told it's bad, a marriage ceremony is not going to change your feeling that it's bad. If you've never been allowed to explore yourself, which is the basis of sexuality, how are you going" to be sexual after marriage?

Eisenstein said that some women fake orgasm to keep their husbands happy. "Most enjoy the contact, and for some this is enough. It's not important for them to be orgasmic, but it may be important to the husband," and that's why they fake it.

Not having orgasm also can be a woman's way of "making the man not feel good about himself sexually," she said. "It can be a way to have power. The woman, in effect, says to the man, 'You can't make me enjoy it if I don't want to.' It's the one thing a woman has that is all hers. She can't have an orgasm unless she wants to."

The workshops seek to help women understand that "it's not up to the man to give an orgasm to the woman. It's something that the woman gives to herself—by being able to tell the man what she wants."

Some other points made by Eisenstein:

From 20 percent to 30 percent of women are able to reach orgasm "just from intercourse." For most women, additional clitoral stimulation is required, and it's difficult to dispel the belief among many men that "there's something wrong with a woman" who can't reach orgasm solely from intercourse. What makes the 20 or 30 percent of women different from the rest? "It could be the placement of the man's pubic bone, which is what the woman rubs against to achieve orgasm. All orgasms are the same—in the sense that all orgasms come from stimulation of the clitoris. It's a question of how a woman gets it."

Unlearning religious taboos that inhibit sexual functioning can be difficult "and some don't. But they may begin to learn to question them. If the clitoris was not intended to provide pleasure, why did God give you one? Because the clitoris serves no purpose except to provide pleasure. It's a question that tends to set religious women thinking."

The number of women who can't achieve orgasm because of organic reasons is so slight as to be insignificant. Some drugs and diseases can hinder orgasm, Eisenstein said, but it's generally safe for a therapist to proceed on the assumption that no organic problem exists.

A wife who for years "was quietly accepting but who now asks" for what she wants sexually can upset the balance of power in a marriage. "It depends on what the relationship was like beforehand," but for the most part marriages are better, not worse, when the wife becomes orgasmic.

Workaholics admiring other workaholics

December 13, 1984

The year was 1981, and Edward H. Kuljian, who once was chief executive officer of a Philadelphia-based corporation that designed and built power plants and industrial projects around the world, was saying that pressure to be a workaholic still abounded in corporate life.

"If you do the job well and lead a balanced life, but if a peer is a workaholic, then I'm afraid that the sentiment in the executive suite often goes with the guy who is there until 8:30 every night—even if your work is as good as his."

The reason for this, said Kuljian, is that corporations tend to be run by workaholics, who recruit people whose work habits mirror theirs and whose craziness validates theirs. "In some ways it's a bondage that pays extremely well. A boss tells you that he'll pay you twice what you're now making if you come to work for him. You say, 'That's great!' But the caveat is: 'Now that I own you body and soul, I don't want any nonsense when I call you at 2 in the morning. I don't want to hear about your going on vacation or planning a free weekend.' ... The consequences are horribly damaging to any family relationship."

In the months after that interview was printed—even today it's still mentioned to him—Kuljian heard from a lot of people, most of whom were "overwhelmingly positive. But several business executives scored me for it and said things like, 'You know, what you said was a rationalization for laziness. You're espousing a take-it-easy attitude, and we don't need that in industry.' But many business leaders told me what I said was true. And many wives [of business leaders] told me they wished their husbands would follow my advice."

●

Kuljian, 51, who heads his own management consulting firm, Edward H. Kuljian Associates, was saying the other day that two aspects of workaholism troubled him above all others:

• The "damaging effect" on other people. "If the workaholic's work style and temperament affected nobody else, that would be one thing, but it's what they do to those around them.... There's a workaholic I know, and his wife was left to do everything—from bringing up four or five kids to balancing the checkbook. She was on the thin edge, and she desperately needed a week in the sun. But, no, he couldn't take her to the Caribbean, because he had an 'important' appointment in Cleveland.

He left, and she came down with nervous exhaustion and was hospitalized.... I see things like this, and it's just not fair.... Now you extrapolate this to the work setting, where the official work time is 8 A.M., but everybody is told, 'We start serious work here about 6:30.' The message is 'You'd better be here by 6:30,' and on and on it goes. It's not only merit that earns points" but also willingness to abide by corporate policy that makes no sense.

• The "unfortunate" selection of workaholics as people to emulate. "Society seems to adopt them as role models. I see that as damaging, the crazy perception that unless you work yourself to a frazzle, forsake all recreation and family life, you're somehow being counterproductive to your own success.... We need to use as role models those who show the value of balance in life, who unquestionably work hard but who admit to enjoying balanced lives."

Sadly, those who strive for balance tend to be viewed as people who don't know what it's like to work hard, said Kuljian. "To hear workaholics talk about it, you'd think that we'd never worked 16-hour days. I've worked many—in Saudi Arabia, Nicaragua, and other places where the environment was hostile. I'm not afraid to do it—when it has to be done. But there has to be a reason. To blindly do it is a form of masochism.

"Whether you're a dentist pulling teeth or a coach watching football films all the time, it may be fun, but there comes a point at which productivity suffers if you don't back off and get involved in other interests.... But they stay at it, because it's 'fun,' they say, and I'm convinced that, once they're beyond a certain age, unless something traumatic or tragic hits them, they go to their graves with that idea, that it was fun ...

"They have money, and the wife and kids would love a cruise, a trip to Europe, a second home in the mountains. But they don't do it, then they fall ill, and life's over for them. That's incredibly sad," and what is equally incredible is that it happens to so many people.

Kuljian asked, "What is the definition of success?"—and then he wrestled with his own question: "Some success we can measure. When Salk finds a cure for polio, that's success. When we send a man to the moon, that's success. But it begins to get tenuous when we try to measure success in a career. You take a man who's a corporate chief executive officer with a high six-figure income. Is he a success? Is John DeLorean a success? Are you a success if you're alcoholic, if your wife divorces you, if your kids won't speak to you, if you have a heart attack, if you're alone at 50? Is that success?"

A problem with society, said Kuljian, is that anybody "who suggests contentment with what he has achieved ... is regarded as a loser. He's copping out. People say, 'Well, he's making ends meet, but who wants to use him as a role model?' The role-model thing bothers me. If you're making big dollars, if you achieve a huge takeover or get to the top spot, it's almost as if there's the feeling that nothing you can do is so damaging that it will impact negatively on you—if you are a 'success.'"

Is it possible for somebody with Kuljian's philosophy of balance to achieve full potential in corporate life? Probably not, he said, because the corporate position, spoken or unspoken, tends to be that long hours pave the only path to bigger and better things. "You're often scored if you take a vacation or even long weekends."

Corporate bosses, said Kuljian, "have a way of putting your vacation on hold forever. He'll say, 'Well, Ed, I realize you missed the summer, but you can take three or four weeks this winter. No problem.' But winter comes, and he says, 'Ed, I'm sorry, but we're in a crunch, and you need to be thinking about that vacation in the spring.' He keeps you waiting, and at some point you may have to get in a shootout with him....

"Life doesn't give you endless chances. The day comes when it is too late."

Kids and depression
December 16, 1984

The entry in the 18-year-old's diary is dated November 27, 1983. Here is some of what she wrote:

"I hate myself.... I am totally self-destructive.... I can't stop hurting me or the ones I love. I am sick. One minute I don't mind living and the next minute I think about ending it all. I keep on thinking about jumping, and I'm frightened. I thought about jumping three stories at Duke, but what if I live? I came up with another idea, and I think it might work. I can jump from an overpass, fall and get hit.... I could go jogging tonight after dinner and easily do it. But what if someone gets out of a car and stops me?"

From the next entry, a day later:

"I'm a bitch; I'm fat; I'm ugly, and I'm no good. I can't do anything right. I feel so sick. Why do I hate myself so much? Why am I so self-destructive? I am crying now."

The next entry, two days later:

"I feel awful, like normal. It looks like a regular day, and everyone's going about it like it was. I know it's not. I feel a little nervous inside, and my plans still are rather shaky. I'll do whatever comes to mind. I don't know where I'll go. I may travel. I just don't know. All I know is that tonight is the end."

•

No, the girl didn't kill herself—although she tried three times. She eventually became a patient of the psychiatrist who made her diary entries available to me, and, the psychiatrist said, the girl, through therapy, was able to stabilize her life.

The psychiatrist, Jean G. Spaulding, 37, who was the first black woman to be graduated from Duke University's medical school, practices in Durham, N.C., and she gets "many referrals" of suicidal children from family physicians and school counselors. Within the last year, she said in an interview, three students in the same regional high school killed themselves, and this has focused, as never before, community attention on what she described as a problem of increasing severity.

Why do kids want to die?

Spaulding, whose patients are 80 percent female and "mostly white," said it's not a simple question to answer, but essentially it shakes down to this:

"The kids are depressed, and depression causes their world to shrink. They feel as if they have no options. Their thought process is slowed down. They feel helpless and hopeless.... The nuclear family has disintegrated ... and they feel they have nobody to turn to. If you look statistically at emergency-room admissions—many of them are attempted suicides—you find that there's a high incidence of fathers who are away from home, either through divorce or business....

"In families that are intact, there is a high degree of mobility. I saw one child of 12 who'd been in 10 different schools.... and had no close friends....

"Young girls feel under pressure to be 'perfect'—in their preparation for career, marriage, and motherhood. At 12 or 14, they don't know how to handle it. Their parents have such high expectations for them—and for their sons, too.... The kids are without support systems or role models ... and many of them are serious about wanting to die. Fortunately, they don't always pick the most lethal way to do it.

"At 12, they think they can jump in front of a truck and 'it'll kill me.' So they start with a truck, a drug overdose ... or they slash their wrists before they progress to more lethal means. By the third attempt they have a gun.... or they drive a car into a bridge abutment....

"I think there are many more suicides than reported. It's thought that 400,000 adolescents attempt to kill themselves each year and that 6,000 are successful. But many of the deaths are hidden in accidents ... or for insurance purposes or to protect the families."

In the troubled young people who come to her, Spaulding finds many who are adopted, and this has caused her to conclude that disruption of the mother-child bonding process, even in the first 72 hours of life, can leave an imprint forever.

"Adoption seems to increase the sense of insecurity in some strange ways. 'If somebody gave me away, I must not be a good person.' I so often hear that. They perceive something bad about themselves. It never occurs to them that the mother was young, unmarried, and couldn't possibly care for a baby. But they have fantasies about it, like 'my mother was a middle-aged married woman who didn't like me. She had other children, but she picked me out as the one to give away.' That's so far from the truth. I happen to know who the mother is in this case—and she had no choice but to put the baby up for adoption. It was a supreme act of love."

Spaulding said one factor that triggers depression in children is the loss of "a loved one, usually a parent.... For parents who are contemplating separation or divorce, it's important for them to speak to somebody about the possible impact on their children. If the children feel closed off from seeing the parent who leaves, they can become depressed and begin to withdraw.... Divorce can be more upsetting than a death, especially if the level of hostility between parents is high, if one parent uses the child against the other parent. Then the child feels like a pawn, totally helpless."

The critical age for girls, said Spaulding, is 15 to 15½, for boys 14½ to 15. "This is in early adolescence, when they're most vulnerable to upset, when they're trying to establish their own identities, when they're going through physical changes....

"These are not marginal kids," the ones who try to kill themselves. "They're functioning at grade level or above. They're popular and involved"—until depression grips them.

Some of the early warning signals include:

• Withdrawal from peers. "They isolate themselves ... and often there are disturbances in their eating and sleeping patterns. They show up at school with dark circles under their eyes."

• Extreme irritability. "They fly off the handle at just about anything.... Small things upset them—like a minor argument with parents. At school, they don't participate."

About one month into withdrawal, said Spaulding, the children may become "absorbed in music out of the '60s, very depressing music. There's often a preoccupation with death and dying. Then they begin to give away their valued possessions—records, books, clothes. At this point they're very close to suicide ... and their mood usually has lightened. They've made up their minds to die."

The classic suicide attempt, she said, comes at home, during the evening hours, in January, February, or March, usually when somebody is in the house. "This shows the conflict. They want to kill themselves, but they want somebody to stop them. Why January, February, and March? Because this is typical for depressed people. For depressed people the holidays are very hard...."

"By the second attempt, the conflict is gone, and they want to succeed. Usually, it's done away from home, in isolation, with more lethal methods."

Therapy, which may include antidepressant drugs, involves "letting them know you care, that you're going to support them, that you're not going to allow them to hurt themselves," said Spaulding. "You do this in part by your manner. A lot come in with a chip on their shoulder, and you get them to relax, to talk about school. You start on the periphery and work in. 'Have you not been sleeping well, eating well? Have you thought of killing yourself?' Often they tell me frankly what they're thinking ... and agree to let me talk to their parents.

"I tell the parents, 'You've got to remove the guns, razors, and pills from the house.' It's amazing that sometimes parents don't want to get rid of the guns. I've never understood why....

"I try to help the children correct the sense of themselves as failures.... One of the problems is that these children take responsibility beyond realistic levels. They feel that they should be able to put the family back together and, if the family remains apart, they think it's their fault....

"With adopted children, I try to help them understand that their parents chose them, that they are special to their parents.... It's important for these parents to understand that they may need to spend more time than normal with these children, that this may not be the time for Mom to pursue her new career or for Dad to go off and work away from home. Sometimes you have to defer these things."

Forgiveness in a vengeful world

December 23, 1984

In the classic film, Shane finally can't take any more insults—and so he straps on his holster and guns down the bad guy in the black shirt. The audience goes wild.

In *Deathwish*, the pacifist architect can't live with the reality that thugs have killed his wife and brutalized his daughter—and so he declares war on the thugs of Manhattan. Again, the audience goes wild.

In the Kenny Rogers song, the coward of the county takes the rifle off the wall and goes after the brothers who have terrorized his wife. Presumably, listeners go wild—if record sales mean anything.

Everywhere, it seems, vengeance is cheered. You sock it to somebody who has it coming, and you're an instant hero. A pound of flesh. An eye for an eye. Is there any place for forgiveness in this world? Is somebody who is trying to peddle forgiveness swimming upstream at this time?

•

If forgiveness is your thing, said Lewis B. Smedes, you're swimming upstream all of the time. Why? Because forgiveness is "so damned unnatural," said Smedes, who is professor of theology and ethics at Fuller Theological Seminary in Pasadena, Calif., and author of the book *Forgive & Forget*.

"It's natural to think of getting even when somebody has hurt you.... That's the moral way. It's fair and just. Forgiving is suspicious, revolutionary, in violation of the moral order.... It comes down to the difference between justice and vengeance—a difference that's tough to digest. I never met anybody who sought vengeance who didn't think that he was seeking justice ... but vengeance is a desire for 'justice' to satisfy your own need for healing. 'I want you to suffer so I will have the satisfaction of knowing you hurt as much as I.' The problem with that kind of 'justice' is that it's a loser's game."

Why?

Because "if I seek the justice of equal pain, I'll never get it. In the pain game, I never get even because I, as the injured person, weigh pain on a different scale than the person who inflicted the pain on me. The pain is not quantified the same way, so I never get the satisfaction I'm seeking."

The only real satisfaction, in Smedes' mind, comes from wiping the slate clean with the act of forgiveness. This is what frees us from the pain of the past, and in that sense we clearly forgive others to benefit ourselves—not those who have hurt us.

What is the step-by-step process of forgiving?

According to Smedes, the forgiveness process is made up of four stages, and "if we can travel through all four, we achieve the climax of reconciliation." The four stages:

• Hurt. "When somebody causes you pain so deep and unfair that you cannot forget it, you are pushed into the first stage of the crisis of forgiving.... The hurt that creates a crisis of forgiving has three dimensions. It always is personal, unfair, and deep. When you feel this kind of three-dimensional pain, you have a wound that can be healed only by forgiving the one who wounded you."

• Hate. "You cannot shake the memory of how much you were hurt, and you cannot wish your enemy well. You sometimes want the person who hurt you to suffer as you are suffering.... Hate eventually needs healing. Passive or aggressive, hate is a malignancy ... it surely hurts the hater more than it hurts the hated. We must not confuse hate with anger. It is hate and not anger that needs healing. Anger is a sign that we are alive and well. Hate is a sign that we are sick and need to be healed."

• Healing. "You are given 'magic eyes' to see the person who hurt you in a new light. Your memory is healed, and you turn back the flow of pain and are free again.... When you forgive, you perform spiritual surgery inside your soul. You cut away the wrong ... and you see your 'enemy' through the magic eyes that can heal your soul. Detach that person from the hurt and let it go ... then invite that person back into your mind, fresh, as if a piece of history between you has been rewritten, its grip on your memory broken."

• Coming together. If the person you invited back into your life returns with honesty, "love can move you both toward a new and healed relationship. The fourth stage depends on the person you forgive as much as it depends on you. Sometimes that person doesn't come back, and you have to be healed alone.... You start over ... in the semidarkness of partial understanding. You probably will never understand why you were hurt. But forgiving is not having to understand."

What happens if we don't ever forgive?

Smedes said he preferred to talk in reference to himself. "When I don't forgive, I find that my resentment and hate get so mixed up with my pain. In not forgiving, I replay the painful tape over again ... and I let the person who hurt me once clobber me over and over again.... I perpetuate the pain, and I spread it to other people. I don't try to get even with the person who hurt me, but I make others the target. I become impatient with my children, surly, unpleasant with my wife....

"When I'm not forgiving, I feel so damned self-righteous. I never feel so virtuous as when I feel hurt," but that's a dead-end road because in the long run, it accomplishes nothing.

How many times should we forgive somebody who wrongs us? After all, even Shane could put up with only so much.

"I can't quantify it," said Smedes. "It's a huge mistake to think of forgiveness as an obligation. It's not a duty, not a way to be nice to the rotten person who's gotten us into this mess. It's a bad mistake to think of forgiveness as toleration ... or to equate forgiveness with putting up with stuff, with being a doormat.

"If we think of forgiveness as willingness to suffer, then that gets us into this kind of question—about how many times you can forgive somebody. But if you think of forgiveness, first of all, as a way to deal with yourself, to get freedom from the past, then the question changes in texture. How much are you willing to put up with and still maintain the same relationship with the other person?

"Any relationship has to have as a basis the element of truthfulness. When I forgive you, I remove the obstacle that you put in the way of our relating fully. When I forgive, do I welcome you back into my life? Only with the condition of truth, only if you're willing to be truthful with the fact that you hurt me, that you feel my pain, only if you're truthful with the future ... and make a believable promise that you don't intend to let this happen again.

"If I'm dealing with repetition of the hurts you give me, there comes a moment when I say 'Hey, we don't have truthfulness here, and if you clobber me again, we'll have to change the ground rules of the relationship.' And we may have to call it quits."

What if the person who is forgiven rejects the forgiveness?

That's the other person's right, and we must respect it, said Smedes.

"Some say that forgiveness is an act of arrogance. In a sense, it always is—because if I forgive you, it means I've already judged you.... It's the other person's freedom to tell me to flush my forgiveness down the toilet, to insist that he's done nothing to be forgiven for.... But I can't let the other person control my life, glue me forever to the past" by refusing to accept forgiveness.

"For me, forgiveness is a way to claim my right to be healed of pain that I didn't deserve in the first place."

Parent-child conflicts
January 15, 1985

A not-so-funny thing happened not long ago to psychiatrist Alan Summers. He was conducting a three-week seminar for parents on how to handle parent-child conflicts, and at first he was playing to a full house. In the second week, attendance slipped, and by the third week, 70 percent of the crowd was gone.

What happened? Was the seminar that bad?

No, said Summers, the seminar wasn't bad at all—but what he was preaching wasn't what parents were buying.

"They wanted to know how to control their kids, how to discipline, punish, and structure. They didn't want to hear anything about looking at themselves, their needs, and how their needs sometimes conflict with their children's needs.... I don't want to put all the blame on parents, but I do want parents to take at least 50 percent of the responsibility for the problems."

Accepting responsibility, said Summers, invariably goes to the point of self-examination—and determining what the real problem is. Quite often the real problem is not what everybody thinks it is.

•

Summers is medical director of the outreach program for Eugenia Hospital, a private psychiatric hospital in Lafayette Hill, and his job, in part, is to provide community education programs. He also has a private psychiatric practice in Wyncote, Pa. In an interview, he said that he's amazed by the similarity of problems faced by parents as their children grow up.

"In early elementary school, the children tend to be shy, not want to go to school, maybe hyperactive, afraid of the dark. By the middle elementary years, the children probably don't want to do their homework. They're messy, fight with siblings, show excessive aggression—or withdrawal.... In adolescence, they are defiant, disrespectful, perhaps achieving poorly in school ... or they're into experimentation with drugs and alcohol or sexual misbehavior."

The problems sound ominous—and indeed some of them are—but, said Summers, "with good instinct, parents often find remedies that work well."

How about some examples?

Well, there were the two brothers, 6 and 8, whose rooms were so messy that the parents were exasperated. But instead of going crazy and forcing the children at gunpoint to clean their rooms, they recognized that conflicting needs were at work. The children "needed" to be messy as a way to establish some control over their lives. The parents "needed" orderly rooms because ... well, isn't that the way rooms are supposed to be?

Their solution bordered on genius, and it went like this: A contest would be held each Sunday to determine which child could most totally mess up his room, and the winner would get a special treat for dinner. But to qualify for the contest the children had to keep their rooms straight all week—which they were quite willing to do.

The problem was solved.

Then there was the 5-year-old who liked to sit next to his 9-year-old brother at the dinner table. Why? Because he admired his brother very much, and it made him feel special when he could sit next to his brother. The problem was that, before dinner was finished, the brothers inevitably got into brotherly conflict, and the 9-year-old always punched the 5-year-old.

The parents could have invoked law and order, separated the two, and told the 5-year-old to shut up, eat, and not cry in his mashed potatoes. But they recognized the boy's need to feel special—and so they created a special place for him at the table, across from his brother, and they served his food on a special plate and his milk in a special mug.

Said Summers: "They met his need to feel special in another way. Parents have to figure out what the child's need is"—and try to meet that need in a way in which everybody wins.

Yes, Doctor, but what about some big-league problems, the things that so often blossom in adolescence?

OK, how about the mother who is ragging her adolescent daughter to stop smoking? This case, said Summers, represents a classic example of how the real problem, which is not the smoking, often gets buried.

What are the daughter's needs? To fit in with her peers, express independence, resist what she views as her mother's attacks on her self-esteem.

What are the mother's needs? To feel that she's doing a good job as a parent, to protect her daughter's health, to ...

All right, here comes the crunch. The mother, when she's honest with herself, knows that she's in a power struggle with her daughter, that her need to control the daughter is in conflict with the daughter's need for independence.

This is the real issue—not the smoking, said Summers, and the solution ultimately will come through their working out the kinks in their relationship—a process that seemingly has nothing at all to do with smoking but that in reality has much to do with it, he said.

Once the relationship is redefined, the problem, whatever it is, "often is resolved in a spontaneous way" because the parent no longer is perceived as clutching and leaning on the child, and the child no longer has a reason to act in defiant ways. The daughter may continue to smoke, for other reasons, but there's not much a parent can do about it—except to explain the potential health hazards. After all, turning loose is a part of good parenting, too.

Summers said that when children refuse to do their homework, parents "have to look at their need for their children to excel." Are they applying so much pressure that the children are rebelling—not against homework but against demands for superior performance?

Children who are experimenting with drugs and alcohol may be reacting to the "overprotective" needs of parents, said Summers. Children who are sexually promiscuous may be reacting to the parents' "exaggerated needs for conformity."

What it amounts to, he said, is a mandate for parents to "sit with themselves, take stock of what their needs are, and consider the possibility that their needs may be in opposition to their children's needs."

This doesn't mean that parents shouldn't enforce rules, said Summers. But it does mean that rules should be based on above-board issues—not on parents' hidden needs.

All this adds up to something that most of us, as parents, already have figured out—that parenting is a tough, tough job.

What do you think?

Businessmen who found God

May 5, 1985

It was a luncheon meeting of the Philadelphia chapter of the Christian Business Men's Committee (CBMC), and 40 men were in the Mirador Room on the ninth floor of the John Wanamaker store in Philadelphia—40 men in flannel suits or the equivalent, most with enough gray in their hair to announce that they'd been around for a while.

The speaker went to the head of the room. He carried a well-known name, Clothier, as in the Strawbridge & Clothier department-store chain. But attorney Isaac H. "Quartie" Clothier 4th was there to spread the word not about the law or the retail business, but about Jesus. Let's listen:

"Eight years ago, I met a guy for lunch at the Racquet Club, and he asked, 'Quartie, do you have a personal relationship with Jesus Christ?' You could have struck me down. This is not the conversation you have at the Racquet Club. I looked around to see if anybody had heard, and I thought, 'Hey, let's cool it.'

"We don't talk much about religion.... We talk about sports, movies, clubs, friends, business, and children, but God is something we don't share with one another.... This fellow Dave at lunch had a loud voice, and he wouldn't quit. He said, 'Quartie, what I mean is—have you asked Christ into your life as Lord and Savior? If you do, you'll have a wonderful, changed life.'

"I was turned off by that. I liked my life as it was. I had a happy marriage to a wonderful woman, great kids, a good job—partner in a major law firm. I had all the material things I possibly could want. I feared a changed life.... Talk about a personal relationship with God was terrifying to me. I thought that God was there and I was here, and maybe we should stay that way.

"I was on the governing board of my church. I'd taught Sunday school. I felt I was doing my share, earning my brownie points into heaven. Why did God need to bother with me? I wasn't sure I wanted Him to scrutinize my daily actions.... But God has great patience: 'If you hear My voice and open the door, I will come in.'

"Six months later, I met a new lawyer, and he asked, 'Are you interested in coming to Bible study? We have a wonderful group. We meet at 6:30 in the morning.' I couldn't believe anything could be wonderful at 6:30 in the morning, but the day came and I woke up at 5 and couldn't get back to sleep. I kept hearing the invitation to come. I drove through a driving rain ... and I found men there, some searching, some who already had committed their lives to Christ. It had changed their lives. I heard that over and over again.

"Three or four months later, I prayed and asked Christ into my life as Lord and Savior. He promises to give abundant life ... and He kept his promise. My life changed....

"Great changes took place in family life. My wife came to the Lord a year and a half later. We'd always had a wonderful relationship—a real partnership, a 50-50 arrangement. But the commandment was 'Love one another as I have loved you.' Was a 50-50 relationship really what He was saying? He gave 100 percent for us. No, we must love each other 100 percent, with total giving—stop counting my 50 percent and her 50 percent. A wonderful marriage became richer and richer....

"In business, too, I have the Lord as part of my life. I turn my problems over to Him ... and let Him direct me.... 'Be anxious for nothing, but in prayer and supplication let your needs be known.' When you ask the Lord to give you peace, amazing things happen....

"It's a matter of faith. I forgot that for years. I said, 'God, prove it; then I'll believe it.' But God says, 'Believe it, and then I'll prove it. You open the door, and I will come in.' We have to take the first step.... God has a plan for each of us if we take the first step."

Applause cascaded off the walls. Men rushed forward to shake Clothier's hand. Later, I asked some of them about their experience of how business and God mix—or fail to mix.

•

Tom McDowell, account executive for Philadelphia's WTAF-TV (Channel 29):

"I see many difficult times in trying to follow the dictates of my mind, my ego, my corporation ... as opposed to what I know to be pleasing to God. I can say without exception ... that the important thing is to follow the dictates of God.... I trusted Him to show me the way out, and He did.... In 1976, I was a functioning alcoholic. I was running one step ahead of dismissal. My marriage was bankrupt.... I turned my life over to Christ, and today I'm one of the top salesmen in the corporation, and my marriage is back together.

"In my business, to be less than ethical is very easy. It's easy to take shortcuts in television advertising, to do what's best for Tom McDowell and the corporation instead of what's best for the client.... I don't hesitate at work to tell the truth because to anger my boss is not such a big deal as angering God."

Payson W. Burt, regional manager, National Alliance of Business:

"It's a dilemma that occurs frequently in business—the gap between what's right for the corporation and what's right for some employees....

"If you take your problems to the Lord, if you're solid in your faith, you're better able to deal with business problems.... I faced a decision in my own career. Is the job all that matters? Just how important is it?

You have to be true to yourself and to God no matter what position you hold. You have to be honest. It's very difficult sometimes. Businessmen are faced with this every day ... but if you maintain your integrity, you'll come up on the plus side.

"The Lord didn't promise that everything would be a bed of roses if we follow Him. He promised to help us get through the troubles. To me, this is a great comfort."

Lee Chapman of Lee M. Chapman & Associates, financial planners:

"Many times what is best for the corporation is not what is best for you and others. If what you're asked to do by the corporation goes against your conscience, explain why you can't do it.... I never had a single person in all my corporate years try to get me to do something that I felt was immoral.... People don't like to fight truth. If the truth is given to a person with humility, he then is defeated.

"We have to make decisions about priorities. If we do wrong, it's not because of corporate pressure but because of weakness in us. We're not strong enough to stand up for what is right. If we stand up for what is right, we can survive the corporate system."

Breaking the workaholic cycle
May 28, 1985

I was back at my old school, the University of Missouri, to speak at a meeting of newspaper editors from around the country. The topic was dear to my heart: how to keep from being eaten alive by the job, how to live with stress or, better yet, how to live without stress.

It was obvious that I had come to the right place because two of the editors I met seemed to be stressed right out of their hides.

One, from the Southeast, accepted the 12- and 14-hour days as "part of the job" and agreed with the publisher that it was important to show the newspaper's flag at community meetings three or four nights a week. Who carried the flag? The editor, of course—and, yes, it was tiring and stressful, but, after all, there was no compelling reason to be at home. Everybody was self-sufficient. Nobody was being deprived of anything.

What about the editor? I asked. Was the editor being deprived of anything—such as a life away from work?

The editor looked at me in disbelief. "Oh, it will be worth it, the long hours. It will be worth it."

I told the editor that I hoped so—and then I turned to the other editor, who was from the West, who seemed relatively in touch with how life ought to be, but who couldn't figure out a way to make it happen. The situation: The publisher believed passionately that the only good editor was an excited editor. "I want you to scream," the publisher had said. "That's how to make things happen—by getting involved."

So the editor had played the game. "Yes, I scream a lot and run around and wave my arms.... It's kind of silly, but that's what they want." Yes, it was anxiety-producing behavior, not only for the editor but also for those who were the targets of the editor's arm-waving. But what could the editor do? What could anybody do?

•

Yes, indeed, what can we do—those of us who know that we're on the ropes and those of us who don't?

If we don't know—and I didn't for many years, when I was a 25-hour-a-day editor—we're in big trouble, and there's probably not much real hope that we're going to change anytime soon. Tragically, the impetus for change often comes when something goes terribly wrong with our lives, when we're felled by a heart attack, when a spouse announces that it's all over, when a child acts out feelings of abandonment in ways that we no longer can ignore, when we're backed to the wall and forced to cry out in agony, "What have I done?"

Is there nothing that can be done before this to increase awareness? That's a question that I've asked many times over the years in interviews with experts in human behavior. What they've said has amounted to this: Listen to what is being said by people around you, by people who matter to you. Are they complaining that you're ignoring them, that you're preoccupied or unreasonable much of the time? Are the children beginning to make jokes about "Daddy Who?" or "Mommy Who"?

It's important to look at yourself, too. Pay attention to your dreams. Are they dreams of hopelessness, dreams of destitution? Is life as much fun as you'd like it to be? Is it difficult to have fun away from the office, even when you're doing things that you used to enjoy, like reading a good book or listening to favorite music? When you look in the mirror, do you feel that you really know the person who's staring back? Or is it the face of a stranger?

•

What can you do if you know that you're being eaten alive by the job? Can you change? Can you get off the merry-go-round—without resigning, shedding the gray flannel suit, and moving to some remote area to build birdhouses or whatever?

Yes, I think it's possible, if we decide that we don't want to live this kind of life any longer because of what it's doing to us or to those we profess to love. It's possible if we change our orientation, if we view ourselves less seriously, if we separate self-worth from what we do, if we reserve life-and-death intensity for the few issues that really amount to life and death.

Here are some suggestions, many of which have worked for me and others:

• Learn to laugh at life's crazinesses, most of which you can't do anything about anyway. I always remember being told by the wife of a man with terminal lung cancer: "You have to learn to laugh—because you can't cry all the time." It's good advice.

• Embrace the words of behavior therapist Andrew Salter: "I do not know anyone who on his deathbed said he wished he had put in more time at work." On my trip to Missouri, I read in the Ozark Airlines magazine a story titled "Midwesterners who love their work." I have no quarrel with people who love their work. I love my work. It's important to love what we spend so much time doing. But it's also important to reserve time for other things—and especially other people.

• Look realistically at your job and ask yourself, "If I left tomorrow, what difference would it really make?" Honest answer: Probably no difference at all. The job would survive, and the person who replaced you might do it better than you ever did.

• Take every day of vacation to which you're entitled—and even try to steal a few extra days. The people who are in the most trouble, I'm convinced, are those who don't take vacations and who seem proud of it, as if only weaklings need vacations. The truth is that only weaklings need to work all the time—weaklings in the sense that they lack the ability to feel good about themselves without daily job demands to make their juices flow.

• Ask yourself: "Why am I working so hard?" If the answer is "Well, it's to give the family the best of everything," scratch that answer and try again. Why? Because you're engaging in self-deception. Nobody ever bought a ticket to ulcerland to benefit somebody else.

• Learn how to be good to yourself—and find time to do it. Play golf. Buy some neckties. Sit in the hot tub. Linger over a second cup of coffee—even if you think that you don't have time. No, especially if you think that you don't have time.

• Focus on what you've done well rather than on what you've done poorly. If you don't enjoy your accomplishments, who will? Answer: nobody.

• Define success in terms of what it means to you, not to society, not to Mother Corporation. What does success now mean to me? Feeling good when I pull the covers over my head at night.

What does success mean to you?

A coach for coping
June 3, 1985

psy-cho-ther-a-py (si ko-ther'e-pe) n. The psychological treatment of mental, emotional, and nervous disorders.
                              —The American Heritage Dictionary

If there's a mission that psychiatrist Richard W. Moscotti feels compelled to pursue, it is to "help neutralize the remaining stigma about therapy."

Yes, it's true that many of our friends and perhaps we ourselves, too, have been in therapy at one time or another, but the stigma lingers—and it's something that we seldom shout from the rooftops.

Why? In an era of so-called enlightenment, why do we so often shy away from revealing that we've been to somebody who has helped us tinker with our lives? The answer, said Moscotti during an interview, is to be found in the very definition of psychotherapy—"treatment of mental, emotional, and nervous disorders." That's the problem—that word "disorders." If you believe that definition, you have to have some kind of disorder before it's appropriate to have therapy....

"I believe the definition is too restrictive, too terse. The world has changed. Most people in therapy today are not crazy or so depressed that they can't function.... Many have existential anxieties or depression or feel lost. They're doing what they thought they were supposed to do, but it's not working out. This leads to pain, lack of joy, alcoholism, drugs, running around, gambling."

These are people who can benefit from psychotherapy, and they need not a therapist but a "life coach."

A life coach?

Yes, indeed, and that's what Moscotti tends to call himself—as a way to "neutralize the stigma that some people may feel in getting help. Most of us need help from time to time. Our parents taught us the mistakes that they were taught by their parents.... Life has speeded up in the last 50 years; it's harder to cope today ... and many of us need help at times. We have coaches for football and basketball, for music and tennis. But we have no coach for life. Where in education did you ever take a course on life? We're poorly prepared for life—and sometimes we get lost. A life coach can help."

Moscotti, who practices at the Institute of Pennsylvania Hospital, which is the hospital's psychiatric branch, said people who were fearful of getting bogged down in years-long therapy should consider the benefits of "short-term, intense psychotherapy. You can have a verbal agreement with the therapist—or coach—for, say, 20 sessions, which may cost from $1,500 to $2,000 ... which is based on an hourly fee of $75 to $100. You can have a contract for six months, or whatever. You spend $1,500 for car insurance. Isn't it smart to make a one-time investment in adult life to see what you're doing right and doing wrong?"

What if 20 sessions turn out not to be enough?

"Then you have the option to renew if you and the coach think that you need more help.... And some people do need more help. Every psychiatrist I know sees doctors, lawyers, high-level executives, businessmen, housewives, truck drivers, and newspaper columnists. These people aren't crazy. They don't have any disorders. They're people who, for the most part, need help with interpersonal difficulties, with marital problems, with ongoing hangups in personality that hurt them without their ever being aware of what's wrong, with unrealistic expectations of the world."

How about an example of a problem that might bring somebody into the coach's office?

OK, said Moscotti, here's a classic one: A "tape" that tends to be played at times in just about everybody's head is "Hey, you're not good enough; you're a fake, a charlatan, and it's only a matter of time until the world finds out."

A way in which a life coach can help shut off the tape is to "help you try some new things and see if they fly. If you've been doing the same thing all the time and it's not working, you have to be ready to try a different way with the coach....

"A good coach should know something else to try—with the boss, the spouse, the kids. Then you can see how you do with that new way. The thing is that success begets success—and your bravery factor goes up with each success. Your trust in the coach goes up, and you start along new pathways. It's scary—trying new things—but the new things are not so maladaptive ... and they help your life work better."

Moscotti said that, typically, some progress could be made in a fairly short time. "Therapy on a good day can help you see things more clearly within two, six, or eight sessions, depending on your education. Educated people tend to see things more clearly more quickly.... So let's say that you begin to see things more clearly in a few weeks. But it takes longer to make significant changes—because first you've got to figure out what to do and if it's possible.... You should be able to see some change within a month or two—if change is going to happen. But you need a competent coach."

What makes for competence in a coach?

To a great extent, it's the rapport that exists between coach and life player, said Moscotti. For this reason, it's appropriate, before committing to therapy, to ask the coach if he or she will "agree to a two- or three-session test run as a preliminary to the contract—to see how the two of you do together. A test run makes sense to me. If you and the coach don't jell, if you can't work together comfortably, then therapy won't work."

Moscotti, who is in middle age, said his bias was toward life coaches who were at least in their 40s and "with their own life experiences. I tilt toward psychiatrists—because we're medical people who can spot a medical problem that might look like an emotional problem. But there are plenty of good clinical psychologists out there....

"Part of the expertise of the life coach is the sense of timing—when somebody can be confronted with an issue.... Sometimes in therapy you go backward and forward—but you can have checkpoints along the way, marks of progress. I really think that therapy pays for itself—by making the person more productive, more buoyant, and creative. It can lift the onus of guilt, depression, and anxiety off your back so you can do better at work."

Moscotti said that coaching was appropriate when somebody felt that "I'm getting the hell kicked out of me, and I don't know what's going on." He said he had seen lives ruined "because people were three inches off base and didn't know why. I like to think that in life coaching, we get in a helicopter and look at the topography of our lives."

A major career shift
July 22, 1985

The year was 1976, and for Arnold S. Relman, M.D., it was decision time.

The University of Pennsylvania asked him to sign on for another seven years as chairman of the Department of Medicine, but Relman had some reservations about that.

"This was a heavy administrative job, and I wasn't sure if I wanted any more of that. I wasn't sure if I even wanted to continue academic work. Maybe I should go back to the laboratory," where he had achieved fame as a researcher in the kidney and fluid electrolyte field. On the other hand, Relman had invested "a lot of skin, nervous system, and heart at Penn. I loved the place, and I'd brought in many good young people who were making names for themselves."

He was torn, and he decided that, at the moment, no decision might be the best decision of all. So he took a sabbatical as visiting scientist in the Department of Biochemistry at the University of Oxford. He had not been there long when he received a message that would change his life forever: The prestigious *New England Journal of Medicine* wanted him to become editor.

•

Arnold Relman, editor? How could it be?

Well, it wasn't as farfetched as it might sound. After all, he had edited high school and college publications, and in academic medicine he'd served on many editorial boards. Once he'd even been editor, on a part-time basis, of a scientific research journal. "I enjoyed doing what editors do."

The previous editor of the *New England Journal of Medicine,* Franz Ingelfinger, had come to the journal straight from academic medicine, so, Relman reasoned, such a move wasn't without precedent. "I once asked him, 'Are you glad you did it?' And he said, 'It is the best job in American medicine, the most fulfilling.'"

As he considered the proposal, Relman was struck by two things: "I wasn't sure there was anything else for me to do for Penn. If I stayed on for seven more years, I'd more or less be presiding over the status quo. But if I left and they recruited a good person to succeed me, that person might be able to do more than I could" because of the new ideas he would bring with him. "I had a visceral feeling that this *Journal* job was right for me."

"Maybe it was time for me to do something different.... To some extent, I'd done the same thing—researching, teaching, consulting—since I was 27. At the time I was 54."

He and his wife talked about it. For two months they talked about it. She was a teacher "and she liked it very much in Philadelphia. I liked it here, too. We had many good friends and a nice house.... We'd come here from Boston, and it had been difficult to leave Boston. Now going back to Boston was difficult—because it meant leaving Philadelphia."

Together, the Relmans made their choice. "She had a lot of input.... We share our lives in a way that makes impossible a major life decision without involving each other."

The year was 1977, and they moved back to Boston. It was editor Relman, if you please.

•

Relman, who was in Philadelphia not long ago to receive the Zubrow Award for humanism in medicine at Pennsylvania Hospital, said in an interview that being editor of the *Journal* was a continuing challenge. "There's nothing else like it in America. I'm getting a chance to use all the knowledge that I've acquired over the years" about medical research, education, practice, and, yes, medical politics, too.

The *Journal's* circulation is now 220,000, up from 175,000 when he took over, and it is the largest "voluntary" circulation of any medical journal in the world—voluntary in that membership in a medical society doesn't guarantee a free subscription.

"Medical research still is the magazine's bread and butter, but we also have a great variety of articles on economics, politics, ethics, law, history, even a little poetry." This may explain, Relman said, why the magazine is increasingly counting nonmedical people among its subscribers.

"This is a university without walls.... I love it. I expect, if my bosses are satisfied, that this will be my last job.... It's hectic.... I have time to write editorials nights and weekends, but it's hard to find consecutive time to write anything serious. I'd like to try to write a book or two and think about problems of medicine."

He is professor of medicine at Harvard Medical School, an appointment that is traditional for *Journal* editors. He teaches "a couple of hours a week, and I meet with students and residents and have a chance to see patients. It keeps my feet on the ground—so I don't float into a make-believe world as editor. I keep in touch with reality."

Has anything about the job surprised him?

"It's as much fun and as satisfying as I expected it to be, but I mis-judged one thing.... All those years at Penn, I worked at top speed. My wife felt that maybe it was time to ease back a little and be at home more. I thought this job would enable me to do that—more time with the family, more time to think. But this has not been true. This is a weekly journal, and it's demanding.... Academic life has a rhythm. You work hard until summer vacation, and then it's time to slow down and think, plan ...

"But with the *Journal,* you're busier in the summer than in the winter. There are no breaks. There are 52 issues a year.... If I'm going to keep my hand on the pulse, I've got to be around."

As a hands-on editor, Relman is as busy as he has ever been in his life. How does his wife feel about that?

"I hope she knows—I think she does—that I meant what I said about being home more. I was mistaken.... I think she's a little disappointed, but she sees that I'm happy in this job—although sometimes frazzled."

A woman's power
July 30, 1985

It's a story that psychiatrist Richard W. Moscotti likes to tell because it makes a point:

For men, entry into heaven is through two gates—one marked for "passive, dependent males only," the other for "assertive, aggressive males only." On this particular day, St. Peter surveyed the scene and found that the line outside the "passive" gate extended into infinity. But in front of the "assertive" gate was not a line but a solitary man.

"Why are you standing here all by yourself?" St. Peter asked.

Answered the man: "Because my wife told me to."

Yes, indeed, said Moscotti, a truly assertive man is hard to find.

•

The couple had come to Moscotti for therapy and, as the sessions progressed, it was apparent that one of the problems was that the woman was frequently beating the man over the head—not with her umbrella but with her words.

"She really was nasty with him sometimes," said Moscotti, "and she tended to tell him what to do and how and when to do it.... One day, I saw the man alone and told him, 'Look, you can't let her talk to you like that. There are times when you have to tell her to shut up.'"

"I should tell her to shut up?" the man asked.

"Yes, by God, the next time she flies off at you, tell her to shut up."

A week went by, and then the woman barged into Moscotti's office. "Do you know what my husband said to me?" she roared.

Moscotti thought that he knew, but he wasn't about to tell her. "No," he answered, "what did he say to you?"

"He said, 'Dr. Moscotti told me to tell you to shut up.'"

How did Moscotti react to that? Well, to be truthful, he wasn't too surprised. After all, a truly assertive man is hard to find.

•

Moscotti, who practices at the Institute of Pennsylvania Hospital, which is the hospital's psychiatric branch, said in an interview that male passivity was everywhere and "has serious influences on both men and women, on relationships, and on marriage.... I feel it's rife in the world. Where does it come from?" Like so many other things, said Moscotti, it comes from our early years, when we were little, physically and emotionally, and when ...

"All mothers are females. Mom is in a very powerful position. The survival of the infant rests in her hands ... and on some level men never outgrow this.... You see a college football player on television and he says, 'Hi, Mom.' He never says, 'Hi, Dad.' It's the power of Mom"—a power that the man eventually transfers to other women in his life.

The result, said Moscotti, tends to be that men are passive and fearful of women, and that women are so very powerful, much more powerful than even they realize.

"I have to be careful how I talk about this," he said. "What I say can be misconstrued by women as 'Here's another chauvinist who's telling us how powerful we are.' But I don't feel that way. I like women. I treat women. I think I understand women," and it's out of this understanding that Moscotti sees the female as all-powerful and the male as, well, as ...

"A little boy needs love and nurturing. He's fearful of losing his mother. Men who as little boys were cut off from their mothers don't do well. The early death of a mother brings increasing psychopathology in children—the kind of psychopathology that we don't see when a father dies. This validates the power of Mother."

This power, said Moscotti, tends to be transferred to the teachers in the early school years—and most of these teachers historically have been women. In his mind, the boy connects women with authority and power that approach omnipotence, and these feelings are forever present, even as the boy, now a man, seeks a wife.

"The man needs her and fears her in the same ways that he related to his mother. He fears that he will disappoint her, lose her love, be rejected, be abandoned by her. He fears that he's not good enough for her and that eventually she'll discover this ... and leave him."

This, said Moscotti, is why the woman in a relationship is so powerful and why a woman "gets superior power in a few years of marriage even if the man started out ahead.... Women are in charge of the sexual activity that goes on in the world. Sexuality is totally in the hands of women. That's a powerful card to hold, and it's another thing that makes the husband afraid of the wife.... I once had in therapy a successful businessman who seemed to be a powerhouse. I said to him, 'You're afraid of her, aren't you?' and he laughed at me. But later he said, 'You're right. We fight and I back down. I'm afraid of her.'

"When I say 'afraid,' I'm talking in generalities and in degrees. Some men are more afraid than others. But this is operational, this fear, much more than people think."

Moscotti said that men disguised their fear of women with a macho veneer. "They gather at pubs and avoid women. They run around with other women to neutralize fear of their wives. They drink too much, gamble, retreat, watch football on TV. Silence keeps up their defenses."

In no other area, said Moscotti, is the man so fearful as in the area of sex. "The question almost always is 'Am I good enough?' He's afraid that he'll be too fast, that he'll hurt her.... I'm pro-woman, as I said, but a woman can't understand what it's like to be a man—any more than a man can understand what it's like to be a woman. No woman in the world knows what performance anxiety is like in a sexual way, knows the fear of impotence or premature ejaculation. A woman can't get a penis and trade places with a man."

Do women like passive men?

No, they don't, said Moscotti, and they tend to show it in their behavior. "Some women I thought of as aggressive were frustrated women stuck with a passive male as a husband. They were forced to take over" and make every decision because the man "wimped out," which is what can happen if a man's fear of the woman overwhelms him.

This concern about being regarded as a wimp is a major barrier to men's being able to reveal their gentle qualities, said Moscotti. So men beat their chests and holler like Tarzan even though, under their loincloths and gray flannel suits, they are shaking like jelly.

What do you think?

"Stand in the longest lines"
August 4, 1985

The homework assignment, psychologist Richard McKnight is saying, is for the next three weeks to "look for and stand in the longest lines—in banks, supermarkets, everywhere ..."

"Look at people in the long lines ... and you see how ugly are harriedness and tension. But you always see one or two who look peaceful. How ... do they do that?"

•

You're sitting in on one of the hottest corporate acts in Philadelphia, Rick McKnight's program "Stress Management and Beyond: Living Your Life Above the Line." He's a self-employed consultant, and stress management is his thing. Dozens of times each year, he presents variations of the program—from two hours to five days.

On this sunny morning, he's performing in a basement room at the Faculty Club at the University of Pennsylvania in Philadelphia. His audience is made up of 20 managers from the Hospital of the University of Pennsylvania, and they will be with him from 8:30 until 4:30 with a one-hour break for lunch. McKnight is dressed casually, in tan jeans, off-white shirt, pink necktie, and shoes with white rubber soles. His manner is just as casual.

"Vacations can be really stressful—because you have to go back to work when they're over.... One year, I was off the whole month of August. It was great. I went to the shore, read tons of books, did whatever I wanted. Then September came, and I had to go back to work. I was like a little kid who refused to leave camp. I had to put on a tie ... and it was awful."

•

"The line"—as in "living your life above the line"—is the midpoint that is considered normal. Most of us, McKnight is saying, "hover somewhere around the line—with normal spiritual, mental, physical, emotional health. The possibility for optimal functioning is not considered.... Most stress-management programs try to get people up to the line, to normal. They're designed to take away something—tension. What about adding something? What about getting above the line?

"The people below the line have the motto 'Life is tough; I am a victim ... I am a punching bag.' Cynicism is their primary stance regarding life.... Above the line the motto is 'Life is fascinating, wonderful. I am the creator of my own life; I make it fascinating.... Sure, there's a lot of stuff I can't control, but there's a lot I can control—and I'm willing to take responsibility.'"

The people above the line—"How did they get there. What do they do? They're not magicians, not saints. What they do is teachable and learnable."

That's why we're here today—to be taught and to learn.

•

"People say to the doctor, 'I'm very upset. I think I have a brain tumor.' The doctor thinks, 'Gee, this sounds familiar.' The doctor says, 'Why do you think you have a brain tumor?' The patient says, 'I have headaches that won't go away.' There's an examination and then a diagnosis: tension. The doctor says, 'You got to slow down, take it easy.'

"There are two reactions from the patient. One is immediate, enormous relief: 'Thank God, I don't have a tumor.' But the delayed reaction is, 'How ... do I slow down?' More tension comes from being told to slow down—and not knowing what to do.

"As kids, we knew how to relax. But, as adults, we often forget.... Relaxation is a learned skill.... In a sense, the diseases we give ourselves are a learned skill, too. We tense up. If we do it chronically, unless we're among the very few lucky people, we're likely to develop symptoms because our system is being overtaxed....

"The doctor may prescribe a tranquilizer.... Everywhere, we're taught that the way to deal with stress is plop, plop, fizz, fizz. Or to drink another cup of coffee. We're encouraged to consume something to relieve stress.... But we need to look at the sources of our stress....

"What's the leading cause of death? We all know that—heart disease. What's the leading risk factor in heart disease? It's Type A behavior, a response to life, and it's more of a risk factor than high blood pressure and smoking. But it's a risk factor over which we have total control."

We can choose, says McKnight, not to be the hard-charging, impatient, Type A person. What do we have to do?

Try standing in those long lines, and ask ourselves, "Why am I so harried? Why am I so tense? Why am I so ... ugly?"

•

McKnight is telling us, "Your greatest ally in relaxation is also your greatest potential enemy—your imagination. You're in a stressful situation, and your imagination either can put a magnifying glass to it ... or it can take you to a pond, a beach, a forest.... You can breathe, let go, stay open, use your imagination constructively—even in those long lines.

"If you're tense a lot, you're imagining the worst. Misery by and large is optional. Imagine things to keep you peaceful."

•

What are the sources of our stress? McKnight asks us to draw a box and divide it into four cells and to label them: recent events on the job, recent events off the job, ongoing conditions on the job, ongoing conditions off the job.

"All sources of stress pretty neatly fit into these areas.... All stressors require energy to cope with. In that sense, because we have a finite amount of energy, we decide how long we will live. If we're faced with a lot of stressors, we wear out faster. That's all there is to it.

"The more complicated life is, the more at risk you are for stress. The most potent stressors are chronic—a job that grinds you down, an unreasonable boss, a marriage that's not working, a child with health problems.... Chronic situations tend to grind people down ... if they are without some way of dealing with them."

There are three basic ways of managing stress, says McKnight:
• Leave the situation.
• Alter the situation.
• Change your perception.
"The primary variable is inside you, not out in the world."

•

McKnight says he doesn't believe that stress is necessarily bad and to be avoided.

"As stress goes up, so do health, happiness, and productivity—up to the point of optimal stress.... With too few stresses, you're in the drone zone. With too many stresses, you're in the burnout area.... You need to find your optimal level of stress and flirt with the edges of it. Life is exciting on the edge of your competence to manage it."

How do you know if you're in the optimal stress zone?

You'll know, says McKnight, if you:

• Enjoy your work.
• Are healthy.
• Feel vital and alert.
• Feel optimistic.
• Smile frequently.
• Enjoy others.
• Are patient.
• Roll with the punches.

If we're in the drone zone, we need to take a bigger bite out of life. If we're at the other extreme, in the nail-biting area, we need to "find some ways to honor ourselves.... To add a sense of control, find a graceful way of saying to people, 'No, thanks, I'd rather not.' You've got to start saying 'no.' It's a sickness in our culture to try to do more all the time, to try to impress people who don't care anyway. If you want to impress people, find ways to say, 'No, thanks.'"

•

We've all heard about Murphy, the inventor of Murphy's Law, which says that anything that can go wrong will go wrong. But now McKnight introduces us to Thomas' Theory of Composition of the Universe: 90 percent of everything is stupid.

If we believe Murphy and Thomas, we're traveling a bumpy road.

A common assumption, says McKnight, is that "stimulus brings response. If it weren't for X, I wouldn't be feeling Y. But it's not this way at all. Events occur ... and we make judgments. Only then do we respond ... and we tend to create what we expect to experience. If we don't expect things to work out, things won't work out." If we expect everything to be stupid, everything will be stupid.

"If we view the world as hostile, we can find evidence everywhere that the world is hostile. If we view the world as usually trusting, we can find evidence of that, too. What we're prepared to see, we see."

We can reduce stress by changing the way we experience the world. It's within our power to do this.

•

The Type A person, says McKnight, is three times more at risk of developing heart disease than the laid-back, easy-going Type B person. The major Type A characteristics are these:

- Hurry sickness.
- Doing many things at once.
- Insecurity of status.
- Excessive competitiveness.
- Concern for having versus being.
- Impatience.

Type A seems to be learned behavior, says McKnight, and it can be unlearned.

"The Type A person is more likely to live in the Northeast, to be employed in a corporation, to be an oldest child.... Type A emotions are aggravation, irritation, anger, impatience.... Underlying the Type A are insecurity ... and anger.... The Type A person lives life in an 'against' state—against time, against other people." It's a miserable way to live.

•

What can we do?

We can change perception; we can strike a bargain with ourselves not to sweat things so much; we can stand in long lines.

We also can practice relaxation techniques, one of which takes just six seconds. It's called "the Quieting Response," and it goes like this:

Make a great big smile.

Draw a deep abdominal breath.

Say to yourself "I can leave my body out of this."

Let the breath go, feeling warmly relaxed from your face to your feet.

All you need, says McKnight, is self-awareness. The Quieting Response is best done when you are tense—so you first must be aware of your tension. It can be and should be done during stressful experiences such as traffic jams, bumpy airplane rides, important meetings ... and long lines.

The performance review
September 1, 1985

Well, here it is, that time again, when the boss schedules you to be in his office at 3 o'clock sharp for your performance appraisal.

What's he going to tell you? That your work is superior? No, probably not—because he's the kind of guy who doesn't express a whole lot of good words about anything.

That your work is "good enough"? Gee, if he says that, what exactly will he mean? Good enough to keep from being fired?

That your work is borderline? How could the jerk possibly think that? But then, facts don't matter to a jerk. That's why he's a jerk.

At any rate it's a minute before 3, your hands are slippery with perspiration, and the secretary is motioning for you to go in. Good heavens, she's not smiling. Does that mean that she knows something? Well, here goes ...

Has this happened to you—and have you wondered how the boss might be feeling at this exact instant?

If there's one thing you can count on, said Wallace R. Johnston, it is that the boss probably is more anxious than you are, more concerned, more fearful.

Ah, you ask, what is the boss afraid of?

Ah, said Johnston, the boss is afraid of you—or, more precisely, he's afraid of how you may react if he gives you a not-so-hot performance appraisal. It's possible that the boss is so anxious that he might blow the smoke of appeasement in your face by telling you that you're doing better than you really are.

Who is Wallace R. Johnston and how does he know so much about what's going on inside bosses?

For those of you who are concerned about credentials, Johnston is a management consultant in Richmond, Va., where he also is associate professor of management in the school of business at Virginia Commonwealth University. Much of his work is with corporate bosses, and one of the things with which he often deals is performance appraisal, a responsibility that many bosses would like to delegate to somebody else—if everybody else didn't run and hide whenever the subject came up.

Not long ago, Johnston spoke in Philadelphia on "effective performance appraisal." He appeared at the 66th international conference of the Administrative Management Society. I asked him why bosses are so chicken when it comes to laying it on the line.

"A lot of the anxiety stems from the things we've been taught, like 'Don't say something bad unless you can say something nice, too.... Do unto others ... Silence is golden.' It seems safe to say that appraisal is harder for the evaluator than for the evaluatee.... It's because we're hesitant to tell people what they need to hear, if it's unpleasant. We fear the type of response we might get. The greatest fear is negative emotional response that is directed toward us."

But, said Johnston, his experience in the workplace and in the classroom has convinced him that most employees are not surprised by the evaluation that they receive. Any anger that employees display probably is rooted not in surprise but in the boss' confirmation of what they already know—or at least suspect.

"Most of the time when you talk to people about performance, the only time you surprise them is when you lie to them. My feeling is that employees know how they're doing, and if they're doing poorly and you don't tell them, they know one of two things—that you're deceiving them or that you're pretty dumb. If you're that dumb, they know that they can go on deceiving you."

Despite grumbling about appraisals, employees do want to be told "how well or how poorly they're doing and how they can do better," said Johnston. "People want strokes—positive or negative, but, for God sakes, give us strokes. That's how people feel," and, as a result, even a bad evaluation is better than no evaluation at all.

Employees need to be evaluated continually, said Johnston, because concerns are "magnified if there's no feedback until a formal appraisal is scheduled once a year or whenever. If people are evaluated continuously, there are never any surprises. If you do it once a year, you do a disservice to the process ...

"Imagine telling your child, 'Well, we're going to sit down tomorrow for your yearly performance review.' Or telling your wife, 'Next week, we'll do your review.' My wife gives me continuing performance reviews," and this is what good companies and good bosses tend to do for their employees. "People may not always like what they hear, but it gives them notice of their standing in the organization."

It's possible, said Johnston, for employees sometimes to turn the boss' anxiety to their advantage—at least temporarily.

"Most bosses are intimidated by signs of anger" from a man or by crying from a woman. "The woman cries for the same reason as the man shows anger—to try to get the boss to soften it, to back off." If the boss isn't made of firm stuff, he can crumble at this point and offer an unrealistically positive review.

However, Johnston recommends neither shouting nor crying as an appropriate response for somebody who is trying to con the boss. "The best thing is to hang your head and say, 'Yeah, boss, I know I'm bad. Just don't hit me too hard.' Then you think, 'Hey, I fooled that sucker again.'"

None of this works with a good boss, said Johnston, because the good boss knows that it's a disservice not to tell people what they need to hear. "It can be cold and hard, but this is what the manager gets paid a slight differential to do."

The response that Johnston favors at appraisal time is for the employee to ask the boss what he or she can do to improve. "Or you can evaluate yourself and give it to the boss before he evaluates you.... This forces the boss into giving you feedback" that may provide more insight into his opinion of your work than you otherwise would get.

"You could say something like 'Look, boss, I've worked here for three years. I think this is the area I'm strong in, this is the area I'm weak in. What I'd like to do is improve. Here are some options. Which do you think are best?' This forces the boss to think hard about your performance and options for improvement.... From the boss' perspective, your sole purpose in the company is to make him look good. If you give the boss options and opportunities, he's more apt to take them" and to help the employee get what he or she needs.

What if the boss consistently rates an employee lower than he or she thinks is appropriate?

"If you disagree regularly with feedback, you may need another job."

Coping and the Catholic clergy
November 21, 1985

Her name is Anna Polcino, and her title is sister-doctor because, as a member of the Society of Catholic Medical Missionaries, she is both nun and physician.

For more than a decade, after her training in Philadelphia, she was a practicing surgeon, performing about 6,000 operations and delivering about 5,000 babies at hospitals in Pakistan and Bangladesh. Then, when arthritis threatened to cripple her hands, she returned to the United States and went into training to become a psychiatrist.

Today she is international psychiatric director for House of Affirmation, an international therapeutic center for Catholic clergy, which was founded in 1970 and now operates residential centers in Massachusetts, California, Missouri, Florida, and England. These are places to which priests, monks, and nuns come for stays that average six to eight months. They receive treatment for problems that range from alcoholism to depression and include just about everything in between.

Let's listen as she talks about the problems and the people:

"It's important to understand that religious life didn't cause these problems; it reinforced them.... The kinds of structures we had [before the liberal reforms set in motion by the Vatican II Council of 1962-65] enforced the behavior of a passive-dependent personality.... Religious life also enforced infantilism. People were told to do a job and sometimes could not use any creativity.... People were not allowed to develop friendships or to relate to the opposite sex.... These factors stunted the growth and development to maturity.... In a sense, priests ... lived a life of emotional poverty."

Sister Polcino, who is headquartered in Whitinsville, Mass., returned to her native Philadelphia to receive the Philadelphia County Medical Society's annual award for "humaneness in medicine." In an interview, she said that problems of Catholic clergy today were not any different from problems of the general public.

A common problem among middle-aged priests is, well, what else but midlife crisis? "Some lay persons in midlife have affairs ... and sometimes this happens with priests, too. It's a time when people begin to review their life choices, to wonder if they did the right thing, to regret what they haven't accomplished.... Some re-evaluate their commitment [to the priesthood] and realize that maybe they made the commitment for the wrong reason. In therapy, they discover that perhaps they chose the priesthood not because it necessarily was what they wanted but because their mother or father wanted it."

Not many priests drop out in midlife, she said, and one reason is that through therapy they come to terms with their doubts and pursue their life's work with renewed vigor.

Celibacy, she said, does not cause emotional problems—although a lot of people on the outside seem to think so. In the years before special services were set up to handle the clergy's problems, priests tended to go to therapists who typically "didn't understand the celibate life. Instead of realizing that the priests were going through a transition phase, the therapists suggested things like 'Leave the priesthood and get married' or 'Have you thought about going to a prostitute?'

"In our psychotheological approach ... we emphasize that people make a free choice to live this life [of celibacy]. To choose celibacy is not abnormal.... The problems are caused not by celibacy but by repression and their not being in touch with their emotions.... We stress that they are not repressing their sexuality, but choosing to avoid the genital aspect of sex.... They still are called to love people, but not just one particular person."

People who enter the priesthood or sisterhood bring with them the same baggage that burdens so many people in all areas of life, Sister Polcino said.

"A number come from broken homes with alcoholic fathers or mothers. Some sisters have been sexually molested and raped. They've never disclosed this to anybody," but a time comes, often in midlife, when these traumas surface and must be dealt with, therapeutically and spiritually.

Here are some other points made by Sister Polcino:

In the years before the Vatican II conference, "many priests had little or no understanding of relationships. It was because of the way they were trained in seminaries. They were told to stay away from women because women would try to seduce them. There were no women in the seminaries.... But a lot has changed since Vatican II. Now women teach in seminaries ... and the men get out of the seminaries and go to other schools to continue their education.... There's much healthier communication between men and women."

It's not possible to present a psychological profile that fits most men who want to enter the priesthood, but "a number we see are introverted. They want a place to which they can retreat. But the vast majority are not like this.... People who are very introverted or who have schizophrenia may be attracted to religious life because it looks like a place of security and quiet. They break down eventually—but they would break down" no matter where they were, and the religious life is not a factor.

Candidates for the priesthood are given assessment tests, interviewed, and asked to write essays about themselves and their relationships with their parents, siblings, and God. For young men who are "immature and psychosexually underdeveloped ... we recommend that they undergo therapy or live life for a while before entering the seminary.... Some have not firmed up their own identity, and they question if they have homosexual orientation. They aren't sure how they feel about women."

Sister Polcino's decision to leave surgery and enter psychiatry was difficult. "I loved surgery. I was self-confident.... But it was obvious that I had to quit because of the arthritis. It took me several years to come to terms with that.... The hardest thing was learning that I had to be patient.... As a surgeon, I operated on people, and they were cured. But in psychiatry, you don't see results immediately."

The parent-child dialogue
January 7, 1986

Ever since Day One, it seems, we, as parents, have been told that our children will ask for the information they want and need. If we sit back and wait, we will be rewarded because the questions will come, and we'll have the opportunity to ...

I think that's wishful thinking. It never worked that way for me, and

I never met any other parents whose waiting for questions resulted in much of anything except frustration. What about you?

If we don't want to wait, if we want the dialogue to begin now, what can we do?

Let's listen to psychologist Erich Coché, who has a 7-year-old daughter and whose nephew lived with him and his wife, psychologist Judith Coché, from age 12 until he went off to college:

"If you come head-on and say, 'Tell me what's on your mind,' the child is not going to talk. You have to create the opportunity, the mood.... With teenagers, especially, you have to wait until you sense that the moment is a good one, and then you start talking.... Sometimes you have to take the leadership by sharing something of your own. You set a model of faith and indicate that this is the time to exchange personal information....

"You can say, 'I'm concerned about you, about some of the things you've been saying.' A kid may drop an offhand remark. You don't have to pick it up then. You can tuck it away and bring it up later, when the time is right."

When is the time right?

"You feel it, sense that this is a good time. The atmosphere and mood are there. It may be when you're away from the normal environment— walking on the beach, traveling in the car, camping....

"It's important to understand that with a teenager, the parent-child relationship seems to come and go almost with wave-like motions. There will be a week or two with tension and suspicion, when the parent is seen as an enemy. Then somehow it changes, and there'll be two good weeks, with openness, willingness to listen and be friends again. The suspicion is sufficiently removed to allow openness to communication, and this is a time when a parent can share concerns.

"You can say, 'Listen, a few weeks ago you said something about smoking grass at school. Can we talk about that some more?' You're coming out of a sense of concern, not heavy authority. Personally, I make the assumption that if a kid is smoking grass, he's probably unhappy about something. It's a risky assumption, but there's a high probability of being correct. I'd let him know that I'm worried. 'If you're unhappy, will you tell me about it?' It's important that this be extended as an invitation to talk—with no force behind it."

For a long time, Coché said, parents were told that it was important to let their children know that they "understood" whatever the problem was at the moment. "Some parents exaggerated this and 'Oh, yes, I understand' came across to the children as a brushoff. Much of the time it may be wiser for the parent to say, 'No, I don't understand. I'd like to hear more. Why are you upset? How do you feel?' Then, if the kid gives you an opening and if the mood is right, go for it. Ask more questions, leading questions. Encourage the kid to open up."

It's important, said Coché, for parents to praise their children for sharing their concerns. "Let them know that you appreciate their openness. As a parent, you are the person with authority. It's not easy for a child to be open with a parent. Everything the child says may be used against him. The kid shares, and the parent says, 'Hey, I've got to punish you for that.' It is risk-taking to share with parents. Let's be honest about that."

How can we, as parents, get our children to be receptive to what we want to say to them?

It depends, said Coché, on our parenting style, and "there is no right answer for all situations. You have to use your best judgment. What is right for one parent at one time is not necessarily right for anybody else at any other time." Here are some of the options:

• Share your own feelings. "You don't do it in a fault-finding, vituperative way, but in a concerned way: 'Look, I'm worried about your driving record, about your safety.' You talk about how you feel."

• Work as a problem-solver. "You're not out to punish the child because of his driving record. You might say, 'You can harm yourself if this keeps up.... This is our problem and we must work on it together. Let's look for a solution that we're both comfortable with.' You don't get hot and bothered. You want to be cool and rational, very unemotional."

• Act as an authority figure. "This is not, in itself, bad. The '70s are over, and it's OK again to be authoritarian. 'Dammit, I'm your parent and I won't permit this! There will be no illegal substances in my house!' You can be authoritarian for your child's welfare. 'Look, you got another ticket. I'm taking away the car keys for two months.' Then you wait until the kid wants to talk about it."

Without doubt, Coché said, it takes time to communicate with children, to create the environment that encourages sharing. "But you can postpone things ... to say, 'That's a good question, and I'm concerned, too, but I can't talk now. How about tomorrow?' The kid then knows you're interested—if you do it in a way that isn't interpreted as a brushoff. But you have to follow up. When tomorrow comes, you've got to be available."

The rules of business, such as they are

February 3, 1986

It was an interview with Edward Mazze, dean of Temple University's School of Business Administration, and he was saying that the true nature of business seems to shock students.

No, said Mazze, business "is not perfect. It's highly competitive ... and lots of decisions are made by intuition instead of by computers or by reasoning.... There are no real rules of doing business. Nobody plays by any sense of fairness."

Mazze said that a "great indicator of interest in the job—for right or for wrong—is the time you get to work and the time you leave work." He wasn't saying that long hours must be the rule forevermore, but "a problem I see is that schools are preparing a lot of people for soft, safe jobs rather than to be competitive."

Numbers of readers told me what they thought about that column, and reaction ranged from disbelief to total agreement. Let me share with you parts of one letter that I thought was especially interesting:

"The column was right on, but I think there's more to say on the subject of business. Here are some thoughts of mine, based on personal experience....

"No rules. Students need to learn this existentially, not as an abstraction. Such as: teacher suddenly flunks all who give right answers, passes all with wrong answers, suddenly gives test questions in ancient Egyptian history—or does whatever it takes to make it very clear that 'of course, it's unfair; you handle it....'

"Extra hours. This can easily be misunderstood as 'be a good old Bob Cratchett,' which I was. Work from 7 A.M. to 9 P.M. and you burn out, which I did several times over. Someplace in there you have to balance in 'no more Mr. Nice Guy' or 'no more patsy.' But how? When?

"Mentors. That's fine, but you have to pick the right mentor. I had a couple of great ones—one retired, one moved on, and I was left like a Democrat in the White House at the Reagan inaugural....

"Ethical questions. These can be very complex, not merely a matter of company pollution and whether an employee should report it or not, which was the example that Mazze used. I worked on a tobacco company account for years, and I knew people who quit rather than do that. I admired them. It didn't bother me that much then, but it would now. Today I'd quit, too. I worked for 10 years on Army recruiting—and that still doesn't bother me. I think it's a good option for some people. But I had a friend, with a daughter, who quit because he decided he wouldn't want his daughter to become a WAC. Things can get very complex, can't they?

"Tough. In the "Mary Tyler Moore Show," she almost doesn't get the job because she isn't 'tough enough.' So she has to prove it. This is a good lesson for men as well as women. I had a boss who once warned my wife: 'They're killing your husband.' And they were. But how to be tough, with whom, when, without getting fired. That's a tough one. It would require a lot of role playing, or something, to work that one over....

"All of these things, and many more, require experiencing, not abstract statements. Students go in—as I did—as babes in the woods, unless they grew up with real street smarts."

•

What would I say to young people leaving college and entering business? Let me share with you some of the things that I've said to my two sons who are deep in the wonderful world of work—Jay, who is in the wholesale food business in Charlotte, N.C., and Grant, who is an accountant in San Diego, Calif.

What you think of yourself is far more important than what others think of you. What this means is that you have to be true to yourself, to your value system, to your world view. The world is full of folks, many of them bosses, who think that cutting corners to get the job done is not only acceptable but also prudent. People who say, 'No, I can't do that because I don't think it's right' may lose in the short run, but eventually they win. I recalled for both Jay and Grant a story told me by my father, who lost his part-time job in a grocery store during the Depression because he refused to do what it took to make stale meat look like fresh meat. "Being able to live with myself was more important than the job, even though I desperately needed the job," he said. It's a lesson that I never forget, and I hope that Jay and Grant never forget it, either: When principle and expediency clash, principle wins.

• Work should be one of many important things—not the most important thing. It has to be kept in perspective if life is going to amount to anything, if a person is going to discover himself and honor himself. Anybody whose primary identity comes from the job is on shaky ground—because the job eventually ends, but life goes on.

• Balance is an admirable goal for which to strive, the kind of balance that brings us back to reality when the demands of work temporarily get us out of kilter. We all have to work brutally long and agonizingly hard at times, but we have to be able to recognize when those times have ended and it's appropriate and necessary for us to reclaim other aspects of our lives. As behaviorist Andrew Salter said: "I know of nobody who on his deathbed wished that he had put in more time at work."

• Enjoying what we do for a living is essential, and it's important to try to keep the kind of flexibility that enables us to change jobs if we reach the point at which work is no longer fun. Grant, at age 25, told me something very profound not long ago: "It's important to work for more than money." A lot of people never figure that out, and their lives turn brown from lack of nourishment. It's important to have fun, both on the job and off the job.

What do you think?

In the wake of Vietnam
March 16, 1986

Have you ever wondered what it is like in a therapy session when the issues are very, very heavy—as when a Vietnam veteran is struggling to come to terms with his remorse and guilt and, most of all, with himself?

What I am going to share with you provides an opportunity to hear about—and, I hope, to understand—a slice of life that rarely is exposed to the public. Psychologist David A. Grady, who lost a leg in combat in Vietnam, made available to me a tape recording of a session in 1982 with a young man who was a tank commander in Vietnam in the early 1970s. We'll call him Chuck. Let's listen to part of his story—and some comments by Grady:

"When I first got home, the atmosphere with my peers—guys I'd grown up with—was that we couldn't communicate.... Because I'd done time in the jungle and I was in the hospital, they couldn't understand what I was talking about.... What was important to me was not important to them. I didn't fit in....

"I got married ... and I started to associate with my wife's friends because I couldn't get along with my friends.... But I had the same problem with them. Something inside me started keeping me away from people.... I was isolated. I had nothing in common with anybody.... I had three years in Vietnam ... while they went on with their lives, went to movies and to parties. There were no parties for me. It was survival.... They'd asked me what I did, and I'd try to explain, but they weren't interested.... My wife said I couldn't get along with anybody....

"My attitude changed. I didn't care about things that used to interest me. Our first son was born, and I spent some time with him ... but my wife said I wasn't taking enough interest in him.... I couldn't seem to get in the frame of mind to participate like other fathers. We started to have some marital problems over that.... She said, 'There's something wrong with you.'

"... Every time I shave, I look in the mirror and I see my scars. Holes, scars on my body. How can I forget about Vietnam and try to live with all these memories? Even at work ... I'll be using a blowtorch, and I'll put it down and just sit there. What's happening is that the smell of the burning ... puts me back to when I was a tank commander....

"It was August 21, 1970.... We got ambushed. My tank was hit bad.... I managed to get off and yank the gunner with me. But my loader and my driver didn't make it.... They burned up.... Later we went back to the tank ... and the smell of flesh or whatever ... when I'm using a blowtorch at work, it's the same thing.... Things like this react in my mind. I'm in a daze. The foreman comes up and says, 'Are you taking a break?' And I say, 'Yeah, it's hot.' He doesn't want to hear that this reminds me of this or that. He's there to get the job done....

"Instances flash through my mind. I recall incidents that happened 11 years ago. That's crazy.... Other guys who were not in Vietnam can't remember five years ago. But to me, it's like it happened a week ago, like the 11-year gap is not an 11-year gap....

"The smell of diesel fuel.... We clean parts at work with diesel.... There are so many things to refer back to. It seems like I'll never forget. We topped off the tanks with diesel every morning. I work now with diesel every day, and it reminds me of working with tanks....

"I watch TV with my two sons.... They have guns, and they run around the neighborhood. If tanks are involved in a TV movie, there I am, plain as day.... I get up and leave the room. I start remembering too much...."

Chuck tells Grady that he tries not to think about the guilt that he feels about the death of those in his command.

"I really get upset. Maybe there was something I could have done to prevent them from being killed.... I almost feel ashamed ... that I'm alive and they're not. I keep on reliving certain experiences when men were killed. I was in a command position to make decisions. A tank commander has five tanks, four men to a tank. That's 20 men. Several instances we lost men. Could I have done anything different? We were ambushed. We got hit.... I was worried about self-survival. I tried to make the right decisions. The decisions I made I felt were the best I could make at the time....

"But I didn't bring them back alive. They were kids.... Kids ... they were older than I was. I was the kid.... But I really wasn't the kid. I was the platoon sergeant, and I was supposed to have the answers. I was supposed to take them out and bring them back alive. Sometimes they didn't come back alive. I feel guilty, and sometimes it gets to the point that I wish it was me who was dead and they were back here alive....

"You spend so much time in the bush with the guys, and there's no sergeant this, corporal that. You're John, Steve, Chuck, Mark, and Bob.... Rank in the jungle means nothing. In the jungle, you're a family. You become close....

"That's the bad thing. When you lose somebody you're close to, you lose a little bit of you with him, and you never, ever get that back. I don't care what anybody says. You're never going to get that back. When it really comes down to it ... it's a shame. You've been over there to be killed ... for Christ sake—that's my own opinion. I imagine there will be a lot of people who'll say, 'Oh, yeah, we did the right thing.' Not from what I could see."

Grady interrupts Chuck: "In a sense it may seem disloyal to rebound from what you're talking about.... I lost people standing next to me, like brothers. I hear you say you lost a piece of yourself and you never can get it back.... I think about what they would want.... When I think of the people I lost, it's important for me to feel sadness and sense of loss. This shows how much I cared about them.... I also know they would want me to enjoy life as much as possible. They'd not want me to feel I'd lost a piece of myself that I never could get back."

Chuck: "But it's my fault. They died and I'm alive. I was in charge."

Grady: "Did they expect you to make sure they stayed alive?"

Chuck: "There are no guarantees over there.... No damn guarantees."

Grady: "You were right there with them. You did the best you could."

Chuck: "I don't know.... I feel better.... It's crazy, but this is the first time in 11 years I've actually talked to anybody about this.... Crazy ... 11 years and not say anything to anybody."

Grady: "You lose somebody close, and you almost want never to get that close to anybody again—so you won't get hurt, never get burned like that again...."

Chuck: "I got two boys at home.... If there's ever a war.... I actually feel better talking to you about this than I've felt in a long time.... Can you imagine talking to somebody who has never experienced something like this?"

Grady: "It probably would be different. But if you only talk with people who were there, you cut out a great majority of the people of the world. The vast majority of people were not there.... I'm not saying you should talk to everybody.... You will run into a lot of people who won't understand, who will interpret what you say wrong, who will be scared by it.... You've reacted in the past by deciding never to talk to anybody about anything.... You can't carry it all around by yourself the rest of your life....

"I was in charge of 12 men in a rifle squad. I lost some.... One day I lost half of them and the other half was wounded.... I think back to the war. It's completely crazy. Nobody knows what the hell is going on....

You go on reflexes....

"You have to be honest with yourself. All you ever can expect out of other guys is that they do their damnedest.... What you're telling me is that you did your damnedest.... You're awfully hard on yourself for something you had no control over. You're still kicking yourself because not everybody got out. Lots of guys do the same thing. I've done it myself.... You're still paying for the fact you didn't do something you couldn't have done anyway.... You're not allowing yourself to have as good a life as you could have....

"I feel my guys are up there looking down, saying, 'Hey, have the best life you can have.' It would be a bigger tragedy if you don't go after all you can get. You made it back.... It's painful to accept what you need to accept. There's not a damn thing you could have done differently. Fate decided it would happen to you.... I try to live each day as best as I can—as a tribute to the guys who didn't come back.... I try to have a little fun for them."

Chuck: "I feel better.... Now I can look at it in different perspective. What happened in the past has no bearing on today.... What happened then was going to happen—to whoever was in that position. I have to go on with my life.... I'm not going to blow it now.... Eleven years have passed. That's a long time."

The seasons of depression
May 25, 1986

While British-born psychiatrist Peter C. Whybrow taught at Dartmouth's medical school in New Hampshire, he lived on a farm and became "intrigued by the seasons and how people adapt to a cold climate....

"Living creatures are enormously adaptive. They live in Center City Philadelphia and also in the middle of Iowa and, as far as we can tell, the health statistics are not too different."

His interest in the subject prompted a Dartmouth alumni group to invite him to speak on how to survive a New England winter, and after that he was asked to write something for *Yankee* magazine—a tongue-in-cheek article that was headlined "Where there's mud, there's momentum" and that offered such bits of advice as "eat a lot, especially fattening foods" and "avoid at all costs totaling up the winter oil bills. Your calculation may put you into a melancholic decline."

It was all fun and games, of course, but then, in 1979, Whybrow was awarded a scholarship to serve as visiting scientist in the clinical psychobiology section at the National Institute of Mental Health in Bethesda, Md. This was where he became involved in fun and games of another kind.

He long had been interested in physiology and endocrinology, and his new colleagues were heavily into how light cycles affect human behavior. So, in Whybrow's words, "one thing led to another, and we decided to study normal behavior through seasonal cycles in northern New England ... to see if seasonal depression really was a pathological entity or a dimension of human behavior that we all experience."

Seasonal depression?

Yes, said Whybrow, who now is a professor and chairman of the psychiatry department at the University of Pennsylvania. "We've known for a long time that depression and other psychological illnesses have seasonal variations. You can tell from hospital admissions.... Mania is more common in late summer, depression in winter. Suicides are more numerous in spring and fall.... Other countries have similar patterns," so it's not something that applies only to the United States.

A fascinating finding is that "the farther you get from the equator, the more precise are these variations"—as long as you remain in the temperate band of seasonal changes. "The peaks and valleys are precise, but as you move toward the equator, the profile flattens.... The Southern Hemisphere is a mirror image of the Northern Hemisphere ... so clearly what's happening—the peaks and valleys—has to do with the angle of the earth and its rotation around the sun."

In other words, said Whybrow, there is an obvious relationship between the way people behave and the season of the year. The relationship, he said, is keyed to the light cycle, which in the Northern Hemisphere is longer from March through September, and in the Southern Hemisphere, from September through March.

In simplified terms this is what happens: The eye, which is sensitive to light, takes in a signal that the sun is up, and the signal, through a complex route, eventually connects with the pineal gland, which is between the two hemispheres of the brain and which is "like a barometer. It's sensitive to light and maybe to temperature and humidity, too."

The pineal gland produces various hormones, including melatonin, which influences the behavior of other glands, including the thyroid. "If there's a lot of melatonin about, sex hormones are inhibited," said Whybrow, and because melatonin is produced more heavily during darkness, there tends to be less interest in sexual activity during winter than during summer.

"Then summer comes on, melatonin is inhibited," and sexual activity increases. "The whole cycle is coordinated through light," and this explains how the reproductive cycle of animals in the wild tends to be timed so that birth comes in the spring, when conditions are optimal for survival and growth.

Essentially, a similar kind of thing is at work in people who suffer from seasonal depression. Lack of light triggers some sort of chemical reaction that produces depression in some people who, for whatever reasons, don't adapt as easily as others to shorter days and longer nights.

So-called light therapy, exposing seasonally depressed people to the intense light of heat lamps or sun lamps, has been shown to be effective treatment.

Knowing all of this, Whybrow and his colleagues wondered if "normal" people had seasonal cycles, too. "It made sense to think so," he said. "Bears hibernate. Squirrels sleep a lot in the winter. Birds go south."

The study was focused on a geographical area that Whybrow knew well—northern New England—where about 100 people were selected to fill out a daily record of their cycles of sleep, energy, mood, and sexual activity for 12 to 15 months. "A high percentage of them were as normal as anybody in society. They were not depressed. They didn't see psychiatrists."

Results of the study, which ended early this year, were presented by Whybrow and the others at a conference on brain research in Keystone, Colo. What they found indicated that normal people, like animals, do indeed have seasonal cycles and "tend to change in all sorts of ways....

"People who are seasonally depressed say that they sleep more in the winter. Well, normal people sleep more, too.... They tend to nap during the evening to supplement their sleep in winter. They feel they need more sleep in winter—but not at other times.... We presume that the endocrine cycle changes in winter" and promotes a kind of hibernation.

Among the other findings:

• Fall is the time of year when people are most active sexually.

• Energy is highest in late summer—in August and early September.

• People are happiest in summer, less happy in winter, and eat more in winter than in summer.

• While both mood and energy increase in summer, mood is "a bit ahead" of energy, which means that mood is beginning to decrease at summer's end, while energy is still high.

•

If light is the key to the cycles, why aren't people who live near the equator more energetic?

That's a good question, said Whybrow, and he wasn't certain that he had a good answer. Apparently the change of seasons is a critical factor in all of this—and people who live where the weather is extreme, either hot or cold, don't react in the same way as people in the temperature band that contains "the major civilizations of the world. The lack of change must have impact."

Why is spring a time of more suicides than winter? Seasonal depression presumably is on the way out by spring—and wouldn't that suggest that suicides would wane, rather than increase?

That's a good question, too, said Whybrow.

"The theory is that there are two types of depression—one that gets better in the spring, one that gets worse. Those who get better in the spring are seasonal. The ones that don't get better, these are the ones where people kill themselves....

"Probably we're talking about two different illnesses. The one that persists in the spring is sort of a malignant melancholia.... Spring is a bad time. They see others feeling energetic. It doesn't happen to them, and they feel driven to kill themselves. It's not seasonally related."

Two sexes, two viewpoints
June 19, 1986

Robert Bly, who lives in a log cabin in Moose Lake, Minn., earns his living as a poet and essayist, but he prefers to be identified as "a student of male initiation in ancient times."

Bly and his poems have been around for a long time, but his name became familiar a few years ago to many of us who don't read poetry with the publication, in *New Age* magazine, of an interview in which Bly gave his views "on being a man." Bly took the position that the problem with men today is not that they have ignored their feminine side but that they have failed to develop their masculinity.

It was a controversial piece—because Bly, in his fatherly, white-haired way, is an outspoken, controversial man.

•

Here is what Bly calls a classic "dilemma" story:

The father and son go hunting together, and the father kills a wood rat and tells the boy to keep it. But the boy throws it away, without telling his father, and the hunt continues.

The day wears on until sunset, and no other animals appear. The father tells the boy, "Go fetch the wood rat, and we'll cook it and eat it."

"I threw it away."

"What?" The father is furious and he hits the boy, knocking him unconscious. Then the father leaves to go back to his village. It's dark when the boy wakes up, but he pulls himself together and walks to the village, where everybody is asleep, including his parents. The boy gets his clothes, leaves the village, and walks into a dark forest.

After a while, he finds another village, where everybody is asleep except the chief, who hears the boy's story and who likes the boy very much.

"Can you keep a secret?"

"What secret?"

"I had a son who was killed in battle. I want you to be my son. Can you keep that secret?"

"Yes."

The chief beats his drum in joy. When his wife appears to inquire about the noise, the chief exclaims: "My son has returned!"

The villagers wake up. They, too, are overjoyed, and they beat their drums. The boy is accepted by everybody as the chief's son. He learns many new things, and he gains many fine gifts of clothing and horses. He is very happy.

But then one day the father appears in the village. "Has anybody seen a boy here?"

He is directed to the chief's hut, where he sees his son, well-dressed and fit-looking.

"I want you to come back with me and hunt rats again," the father says.

The chief is distressed. "I adopted him as my son. I want to keep him here.... If you let him remain with me, I will give you gold."

The father is adamant. "I want my son."

The chief turns to his right-hand man and tells him to "get three horses and a sword."

The chief, the father, and the boy ride the horses through the forest and into a clearing, where they dismount. The chief faces the boy and says, "You can kill your father and leave with me—and remain as my son. Or you can kill me and take my gold and live with your father."

Then he hands the sword to the boy.

●

His telling of the story completed, Bly turns to his audience and asks: "If you were the boy, what would you do at this very moment? Would you kill the father or would you kill the chief?"

●

Bly was a keynote speaker at a symposium on "Fathers and Sons" at Horsham Clinic, a private psychiatric hospital outside Philadelphia. The audience of about 125 people was made up, for the most part, of therapists, who by attending qualified for continuing-medical-education credits from the Temple University School of Medicine.

About two-thirds of the group was male, and when Bly asked for a show of hands on whom they would kill, almost everybody pointed the sword at the chief. Why? Because blood was thicker than water. The reaction surprised Bly, who speaks at a lot of male conferences and who later said that many men vote to kill the father—because of the bottled-up rage that they feel toward their own fathers.

I was a member of the symposium's faculty, and Bly asked me to meet separately with the women in the audience to find out how they reacted to the story. Would their view be similar to the men's?

No, not on your life. Women's traditional role of peacemaker surged to the foreground and they sought a third option, in which nobody would be killed. Some of their comments:

"I'd try to find a way to get the chief and father to reconcile. If I couldn't do that, I would simply leave."

"I would run away if I had to. I wouldn't let anybody limit me to options that I couldn't live with."

"Before I'd kill either the father or the chief, I'd kill myself—if it came to that."

"I would refuse to accept the chief's terms. I'd take the sword and put it away."

"Both the chief and the father represented parts of myself, and if I killed either, I'd be killing a part of myself. I wouldn't do that. I couldn't."

•

I told the women that my interpretation of the story was that the son had rejected the family's lifestyle and had gone off and made a successful life for himself. When the father appeared and asked to reconcile, the son was torn between giving up his new life, which he enjoyed, and getting back with his mother and father, whom he loved. He viewed the situation as either/or—and he was ambivalent, as are many adult children in 1986.

The story, I said, was symbolic of the adult child's split from parents, who also are torn—between their sadness about what they view as the child's rejecting their way of life and their desire for the child to be successful and happy.

What do you think the story means? And what would you do if the chief handed the sword to you?

The therapist is part of the therapy

June 29, 1986

The stigma that is attached by society to those with mental illness—and even to those who seek therapy because of garden-variety problems of everyday living—extends to "the people who treat it, particularly psychiatrists," said John L. Bulette.

Let's listen as Bulette, who is chairman of the department of psychiatry at Abington Memorial Hospital in Abington, Pa., talks about it:

"The interesting thing about stigmatizing attitudes is that the people who do it usually know very little about mental illness or psychiatrists or what psychiatrists do. So how do we account for this contradiction?

"Unfortunately, my profession has unwittingly played a role in fostering this mysticism, particularly psychoanalysts—with the idea that what went on had to be very guarded and that descriptions of the activities had to be phrased in impossibly abstract terms, unintelligible to anyone outside the field and frequently to many in the field."

What causes psychiatry to operate so much in the shadows instead of in the sunlight?

In an interview, Bulette said that a primary reason is that psychiatrists may approach a problem from many different perspectives, and often they don't even speak the same language.

"When it comes to language to describe psychological symptoms and treatment, you've got a tower of Babel. You have two psychiatrists talking about a depressed person, and if they're oriented differently, they're going to see different things. When you ask them to try to explain what they see and what they're going to do, things can get very confusing."

It's not like this in other branches of medicine, he said.

"When surgeons talk about a stomach ulcer or appendicitis, there's not a lot of ambiguity. It's pretty much cut and dried. But when psychiatrists talk about depression, say, you can get a spectrum of viewpoints....

"You have a psychiatrist who is from the biological school, and he thinks that if you define and rectify the [chemical] imbalance, the depressed person will feel better.... You have a psychiatrist who believes that depression is a psychological response, and his position is that you can talk about the impairment in the functioning ... and rectify the problem. Most psychiatrists are someplace in between," and it's difficult for the public—and even for many doctors—to make sense out of what is going on.

Psychiatrists also may be their own worst enemies by exhibiting, at times, attitudes that suggest runaway arrogance.

Said Bulette: "I was sitting at a hearing where a psychiatrist was testifying about committing somebody involuntarily. He described the person's behavior, and the hearing master asked, 'Why does this mean that he should be committed?' The psychiatrist puffed up and said, 'I am a psychiatrist. I am an expert. Why are you questioning me?'

"There's a kind of omnipotence attached to this," and it's not difficult to trace the roots if you understand that psychiatrists spend much of their time in the company of patients who tend to view them as bigger than life, if not omnipotent. Sometimes psychiatrists accept that view readily—and that's when the trouble starts.

●

What causes the stigma that society pins on those who seek help for emotional problems?

Bulette's answer is as good as any I ever heard—and better than most: "When people begin to hurt and they have a sense of where it's coming from—some emotional involvement—they struggle because it's hard to say, 'Hey, something's going on; I need help.'

"So they go to the family doctor. They're an interesting group, family doctors. They vary, depending on their training, but I'm not at all sure that they're not part of the issue of stigma.... Many of them feel that they would stigmatize the patient if they recommended psychiatric help. This is a generalization, but it's my feeling that this is more the rule than the exception....

"One of the things that happens when you become symptomatic is that you feel weak. In fact you are weak. The brain is the most adaptive organ in the body, and if it's not working up to capacity, you're really in trouble. If you can't use your memory, interpret the environment, formulate appropriate responses ... well, this is what Alzheimer's disease is all about....

"You feel weak and vulnerable ... and this is not in keeping with society, which says that adults should be self-sufficient and independent and keep a stiff upper lip. Society says, 'If you made up your mind, you could will your way out of this mess,'" which, of course, is like trying to will your way out of diabetes.

●

How does somebody who's troubled know if he needs professional help—or if talking out the problem with friends will be sufficient?

"Talking with friends doesn't happen enough. It's an enormously powerful thing, to clarify things and talk about what's going on, to express things you weren't sure were there. This is enormously relieving—and it's better to do it with more than one person, hopefully with a network of friends, if you have relationships that are open to this kind of talking...."

"But in the course of doing this, if you don't feel much relief, if you don't clarify the source of distress, if the distress begins to intrude into your capacity to function, if you've cut yourself off from having fun, then, clearly, it's time to get professional help....

"The whole thrust is that the therapist doesn't have the answers, but he knows how to get to the answers.... The answers always are in the person, but sometimes the person has mud in his ears and can't hear the answers. Sometimes the therapist has mud in his ears, too—and that's a biggie."

How do you know if the therapist has mud in the ears?

"It's a gut reaction ... if the therapist has his own agenda, if he tries to impose something that doesn't make sense or that seems against your values, if he doesn't seem to relate to what you're talking about, if he doesn't respond to indicate some understanding. Interest in you as a person with a problem is what you're paying the therapist for. The therapist has to care about what happens" and has to communicate this to the patient for therapy to be successful.

"The major issue in therapy is the therapist's capacity to understand what's going on—the recognition and ability to give feedback to the person in a way that the person can use."

It's helpful, said Bulette, to know the therapist's orientation—to know if "the therapist sees things biologically, interpersonally, within the family. Most people don't know this, and they should ask. You have a person who needs to understand himself, and you have a doctor who's trying to convince him that he should take drugs. That makes no sense. Or you have somebody who could be helped by drugs, and the doctor's giving him only psychotherapy.... That makes no sense either....

"Some therapists may not want to answer these questions ... but it's not in the patient's best interest to avoid asking them."

The pain of healing
July 13, 1986

Sidney M. DeAngelis already was established as a successful divorce lawyer when he ended his marriage 27 years ago, when his daughter, Barbara, was 8, and his son, Michael, was 7.

In the years that followed, DeAngelis' career zoomed to even greater heights—in his words, he was "traveling all over" and representing everybody from prosperous businessmen to European royalty.

"I was doing all kinds of things to get satisfaction," he said, even writing a screenplay on which Warner Bros. bought an option. When Pennsylvania's new divorce code went into effect in 1980, DeAngelis became "busier, if you can believe it, and even more successful," because he studied accounting at the Wharton School, and "the new divorce law is all accounting."

But it was not a happy time for DeAngelis because "no matter how successful I was, I couldn't succeed in getting close to my children. There was a barrier.... When we were together, we talked only about 'nice' things.... We'd go to Bermuda or Disneyland, but it just wasn't right because we were not able to talk about our real feelings."

The barrier that kept DeAngelis from his children was "my guilt from leaving their mother. I found my way in life, but I left them as young children with their mother. I couldn't get over my guilt. I couldn't forgive myself"—and because they couldn't talk about it, the DeAngelis children, now adults, couldn't forgive him.

"I'd call Barbara on the phone and ask how she was, and she'd say 'fine,' and that would be it. We had nothing meaningful to say.... I'm supposed to be smart ... but nobody taught me how to be a parent. Nobody told me what would happen if I fell out of love with my children's mother. There's nothing in the law books about that. I goofed up."

And over the years he paid a price—in the anguish that so often engulfed him and in the longing that persisted for a relationship that seemed impossible to consummate.

"I couldn't get beyond my guilt. That was what was keeping us apart," and it was so powerful that even DeAngelis, "tough lawyer that I am," was fearful of confronting it.

By now his daughter, Barbara, was into her 30s, herself divorced, and a celebrity psychologist in Los Angeles with a doctoral degree, her own radio program, television appearances, and the directorship of the Personal Growth Center, which offered weekend workshops on relationships.

One day, she called DeAngelis at his office in Norristown, Pa., and told him about the workshops.

"That's nice, Barbara." It was the only response that he could utter at the moment.

But she persisted and called again. "Daddy, please take my workshop."

"Sorry, it's not for me." What he felt, he would say later, was that "I didn't believe in what she was doing. I thought it was West Coast hocus-pocus."

But in November, she called again. "Daddy, I know what you do for a living, and I'm proud of you. But you don't know what I do. Please come to a workshop. I'm writing a book (*How to Make Love All the Time*, which will be published this fall), and I'm able to heal relationships between parents and children. Why can't I heal ours?"

It was an offer that DeAngelis couldn't refuse. So he accepted reluctantly, after his daughter told him that Michael, her brother, would be at the next workshop. "I told her, 'OK, I'll give it a try, but I don't expect much, and I'm not going to stand up in front of a hundred people and tell them what I'm feeling.' I was afraid. I didn't want to face my feelings.... It was time for us, she said, to put our old hurts aside, and I certainly agreed with that. But I was afraid."

•

The workshop began on a Friday night, and 100 people were there.

DeAngelis: "My daughter was on the stage. I sat there, with my show-me attitude. She said there were many parents and children there, all having difficulty in relating. She said that by Sunday night our lives would be changed. I didn't believe it."

But something happened on Saturday morning to put a dent in his skepticism, DeAngelis said. "Barbara was up there with the father of a 17-year-old girl, and he said, 'I love my child. But we haven't talked in five years. I can't get through.' Barbara asked, 'What would you like to tell her?' He said, 'I'd like to tell her I'm sorry,' and Barbara said, 'Well, there she is. Tell her.'

"This girl walked up, and the father looked at her and said, 'I'm sorry, darling. I love you so much, and I miss you.' They put their arms around each other and cried. Everybody cried, including me."

At that point, DeAngelis felt "compelled to walk up to the front and say to the group: 'I want to share my feelings with you.... I love my daughter, and I want to be closer to her.' Barbara said, 'Would you like to tell that to your daughter?' I turned to her and said, 'Barbara, I'm sorry. I didn't want to leave. I had to leave. I feel I let you down. I'm so sorry.'

"She said, 'Daddy, you didn't let me down. You gave me the best gift of all—life. You gave me intelligence. You helped me to be successful. Look at what I do for other people. How can you be sorry?' And we cried and hugged.... A stone I had carried around for years was gone—as if it never had been there....

"I began to see my daughter as a healer. I saw the healing between husbands and wives, between lovers, between parents and children. It was amazing."

This spring, DeAngelis wrote for *New Woman* magazine a story on "how to get the best possible divorce." His daughter read it and called him. "Daddy, it's a wonderful article, but it doesn't contain anything about the emotions of divorce. It's time for us to complete our healing.... You and I are going to write a book about the economics and emotions of divorce. We owe it to the people out there."

The two of them now are working on the book "as father and daughter. We have succeeded in bridging the emotional gap. Now I can call her, and we can talk for hours." The relationship with his son, Michael, has not "had as much breakthrough as with Barbara, but it's almost complete," DeAngelis said.

Where does the healing power of the workshops come from?

DeAngelis: "I went back a second time in the spring.... We sat there, in small groups, paired with a stranger, and they asked, 'What are you sorry about? Who would you like to apologize to?' Even people who no longer are with us. And so you say it to the person you're sitting with, this complete stranger, just as you'd say it to the real person. Something happens to you. People break down. 'Daddy, I'm sorry I didn't tell you I loved you before you died.'

"In watching it happen to others, you feel safe in letting it happen to you.... I was able to stand up in front of a hundred people and say, 'I don't feel guilty anymore. I love you, Barbara.' And she hugged me. I feel free. I've paid my dues.... When I got back, I called my mother, who is 80, and said 'Mom, let's see more of each other. Let's have dinner together more often.'"

•

DeAngelis said that his practice of divorce law has changed since he has changed.

"The first thing I do now with a woman is tell her, 'Look, your husband may be a [no-good], but you must put that aside to help your children.' I tell her to work at helping the children have a relationship with their father, to take them to a store to buy a necktie for Father's Day, to have them call their father. I say, 'They can't be happy without a father, and if they're not happy, you can't be happy. This is something you can do for them—and for yourself.'"

How do people react?

"It's not easy. People are angry. Maybe the husband has taken the wife's car away; the phone has been shut off; the maid doesn't come to the house anymore. I tell them to let go of the anger for the sake of the children, and they look at me as if they think I'm crazy. But I know I'm right....

"Sometimes a husband will snicker, 'Ha, I took away her Mercedes.' I tell him, 'Man, that's dumb. What will your kids think? I'll tell you what—that the [jerk] has made it hard for them to get to school. What are you accomplishing? Don't do it.' For the most part, men listen, and they get the car back to the wife.

"Sometimes, if the parents are really fighting, I'll ask to talk to the kids alone, if they're old enough, 10 or 11, and I'll tell them, 'Stay out of the fight between your parents. You love them both, and they love you.

Don't take sides. Don't play one against the other. It's tough, but you can do it.' And they freeze and say some polite things.... When kids talk, you can see how much they feel the hurt."

DeAngelis said that he worries "about the kids. The kids feel there's a war going on," and they don't know what to do. They are the real casualties of divorce.

When a client first comes to see him, DeAngelis may try to discourage a divorce proceeding, he said—or at least defuse some of the rage. "Divorce is expensive. Nobody can afford it.... It's not so bad for a young couple with no kids, a little apartment, a Volkswagen, and a pair of skis. But when you've been married for 25 years, and you have kids and a big business with profit-sharing, it's different." The stakes are higher and the potential for rage is greater. "At first they don't want to settle things. On January 1, they want blood. By July 1, they're getting the bills, and they realize how costly it is—and how damaging. By December 1, they're more ready to settle things.... But divorce is so much more than a financial settlement."

That's something else, he said, that the law books never taught him.

Dealing with the rotten mood
July 14, 1986

It was the kind of Friday of which nightmares are made—and, as usual, I'd done it to myself, by scheduling more than I could handle.

I had to get the car into the shop for maintenance by 8; then I had an appearance on a radio talk show, an interview, a noon speech, another interview, a stop at the office to go through the mail and return some telephone calls. Then I went to the bank, retrieved the car, hurried home, packed, and picked up my wife at her office for our weekend trip to the beach.

I was tired, hot, and fuming as I nosed the car into expressway traffic, and I said with as much civility as I could muster: "Look, I'm in a rotten mood. It's been a rotten day. Just leave me alone for a while, and I'll be better."

"What happened?"

"I'd feel better if I had somebody I could blame it on, somebody I could yell at. But I did it to myself, and it doesn't help to yell at myself."

Sound familiar?

•

Sidney J. Cohen is a psychologist in private practice in Cherry Hill, N.J., and one of the things he does is help people learn how to deal with people who are moody. It's an area in which Cohen has a personal interest, he said, because "I feel as if I've lived my life with a moody person—the one I see in the mirror every morning."

During an interview, Cohen said there were two varieties of moody people: those who attack and those who withdraw. Either way, those who are on the receiving end tend to make a big mistake "by taking it as personal rejection. That's at least half the problem. It's easier said than done—not taking it personally—but if you can teach yourself not to react that way," you'll be several steps ahead of the rest of us, he said.

The moody person, said Cohen, "by nature tends to be somebody who needs to be loved and appreciated, although he may not look like it when he's moody.... A lot of people feel guilty when they're in a bad mood. They know they're making people around them and themselves miserable, but they feel it can't be controlled."

The result of this inner conflict is that a "vicious circle is created. Actually, two vicious circles—one within and one that's external. The circle that's within—the more the moody person prolongs the mood, the more guilt he feels, and the more guilt he feels, the worse the mood gets.... With the external circle, the worse the mood, the more other people are turned off, and the more they're turned off, the worse the mood gets."

Cohen's method of helping people is to teach them ways in which these circles can be broken.

"The two most typical questions a moody person is asked are, 'What's wrong?' and 'What's the matter with you?' The people who ask are well-intentioned, for the most part, but their tone of voice comes across as attacking or critical. So the moody person is put more on the defensive and either attacks or pouts more. So drop those two questions," and experiment with what Cohen calls his "three tools" for dealing with a moody person:

• Ignore-plus. "This is used mainly with the pouting person, not somebody who attacks. You ask, 'Is there anything I can do?' or 'Do you need me for anything?' This conveys concern, but it's not critical of the person. If the person doesn't want anything, you say, 'OK, please come talk to me when you're ready.' This is the most important step. It lets the moody person know that you'll be there, ready to help. Then you ignore the person. You don't pout, but you go do something—read, cook, whatever." The process is repeated at 15- or 20-minute intervals for up to an hour—and often the moody person has snapped out of it by then and is ready to talk.

• Confrontation. "You can use this under two circumstances—if after an hour you haven't gotten anywhere with ignore-plus, or if there's immediate urgency and you can't wait ... as when the moody person is crassly attacking." Confrontation can be achieved by putting the focus on the moody person: "Will you take a look at what you're doing to yourself? You're making yourself miserable." Or you can put the focus on yourself: "I don't deserve this." If the moody person is especially nasty and saying that you're stupid and horrible, then Cohen recommends a harder approach: "Don't you dare talk to me that way. I want an apology right now." If that doesn't work, it's appropriate to take time out. "Hop in the car and leave for a while."

• Teasing. "This is my favorite. It's also the hardest. It takes lots of self-confidence, and you have to know the other person well enough to understand what that person will respond to.... You can do an imitation of how the person is looking. You can hold up a sign that says I'm here; don't be so mad at me. I love signs. They're a good way to communicate when spoken words fail.... But you can't be sarcastic, or it will backfire."

•

What can the moody person do to help himself or herself?

Cohen has three suggestions: distraction, meditation, and "confession."

With distraction, "you try to do something to distract yourself" from the bad mood. "You could exercise, read, go to a movie"—whatever seems likely to work at the moment.

Meditation simply involves self-relaxation. "Anything you can concentrate on will help," anything that can crack the mood. Unfortunately, when a mood is really bad, a person's ability to concentrate may be impaired to the point that meditation is not possible.

With "confession," the moody person recognizes that he or she is in a lousy mood. It's appropriate to say: "I'm in a bad mood; please let me alone. I need you to respect that." It's important, said Cohen, that the moody person be given space, because this allows time for cooling off.

It's not a good idea, he said, to "yell at yourself if you know that it's your fault that you're in a bad mood. This may prolong the anger."

Living before dying

July 20, 1986

It was March 1983 when Ginny Rich got the dreaded word that her cancer, which she thought had been stamped out by surgery four years earlier, had reappeared.

Her husband, David, described what it was like:

"Casualness was overcome by reality and its accompanying tears, anger, frustration. Why now? A second round of chemotherapy began. This time the treatments required three days in the hospital, days of pills, needles, IVs, X-rays, vomiting, new drugs. This scenario took place every month, with no letup, for more than two years, until May 1985, when Ginny said quietly, 'No more.'

"Now what? What will happen? When? How? It became a time of waiting. How long, oh Lord, how long?

"How does one wait to die? What does one do? The only thing we knew how to do was to go on living.... Our living had its freshness and tender moments, but also its questions, fears, arguments, and disagreements.... Ginny was waiting to die. Not giving up ... but waiting. I, too, was waiting, tired but still waiting."

•

David Rich is an ordained American Baptist minister, executive director of the Pennsylvania Commission for United Ministries in Higher Education, an ecumenical agency of seven Protestant denominations, responsible for developing and carrying out campus ministry in Pennsylvania. His office is in Berwyn, Pa., and five minutes away is the house in which he, his wife, and Martha and Andrew, their college-age children, lived for so many years.

His job involves much travel, but for two years he arranged his schedule so that he always was at home when his wife had to go to the hospital for chemotherapy.

"I want to be with you when you need me," he said.

She told him, "Listen, do what you need to do. I understand."

What would he do ... as the two of them awaited her death?

•

One day the commission's director telephoned. "I'm going to recommend you get a leave of absence. You need to be at home.... You've given us so much through your leadership. Let us give this to you."

Rich: "I didn't ask for it. I didn't even think of asking. But here it was—an indefinite leave of absence at full pay that we would review from time to time.... Is this rare? Because it was a church agency, is that why they thought to offer the leave? Do corporations offer similar leaves to employees? Most people say I was fortunate, and I was....

"I could be present seven days a week, 24 hours a day, as I needed to be.... Ginny was a very private woman. She dealt with a lot of stuff internally. She kept journals.... I needed to talk. She didn't need to talk as much, but at times she'd give a clue that she needed to talk. If I'd been traveling, I would have missed some opportunities. But I was always there.... It was important to be present at those moments when she wanted to talk—whether it was 11 at night, 5 in the morning, 2 in the afternoon."

What did they talk about?

"She talked about the time, in the '60s, when she wanted to pull away from the church. She was interested in communal living. Part of it was to throw off her upbringing, which was very conservative.... It was almost a mild hippie period, and she wondered if she had hung onto her religious roots, would things have been different? Was this, the cancer, some kind of punishment? She didn't dwell on it, but she wondered about it....

"A year before, she had been extremely depressed.... She got lower and lower, and she was asking, 'Who am I, as a woman, a mother, a professional?' She was very talented in arts and crafts, with so many interests. But she hadn't focused on anything in depth, and she worried about that....

"Her mother had died when she was 12, and one day she said, 'I really miss my mother. You're very supportive, Dave, and so are the children. But I miss my mom.' I asked, 'Who could be your mother?' She mentioned a couple of names, including my mother.... So she flew to New York to visit my parents. She looked old and beat as she shuffled onto the plane. It was very sad to see a vibrant woman that way. My parents were shocked. They couldn't believe she looked that way....

"She stayed with them five days ... and she got in touch with something there. I don't know what it was.... But it was a turning point. Her attitude went uphill."

●

In an interview, Rich talked about his feelings:

"I kept wondering how long it was going to take [for her to die]. Everything was coming unglued.... The sexual stuff had stopped six or eight months before. I understood why she wasn't interested.... But she liked to be held, and I held her.... I had some anger.... We had a great medical plan, but all our money was going for her care and for tuition...."

"I didn't feel guilty, but I was frustrated ... and I had some people to say it to, and they said it was OK.... I don't know what people do if they keep it in and when somebody asks about them, they say, 'Oh, I'm fine.'

"I began to say 'I'm not fine.' I'd have lunch or a drink with somebody, and then I could go back home. Ginny knew that.... We were independent people with a ... lot of interdependence.... I could say to her, 'I'm going to have lunch with a friend. Will you be OK for an hour?' She was not possessive. She never said, 'How dare you leave?' She needed her space, too....

"Once she said, 'Dave, I know you care for me, but I don't want you in here now. I need to be alone.' I felt rejected. It hurt so much. I ran from the room and cried.... We respected the mutuality of each other. We would disagree at times and get impatient with each other.... She was a very good friend of mine. I respected her feedback. We had a good marriage, but it was not the myth of two who became one and walked hand in hand into the sunset."

•

It was Ginny who had introduced him to what she called "anticipatory mourning." A year earlier, he had to make a business trip to St. Louis, and while he was at the Philadelphia airport, waiting for his plane, he began to weep.

"It was buckets of tears. I called Ginny and said, 'I don't know what's going on.... I really miss you. I love you so much.' She said, 'It's OK. You'll be all right. Go ahead and take the trip.' And I was to understand that there would be more anticipatory mourning, more tears at unexpected times and places....

"I would think of what it was going to be like without Ginny. Some of my feelings were positive. I'd have a cleaner and more organized house. She left her crafts all over because order wasn't as important to her as to me.... I'd be free to do whatever I wanted. But then I'd break down. Would anything ever be the same again ... without Ginny?"

•

She died on September 29, 1985, at the age of 49, three months before publication of her first book, *Crafts for Fun*. In a series of stories that Rich wrote for the *American Baptist* newspaper, he described the final hours:

"The night is quiet. I find myself waking almost every hour. Her breathing now is more steady, more regular. I awake at 4 A.M. There is a full moon shining through the window on her bed. It is peaceful. Her eyes are closed. Her breath steady. I continue to hold her hand. I watch. I wait. At 6:08 A.M. her last breath is taken. I wait some more. Nothing happens. I call the doctor.

"My best friend, lover, partner is gone after 25 years of life together.... I am quiet. The hibiscus blooms. And God weeps."

•

Rich said that the leave of absence given him by his agency was a precious gift. "From the feedback I get, it's very unusual. I wonder why I never thought to ask....

"Why don't we ask? Does the corporation think about how best to care for a person in this situation? Does the corporation wonder what it can offer? Is something negotiable? Does it take outside intervention— a hospice or a pastor to sit with the employer and explain the situation? 'David is uncomfortable. He needs time. What can we work out?'

"I don't hear this happening.... People feel it's not appropriate. But it is appropriate. I'd be open to asking for somebody else.... My optimistic side thinks that people are more open to dealing with it than we think. I may be naive, but it's where I am."

The meaning of pornography
September 1, 1986

The letter was from a man who wanted to tell me what he had learned after he had gone into therapy to try to rid himself of the compulsion to spend "so much time" in the fantasy world of pornography. Here is part of what he wrote:

"In therapy, I found that my preoccupation with pornography had nothing to do with my sexual desire but was a vehicle for acting out anger.... Real sex is doing with. Pornography is doing to. I'm convinced that it's sick, childish, abusive, and is damaging not only to women but also to the souls of men.... After years of wallowing in that stuff, I can look at it now with no interest, no desire. The girls just look foolish and exploited and sad to me.... I realize how sick I was—and how free and healthy I feel now."

•

Another letter was from a woman who wanted to tell me what it was like to be married to a man who was hooked on pornography. Here is part of what she wrote:

"I've been married to him for 22 years, and he was into pornography before he met me.... Many times over the years, I asked myself, 'What's the matter with me?' I live by my standards, he lives by his. I would have preferred that he raise his standards to meet mine, and I'm sure he's tried. I tried lowering mine to his level, but that didn't work either.... I ask him now not to expose me to it, and he respects my wishes....

"What does this do to a relationship? Is he grateful that I have accepted him as he really is, or does he scorn me for putting up with a situation that I abhor? I really don't know.... I love this man, and yet one of the most basic ingredients to a strong relationship has been badly damaged—respect.... On my best day, I know I'm not going to be enough for him. Is this my fault?"

•

The two letters were among many that I received after a column in which I and an "exotic" dancer I had interviewed took the position that men turn to pornography basically because they feel that they're not getting what they need at home.

I sent copies of the two letters to psychiatrist George S. Layne, who is director of the mental-health unit at the Lower Bucks Hospital in Bristol, and who in a letter to me had been critical of the column because "you always blame the woman for everything." What did Layne think about the whole issue of pornography?

In an interview, he said that "the one thing you can say about pornography is that you can't generalize. It's always very specific to the person. Not everybody who's into pornography is dealing with unresolved anger.... We have to be careful not to say that everybody with an interest in pornography is suffering from some illness or unresolved issue."

Sometimes, said Layne, pornography has a legitimate use in therapy. "Some people get married and don't know how to have sex. They come from homes where it was never talked about. They were sheltered, and they might benefit from looking at pictures. If they're embarrassed by nudity, they might be desensitized by pictures....

"Let's say that a man is impotent but that he can function if he looks at pictures first. We might use pictures first as a step in treatment, then try to wean him off pictures.... Most therapists take the position, 'If it works, do it.'"

But it's important, said Layne, to "differentiate that kind of pornography from the kind that makes a link between sexual behavior and violent behavior.... Some of the detective magazines always seem to connect sex with rape, murder, or torture. That's the kind of connection that has people worried.... Can pornography lead to violent behavior? There's no reason to believe that pornography with sexual excitement leads to violence. But when pornography connects sex with violence, it amounts to tacit approval ... and some naive, immature person is going to get the feeling that this is how you're supposed to behave."

Layne said that in his opinion pornography is not a problem until it becomes a compulsion: "If you assume a compulsive need, you can assume a problem." But even so, he said, it doesn't necessarily mean that the men are "perverted in the common sense of the word.... It can be a way of dealing with anger, sadistic impulses, voyeurism.... Maybe the man didn't do a good job of resolving his impulses, and he needs pornography for that. Like any addiction, it requires a fix."

It's possible, said Layne, that a man can be addicted to pornography but can box it in so that it doesn't interfere with the rest of his life. "He maybe has a wife at home with a decent sexual relationship. But if the behavior interferes with a good relationship, then he has a problem. I would have to hear from the wife that he's not paying attention to her."

•

What would Layne say if the woman with the pornography-loving husband came to him for help?

"I would wonder if she feels there's something immoral about it.... Maybe it's a moral issue. Maybe her father taught her that pornography was a no-no ... and this means that her husband is not matching up with her father.... People need to talk to each other ... and understand their different rates of need for sexual turn-on. They need to be able to come to some compromise.... Most people who are worried about their spouse and pornography probably need to do more talking with the spouse about sexual needs."

It's possible, said Layne, that the use of pornography may be one symptom of a broader problem that should be the focus of therapy: "I would want to explore the relationship. They may not have had a good relationship to begin with."

The business of socializing
September 16, 1986

If you are climbing the stairsteps of success with single-minded devotion, you may be wondering whether there's anything else you can do to boost your career, to be noticed by the "right" people, to put another feather in your cap.

Well, yes, as a matter of fact, and it's in an area that you, with your head buried in the corporate innards, may not have thought much about: the social scene.

Let's listen as human resources consultant John D. Erdlen tells us the reasons why:

"The ability to interact socially with fellow employees and management can be a plus for career advancement," and it's the shrewd person who understands this and puts it to use at social functions sponsored by the corporation.

"Take the time to strategize before a function, as if it were your next business meeting. The dividends may show up at your next performance review and result in financial and professional success."

Erdlen, who is chief executive officer of Costello, Erdlen & Co. of Westwood, Mass., offered these suggestions:

Volunteer to serve on committees, and if it's a corporate picnic, consider cooking hamburgers, slicing watermelons, judging races, or distributing name tags. "These activities offer access to individuals who may be in a position to foster your career."

Introduce yourself to senior executives, if the occasion arises, and express appreciation for sponsorship of the event. "Greet spouses of associates and subordinates and acknowledge their interest and support."

Listen for favorable comments or criticism of your job performance. "This is valuable information to build on later."

Here are some things that Erdlen suggests that you avoid:

• Stay away from conversations that are critical of individuals or company policies. "Negative remarks can be misquoted or taken out of context."

• Don't probe for information that is outside your area of responsibility, nor disclose confidential matters as a means of developing a relationship. "These discussions are often brought to the attention of company management—with severe repercussions."

• Refrain from excessive drinking, inappropriate attire, company romance, and lengthy discussion of organizational issues, "particularly negative ones."

In an interview, Erdlen said that participation in corporate activities outside the office "gives you exposure to people throughout the company ... and demonstrates your attitude of being a total team player.... If your spouse attends with you, it's an indication that she or he is aware of and supports your career ... and fits in with the company environment. This can be important to senior management."

How much should you drink at a company function?

"You have to be yourself. You don't want to patronize your bosses and drink just because they're drinking.... The rule is that you should do what is acceptable within the organization. In some, it's OK to drink. In others, it's not OK. You have to accept whatever the culture is."

What if the boss is a big, big drinker? "Do what's right for you. If you try to match the boss, it may catch up with you—and with him. Don't emulate any bad habits the boss may have."

Do you let the boss win at golf or do you try to skunk him?

"Don't be unreasonably competitive. You don't want to play up to the boss and miss a two-foot putt to let him win, but you don't want to show how good you are to embarrass the boss." Translation: If the boss is seven-down after nine holes, ease up and shank a shot here and there.

Why avoid company romances? Are they still considered the kiss of death in many places?

"If you're going to have a company romance, it has to be done right.... If neither is in a position to do it—if one or both are married— then it should be avoided at all costs. If both are eligible for dating, they should keep it to themselves and not parade it around. They have to keep it in good taste....

"It's not as bad as it once was. I met my wife in an office environment, and when we were married, she had to quit. We've come a long way since then," but it's still wise to be cool about it—at least in the corporate setting. "If romance interferes with either of them, the company is going to be upset. If others are going to gossip and be concerned, the company is going to be upset."

Is it important to go to all or most company functions?

Yes and no, said Erdlen. "You don't want to get a reputation as a social butterfly ... by appearing at everything. People will wonder why you don't have a home life. And, in fact, going to everything can ruin your home life.... It's OK to go to many of the functions, but don't always be the first to arrive and the last to leave. Don't try to take over every function by always being the chairperson. You don't have to be the leader of everything. You can work behind the scenes. You don't always have to make the speeches and hand out the awards."

Is it all right to talk business at social gatherings?

Only if the person in command takes the lead, said Erdlen. "If the person for whom you work brings up something and if you feel that he wants to continue talking, well, OK, but be discreet." Don't pursue it to the point that the other person seems uncomfortable. "If you get a reputation of always trying to find out things, people will begin to shy away from you."

How much success will you allow yourself?

September 21, 1986

Arlene Kramer, who could reasonably be called a 24-hour-a-day therapist, was talking about a problem that, in her judgment, "is running
amok in our society."

The problem is this: "Young women have come to believe that if
they're successful, they can't have home and hearth. It's hopeless,
depressing, and demoralizing.... The message always is that women
have to choose, that if they're too successful, nobody can deal with
them, that men are threatened. I get so tired of hearing that."

It's true, said Kramer, that as a woman becomes more successful in
her career, the pool of available men thins. But "the pool thins in a number of directions—if you're 6-1, if you're 4-10, if you're overweight, if you
can't ski" or play tennis, if you don't exercise or drink wine coolers.

It is a "very faulty premise" that links success and the improbability
of marriage, said Kramer—yet it's a premise into which many women
have bought.

"I see women with tears in their eyes, and they're saying, 'I made it,
and I'm home alone.' But this is such superficial reasoning.... How
come Margaret Mead, Joanne Woodward, and Sandra Day O'Connor
got married? There are men out there," and it's a blatant cop-out for a
woman to put the focus solely on her success.

Rather than success, said Kramer, the heart of the matter is this:

"How much can you permit yourself to have in life? Who do you feel
you are and what do you deserve? I see this directly connected to the
message that mothers give to their daughters, sometimes directly by
words but primarily by how the mothers live their lives."

Most of today's young career women were brought up by mothers
who were housewives or who, at best, had relatively low-level jobs, said
Kramer. "They certainly didn't have the professional careers that
women have today ... and the mothers were not able to convey to their
daughters that it's OK to do it," to go for the gold, to grab for the brass
ring.

"They never said, 'Sweetheart, go out and get your Ph.D., be a physician, get married, be happy.' They never said, 'Sweetheart, I want you to
have it. Feel free to go beyond me.' They never said it ... because they
couldn't. It wasn't in their repertoire."

Typically, the message from mothers was "Stay here with me"—
because the mothers feared abandonment, said Kramer. It was a message that became etched on the souls of the young women, and it crip-

pled many of them.

"It's why some women are so ambivalent about success. They do good things with the right hand and take them back with the left hand. They feel that 'somehow I'm bad if I do it.' As a therapist, I have to cut through that and give them another message."

What Kramer does, she said, is give to the young women who come to her what they never got from their mothers—permission to fly as far and as high as their talents will take them. It's a message that must be repeated and acted out in many ways over a substantial period of time to give it enough weight to override the earlier message from mother.

"Therapy can take a long time—a number of years. It's not something you do in six weeks," said Kramer.

It's also not something that is done once a week during the therapeutic hour.

"You need to be there when they need you, during times of self-doubt, self-deprecation.... I say to them, 'Call when you need to talk to me.' Or I call them, to ask how they're doing. Not everybody can reach out to you, even if you give them permission, because they think, 'I don't want to bother her' or 'She'd get mad at me.' When something upset them, I want them to know that I'm available."

Kramer, whose office is in Center City, creates relationships with her clients. She goes out with them to birthday parties, graduations, and other occasions that are special. "One woman got into law school, and we went out to celebrate. Somebody else moved into a new house she didn't think she'd ever be able to afford, and we celebrated that.... Sometimes we go shopping together. Many girls never were taken shopping by their mothers, and they don't know what to buy."

It is time that never is charged to anybody's bill, said Kramer. She does it because "I want to do it right," and doing it right means that she, in some ways, becomes a substitute mother. Certainly she is an authority figure, a mentor to whom the women can look for direction and understanding.

Eventually, said Kramer, young women come to feel entitled to the success that they have achieved, and they are able to accept the good things that come their way without feeling that they are impostors.

"My message has to come to be as powerful as the earlier messages. I grant permission. 'I want you to do well.... I expect you to do better than I do.... My pleasure is to see you leave me in the dust.... That's how you can pay me back—by being as great as you have the ability to be.' It's a vision that is created over time. 'Knock them dead. You can be great.'

"It's a journey. I take her hand, and the two of us take off.... It's a journey that never ends. I expect her to leave me behind and find another mentor. It's OK to leave people behind—parents, therapists, mentors—and to find other mentors, as long as you need to."

Kramer said that it's a mistake to blame parents for giving out the wrong messages. "You can't give somebody something you don't have. Parents gave what they had . . . and you can't spend your life bemoaning that. You can't forever hate them. You have to let go and get on with life. I don't think parents woke up one morning planning to torture their children," and parents should be given credit for doing the best they could, even if at times it wasn't too good.

"The therapist's job is to help fill in the empty spaces."

•

Must the therapeutic relationship necessarily be woman-to-woman to be most successful?

It's true, said Kramer, that the parent-child programming should come from the same-sex parent, but in therapy, a male "could make it work, too. A man could be nurturing and help women get through it. But female-to-female is very powerful. That I do know."

Kramer said that women who in childhood got their messages of encouragement from father rather than mother often have paid a heavy price—guilt, which has been described as the gift that keeps on giving.

"The daughter who is encouraged by her father begins to feel more special than her mother, and this causes her to feel bad. She's with her dad, and mom's out in the kitchen, and she becomes more the wife [to her father] than her mother."

It's a guilt, said Kramer, that may take the woman many years to outgrow—even with good professional help.

•

The people who do best in overcoming adversity that is rooted in the past are those who possess what amounts to a "life force," said Kramer. "I can't tell you where it comes from. . . . They're willing to fall down and get up, fall down and get up. They are people who say, 'I'm willing to do whatever I have to do to get from here to there.' They have the courage to face the ordeal of change. Even change for the better is terrifying."

Do the clients who are in the process of change keep Kramer constantly on the move? Does she ever have an hour to call her own?

It's not as hectic as it might appear, said Kramer, who has been divorced for 10 years.

"Everybody's not in crisis at the same time. My phone isn't ringing all the time. It's not that I've gone into the jungle like Schweitzer and given up everything. . . . I get around. I have friends. I go to parties. I have vacations. I go out to eat. . . . I enjoy my life."

One family and bipolar illness

September 29, 1986

For 27 agonizing, unbelievable years, Marvin Silverman suffered the ravages of bipolar illness, during which he cycled between the frantic peaks of mania and the bleak valleys of depression.

When he was on a high, he "wanted to control things ... and I always had the sense that I was right. No matter what, I was right." He was verbally abusive to his wife, Shirley, who said that "I felt sorry for him, but at the same time I wanted to strangle him. When he was high, his judgment was impaired, and he couldn't be trusted, but he didn't see it that way."

When he was low, he wanted to bury himself at home and talk to nobody. "It was terrifying," he said. "My worst enemy should get depression." Said she: "It was dreadfully sad to watch."

Between the highs and lows, Marvin Silverman wallowed in "the trough," waiting for the mood swing to begin all over again. For 27 years, his life was in a kind of holding pattern. He worked regularly, as a high school English teacher in Philadelphia, and he paid the bills and parented his three children. But by no stretch of the imagination was he living.

Shirley Silverman: "There were times when I didn't see how the marriage could continue.... Sometimes fear drove me out of the house," the fear of trying to deal with somebody who, although he legally was her husband, was not really her husband at all.

Over the years, Marvin Silverman, who now is 55, sought help from a lot of people.

There was the Freudian psychiatrist who off and on for a dozen years tried to analyze him out of his illness and who finally in frustration said, "That's it. You're going to have to learn to live with it."

There was another psychiatrist who gave him tranquilizers. "I was like a zombie," said Marvin Silverman. "I tried to play tennis, but I couldn't even hit the ball. I was swinging up here when the ball was down there."

There was the physician who prescribed anti-depressants. "I got bloated and constipated, and my sex drive disappeared," he said, but the illness remained.

There was even a "healer" with whom Marvin Silverman, in desperation, conferred about the need to "transfer energy from my toes to my head and from my head to my toes."

Shirley Silverman: "We were very young. We didn't ask questions. We thought the doctors were gods, and we did what we were told. Now, we can look back and say, 'Sure, they weren't helpful,'—but at the time they served some purpose, I suppose. They gave us something to hold on to."

Once, in the late 1960s, he was directed to an outpatient clinic where lithium, which today is considered the treatment of choice for bipolar illness, was being tried out. For 18 months, he took the medication; but nothing happened, and the psychiatrist who was treating him at the time did not seem disappointed, Marvin Silverman said. "I think he was hoping that it wouldn't work, because, if it had, it would have trashed his approach to treatment," which was that the patient's problem was in his head and needed to be treated with psychotherapy.

For some years, Marvin Silverman, in disillusionment, sought no help at all. Then two good things happened:

He met a therapist who understood bipolar illness for what it was—a family problem in which everybody had to be involved.

He was directed to a physician who wanted to give lithium another try.

Today he is, in his words, "like a normal person again." His condition has been stabilized for three years, and his marriage is strong. But the memory remains: "If I had to do it over again, I wouldn't."

Shirley Silverman: "I was on the verge of leaving in the early '70s. I'd gone to school, got my degree, and I was working, and it was economically possible for me to leave.... But this therapist showed me that we had a vital marriage, a long history together, and it was worth fighting for."

The fight, she said, consisted of coming to terms with her husband's illness. "In the beginning, no amount of talk by psychiatrists could convince me that it was real. I thought it was a copout, that Marvin really didn't want to try. If it were real, why didn't he conquer it? It took me many years to accept that, yes, this is a disease. Marvin wasn't copping out. He wasn't mean. He was ill. This is hard to accept. I'm not sure the children truly accepted it, but it's crucial to the victim's well-being for it to be accepted."

●

Nobody can explain why lithium didn't help Marvin Silverman the first time. Maybe the dosage wasn't high enough. Maybe this, maybe that.

He described his life back then: "I never did anything dangerous when I was manic.... Shirley says I was verbally abusive, and I guess I was, but it didn't seem that way to me. Everything I did seemed perfectly normal.... I'd write poetry, and it would seem great. You've heard about how creativity may be enhanced during the manic phase.... It didn't work that way for me. I'd go back and read it later, and it wasn't great. Believe me, it wasn't great."

The depression was much worse than the mania—and it lasted much longer, sometimes three or four months at a stretch.

"The only time I felt relatively comfortable was when nobody was in the house," he said. "At times, I took the phone off the hook.... At school, I managed to make it through the days; I had nothing to do with my colleagues. It was self-imprisonment. If anybody noticed anything was wrong, they didn't say anything. Only my closest friend loved me enough to express concern.... I'd come home and read a book or watch television, anything to keep my mind off my misery.... I was bereft of the world."

His advice to bipolar victims: "Recognize that you're sick, that you've got something that chicken soup can't fix.... Be dedicated to finding a solution. If they tell you that you've got to accept it, don't believe them. Keep looking."

Men, women, and sexual outlook
October 9, 1986

The note from a reader said that she was tired of my "always blaming the woman for everything that goes wrong in a marriage," and she asked that I write a column with the theme of "There are no frigid women, only clumsy men."

Well, what about that?

That's what I asked psychiatrist John Reckless, who was one of the early students of Masters and Johnson and who knows as much about sex, frigidity, and clumsiness as anybody you're likely to meet. Reckless's reaction:

"It's a put-down phrase, an unfair statement. Sex for the female is determined by many factors," only one of which is the male's inability to do the right thing at the right time.

But is clumsiness often a problem?

It used to be, said Reckless. In the old days, 25 or 30 years ago, men "didn't know how to find the clitoris or what to do with it.... Men have more knowledge now," said Reckless, and whatever clumsiness remains can be helped by women's sharing with their men "what they need to be orgasmic."

But, said Reckless, it's important for women to understand that they must be tactful in how they ask for what they want.

"If she acts like a drill sergeant at Parris Island when she tells him

213

what to do, it won't be helpful. There are two things that a woman shouldn't tell a man he can't do well: make love and drive a car."

•

British-born Reckless, former professor of psychiatry at Duke University, is medical director of the busy John Reckless Clinic in Durham, N.C., which is devoted to psychiatry, psychosomatic medicine and the treatment of sexual dysfunction, and relationships that have turned sour. During an interview, Reckless focused on the sexual differences between men and women.

The primary need for a woman is to feel special, he said, and she will feel special and have enhanced sexuality if she is in a relationship that offers these four essential elements:

• Time. Does the man have quality time for her, time when she is the sole focus of his attention? "If she doesn't get the time, she doesn't want sex."

• Touch. Most women "crave to be held," which is distinctly different from being touched sexually.

• Talk. Women feel left out if a man doesn't talk about his feelings. On the other hand, "if a man is in pain and talks about the pain, the woman feels a connection" and wants to hold him and love him. It's very probable that she will respond sexually.

• Trust. She must believe wholeheartedly that the man is committed to her, that he will listen compassionately to her innermost feelings—without automatically providing her with solutions. What a woman needs, rather than solutions, are abstract things, such as a glance, a touch, a poem, warm feelings.

•

What about a man? What does it take to make a man sexually responsive?

Well, said Reckless, it doesn't take much. Not very much at all. A man responds quickly to visual stimulation. "The wind blows up a woman's skirt, and the man whips around and takes a look. A woman doesn't respond the same way. If a man's pants fell down on the street, not many women would 'ooh' and 'aah.' But men are almost constantly sexually preoccupied," and they often turn to sex in much the same way that an infant reaches for the bottle—for comfort.

Men tend to deny certain feelings, such as loneliness and anxiety, and to deal with them by sexualizing them, said Reckless. This is a major reason that many men get involved with pornography, he said.

"A man is lonely, and he doesn't know what to do. So he goes to a pornography shop and buys a magazine. He denies the need for companionship to overcome his lonely feelings" and instead uses sex for relief. "He has a climax, falls asleep, and he's OK." The man has dealt with his feelings of loneliness without ever acknowledging them.

"A man will deny his anxiety. He's worried because the business is not doing well or the kids are not doing well. But he doesn't recognize that he's feeling anxious ... and he may begin to become preoccupied with pornography" as a way to ease his anxiety. "There's a sense of doing something exciting ... and somehow he feels that he beats the system. He can't ask his wife for sex; she wants to talk. So he goes to the porno shop, and he's rather like a conditioned monkey. He pumps $20 worth of quarters into a machine.... He strings out his sexual arousal for 30 or 45 or 60 minutes ... and he really enjoys this intense sexual preoccupation, because he's not worried about anything."

•

What about women? Is there some watered-down version of pornography that appeals to them, even if they aren't visually oriented the way men are?

"Women usually like things that are less explicit. If a woman is lonely, she may get a Jackie Collins book or a Harlequin romance novel ... and replace the heroine with herself. If she looked at a visual image, she would notice that the lady had dirty feet," not that the lady was sexually involved.

Thriving in a two-career marriage
October 12, 1986

It was an interview that stayed with me for a long time because it produced not only a much-talked-about column but also material that I wove into many of my speeches about the eternal need for work-play balance in our lives.

Psychologist Julian Slowinski had talked about his decision to buy a house on the French coast, where he and his family would spend every August. Yes, he could rent a house more cheaply, but "there's a difference between buying a place for an investment and buying a place for fun. People say, 'It's a lousy investment.' I say, 'So what? It's fun.'"

Slowinski had talked figuratively about the importance of sniffing the roses. "We need to take time to have a concept of ourselves and to understand what we see as really important. On the deathbed, we always wish we had done this or that. The trick is to do it while we're alive."

He had talked literally about the importance of sipping the champagne. "I'm always looking for opportunities to celebrate. Years ago, before it became popular, I discovered cheap Spanish champagne ... and I kept the refrigerator full of it and celebrated with it.... The thing to remember is that the more we do things we enjoy, the more we increase the chances of doing them again."

And he had talked about the obstacles to balance. "Materialism and consumerism get in the way. And we, ourselves, get in the way ... because we put our whole ego into the job.... In two-career marriages—I have one myself—the stress often is incredible because people have no time for anything but work.... People often put success in the business world over personal happiness because they equate success with happiness." But it doesn't work that way, at least not for most of us.

•

My first telephone call one morning was from a Philadelphia man who, because of the nature of his work, is mentioned in the newspapers almost every day. It's a high-visibility, pressure-cooker kind of job, he said, and that was part of his problem. The other part was that his executive-level wife was in a pressure-cooker kind of job, too, and when they came together at day's end, they often created not a celebration but an explosion.

Yes, he said, he knew that the rule of thumb was that the person who was the least incapacitated should try to nurture the person who was the more incapacitated. But what happens when both are knocked out, victims of their separate battles against the dragons? What happens when neither has the energy or inclination to take the first step toward helping the other?

I told him that my mail suggested that many two-career couples were in the situation that he described. Yes, I would write something about it. Then I made an appointment to see Julian Slowinski.

•

What is important, said Slowinski, is for work-weary couples "to call a spade a spade," to examine their situation as it really is and decide what, if anything, they can do to make it better.

"We need to periodically appraise the situation and not be afraid to admit that we don't like it. For many people, there's the fear that if they admit they don't like it, they have to do something about it. But that's not so. We don't have to do anything about it. The very act of talking—

'We're in this together, kid; hang on'—can be helpful, acknowledging it instead of carrying a grudge. It's not what happens in a situation but what we tell ourselves about it" that often determines if we sink or swim.

It is essential, said Slowinski, for couples to understand the difference between changing expectations and settling for something.

"I see a lot of this in my office, two-career couples who come in, and they've settled for infrequent, unsatisfying sex because they feel it can't be any other way. This settling is what produces a great inertia" that deadens and often kills relationships.

What people in this situation should do, he said, is change their expectations. "A couple may say 'We'd like to have more sex, but we're too exhausted, and so what can we do about it?' What they can do is negotiate an agreement that says 'Yes, we're tired, and we'll forget about sex during the week, but we'll consider weekend time for romance. At least we're doing something'—rather than settling for nothing. They won't get upset about no sex during the week because they've acknowledged that they're too tired. They have changed their expectations."

Busy couples need to "accept and live with the boundaries of their daily routines," said Slowinski. "But typically what people do is define a situation as unchangeable but then try to change it. When they find out that they can't change it, they get depressed. The idea has to be, 'If nothing can change, I will not get upset. I will cope with it and look for the opportunity to be more flexible.' The weekend schedule does not have to be the same as the weekday schedule."

Does this put such pressure on weekends that, no matter what happens, weekends will be disappointing?

"You've got to be realistic.... A sense of humor helps.... Yes, it's hard work.... Yes, life is tough."

•

Slowinski's Paris-born wife, Betty, has a doctoral degree in French literature, and she is a research specialist in the Wharton School's Industrial Research Unit, which is a worldwide think tank that produces reports analyzing the political and economic climates in countries in which its clients do business. She writes the French edition, and, said Slowinski, it is a demanding job because "if a government falls somewhere, the research is no good, and you've got to start all over."

The Slowinskis' agreement is that he takes "the morning shift" and gets their 11-year-old son, Stefan, to school. She takes "the afternoon shift" when Stefan comes home, and often she and Stefan do their homework together. Slowinski arrives home at 6 on an early day but generally it's not until 7, 8, or even 9.

"What a couple does at home depends on the quality of the relationship. One couple might have some wine and plop down together and unwind. Another couple might want to be alone, separately, for half an hour. It depends on what works for people.... If you have children, there may be no time for anything," except wrestling with the children's demands.

What is life like in the Slowinski household in the evening?

Well, they have their problems, too, he said—like everybody else.

"I come home and want to unwind. I'm very gregarious.... I have a high energy level, higher than Betty. Sometimes she feels pressured ... and the kid gets caught in the middle. I want to talk with him, and she tells me not to interfere with his homework. She says, 'Because you're finished, you think the rest of the world is finished, too.' She's working, too, sometimes, and I can't find anybody to play with."

So what does he do?

"I can have fun doing anything. I can have fun watching a grasshopper." Translation: He amuses himself, generally not by watching grasshoppers but by punching up a fluffy movie on the VCR, listening to music or "sitting in front of the fireplace with a glass of something in my hand. I can do that for hours."

And there is, of course, that time every August in the house in France, that time of renewal and regeneration.

•

Slowinski said that what he sees in many two-career families are women who accept a disproportionate share of household responsibilities. "I do a helluva lot of cooking and nurturing, but some men don't do much of anything.... Even when the husband is cooperative, the wife may feel guilty because she feels that she should be doing more. No matter how much she's doing, she may feel that it's not enough" because, culturally, women have been programmed to do it all.

This is when the woman may feel trapped and helpless, he said, because she feels that she can't do anything to change the situation. "I think the woman feels the stress of her role more than the man."

What's an answer?

Part of the answer may be for the couple to hire a housekeeper and a babysitter—"and not feel guilty about it."

It's what Slowinski was referring to when he talked about the importance of calling a spade a spade. If you can't do it all yourself, acknowledge it and try to change it, if you can.

Would you like to grow old before your time?

October 21, 1986

It could be described as a typical corporate seminar on a subject that touches just about everybody—preparing for retirement.

It could be described as a typical group, too—people from many places in the work force, in golf shirts and slacks and in gray flannel suits and striped neckties, ranging in age from the middle 50s to almost 65.

The topic of the moment was health—and how to preserve it in the so-called golden years—and at the front of the room was Cynthia Livingston, who directs Hahnemann University's community health program in Philadelphia and who was asking what sounded like a strange question: "How many of you hope to get old before your time?"

Not a single hand went up, of course, and a few snickers rose from the 40 or so people who would spend two days listening to speakers on subjects from Social Security to stress, from money to leisure time.

Livingston looked at the people who didn't want to get old before their time and began asking more questions:

"How many of you are overweight?"

It looked as if almost every hand in the room reluctantly drifted up.

"How many of you are relatively inactive? How many of you don't get much exercise?"

More than half of the people acknowledged that they spent a lot of time more or less sitting on their hands.

"How many of you smoke?"

About one-third of the hands waved.

"How many of you don't feel satisfied with life? How many feel that the stressful side of life outweighs the side you feel good about?"

People looked at each other, as if to get permission. Then eight or 10 hands went up.

Well, said Livingston, the four factors that she had asked about all related to premature aging—and it looked as if a number of people in the group were trying with all their might to get old before their time.

Suddenly, her original question didn't seem so strange—and nobody was snickering.

The bad news, said Livingston, is that the way we live can lead us to premature aging. The good news is that "we have control over it," and that statistics show that by changing lifestyles, people can lengthen their lives and remain active and productive in those extra years.

As a nation, said Livingston, "we are dying from heart disease, cancer, stroke, and accidents. These four account for 73 percent of all deaths," and it's possible for us to reduce the odds of heart disease, cancer, and stroke by maintaining ideal weight, getting reasonable exercise, not smoking, and dealing with our daily stresses.

Yet, said Livingston, lots of people continue to live in unhealthy ways. "Why do we do this to ourselves? Are we not too bright?" No, for the most part, the problem is that we don't have the information we need about what we're doing to our health. "We get into patterns of living, and patterns are hard to change. But we can change."

Here are some of Livingston's suggestions for change in the four areas that are critical to good health:

• Proper weight. As we get older, we require fewer calories to maintain our weight. A man at 65 needs 600 fewer calories a day than at 55, and a woman needs 500 fewer calories. If we don't eat less, we will gain weight, but the Catch-22 is that in eating less, we may not get the nutrients we need to stay healthy.

Livingston suggested keeping a 10-week "eating diary" so we can become clear about what we eat—caloric content and nutritional value. As we age, we need more calcium, protein, and fiber, she said.

• Reasonable exercise. "This raises images of people in sweat clothes, jogging and killing themselves. But we're talking about any kind of physical activity, including household tasks and gardening. It's important to have plenty of daily exercise. How often do you use the stairs instead of taking the elevator?"

Exercise, said Livingston, must be fun. "If you don't enjoy it, you don't do it."

A balanced exercise program should include aerobic exercises to strengthen the cardiovascular system, non-aerobic exercises for strength and muscle tone, and stretching exercises to improve flexibility and increase resistance to strains and sprains. Some classic aerobic exercises: running, walking, biking, rowing, swimming, jumping rope.

The key to meaningful aerobic exercise is to get the heart rate up to what is called the "target" rate and keep it there for 12 minutes. The target rate is calculated by subtracting your age from 220 and taking 70 percent of that.

• Not smoking. About 350,000 people die every year from smoking-related problems, said Livingston, and smoking is "the leading cause of preventable deaths."

One-third of the population still smokes, she said, and the bad news is that the death rate for smokers ages 45 to 54 is 150 percent higher than for non-smokers of the same age. The good news is that "of those who quit smoking every year, 90 percent do it on their own." This means that it's not necessary to go into a formal program to stop smoking if you're sufficiently committed to stopping. But if you need help, don't be hesitant to seek it.

• Managing stress. "You can approach a neutral event as stressful or as a challenge. What you say to yourself determines [to a great extent] if an event will be stressful or not." So it's important to monitor your internal dialogue.

It's also important to find out what helps you to shed stress and to feel peaceful—and to engage in as much of this as you can. Activities can range from listening to music to deep breathing to stroking your pet. What works for you is what you should be doing.

Healthy talk, unhealthy talk
November 18, 1986

To every thing there is a season ...
                                        —Ecclesiastes 3:1

Not long ago, I spent three days in a management seminar—after all, I write a lot about management—and in one exercise, the eight people in the group to which I was assigned were asked to evaluate each other on a variety of points.

A woman said she found it virtually impossible to evaluate me because, as she put it, "I don't feel that I know you."

"Why not?" I asked.

"Because you only talk when you have something to say."

I thanked her for what I regarded as a first-rate compliment.

•

The problem, psychologist Edward B. Fish was saying, is that in this time of heavy emphasis on communication, more people are talking more but saying less than ever before.

"We've reached the point of overkill. We talk so much that it becomes part of the problem—instead of the solution. Up to a point, talking makes sense. But like anything else, it can be overdone to the point of absurdity.... We start to intellectualize our relationships and analyze them excessively. We have sexual difficulties, and we talk about sex instead of making love....

"I believe in Ecclesiastes.... There is a time to talk, a time to be silent. Both can be meaningful. The trick is to know when each is appropriate and inappropriate."

There is healthy talk and there is unhealthy talk, Fish said.

"Healthy talk is when you talk because you have something to say to add to the relationship, to help make the relationship more interesting.... Unhealthy talk is when what you say is meaningless or destructive, when you try to overpower the other person with words. You're not trying to convey information; you're trying to gain power....

"If you're an oral person, you have an advantage over the person who is less oral and you learn to use words as weapons. You never give the other person a chance to interject....

"Good talk is a dialogue. Bad talk is a monologue. In good talk, you listen and respond. In bad talk, you're into your own agenda and you don't listen.... In good talk, you hope to show the other person a reason to change. In bad talk, you insist that you're right and that the other must recognize it.... In good talk, you stay with the issues. In bad talk, you ramble, talk around the issue, attack the other person....

"In good talk, you show respect for what the other person says. There's an exchange of ideas, a parity between talking and listening. The stated purpose is to enlighten. In bad talk, you don't listen ... and the unstated purpose is to indoctrinate. 'You got to believe what I want you to believe.' It's the difference between education and propaganda."

A barrier to good talk is what Fish calls "psycho-babble," and it not infrequently is employed by people who have gone to a seminar "or read a few books and don't quite understand it all but throw it around anyway. They try to play therapist. They can talk a good relationship but can't do it....

"They tell another person, 'You're insecure,' and if you disagree, they say, 'Now you're defensive.' They say that you rationalize, that you deny, that you project, that you're threatened. They use these terms to get away from the issue," and what follows becomes a debate instead of a discussion.

How can this be stopped?

"It takes two to play. You can end it by asking, 'Hey, what kind of game are we playing? What the hell are we doing? Come on, let's stay with the issue and try to look at it objectively.'

"You need a *Robert's Rules of Parliamentary Procedure,* or whatever it's called. When you're on old business, you stay with old business. When you're into new business, you don't talk about old business."

Sometimes it's possible to put a stop to the game by appealing to a point that's near and dear to the other person's heart. A true story from Fish's casebook:

"This lawyer treated his wife like he treated a witness in court. He was far more verbal, and she never had a chance. Finally she said, 'All I want in this relationship is justice. I want you to be fair. You're more articulate, but that doesn't mean you're always right. Is what is happening just? Is my case being represented as well as yours? If you represented me, would you accept what you're doing to me? You don't want me to use sex as a weapon, and I don't want you to use your tongue as a weapon.' She appealed to him as an attorney, and he responded to that."

When is a good time to talk?

When both people want to talk—but sometimes, in a crunch, "you may have to do it now, whether everybody is ready or not." But, as a rule, talk is not especially wise when:

• One or the other of you is hurrying to get off to work in the morning.

• You're together in a car and try to take advantage of a captive audience.

• One of you is asleep. It's almost never productive to wake up somebody to talk.

• You're tired and your defenses are down. "This is when you say things you don't mean."

When do you end a conversation?

"You have to distinguish between ending and tabling. Some things may require several conversations....

"But you have to know the difference between talking and rehashing. You have to know when you've said it all and when you have something else to say.... You stop when the other person wants to stop—when it's conveyed by words, body language, or fatigue—and you resume later, if that's appropriate.

"You have finished business and unfinished business, and you have to know which is which."

Spirituality and healing
December 14, 1986

The Rev. Lynwood Swanson, who is director of pastoral care for the Wilmington-based Medical Center of Delaware, was talking about how medicine is "recognizing as never before the spiritual dimension and how it reacts on the body ... and its role in the healing process.

"I see great interest in hospitals generally for the ministry, beginning with the hospitals' own staffs," he said. "You go into the intensive-care units, where the patients are very ill, where treatment is highly complex.... The dynamics there, even on a slow day, sap energy and resources. The problem of burnout is raised, the will to go on, the purpose and meaning of what is being done....

"Ultimately, these become deeply spiritual questions, profoundly theological ... and hospitals turn to those disciplined in matters of tension and faith. In the best terminology, 'faith' means to walk where there are no easy answers, where there is no clearly defined way. The journey is begun fraught with dichotomies, ironies, polarities....

"This is where medicine finds itself today in so many ways ... and medicine is turning to whose who symbolize that it's OK not to have all the answers, that sometimes the point is just to help people stand where they are, that the immediate purpose may be to do the very best you can at this time. A pastoral person is good at that. 'Oh, God, help me make this moment, this day, this event.'

"When I was getting divorced, I didn't need help in what to do. I needed to hear from people who said, 'Hey, we know what it's like. Let's focus on where you are, what's happening now.' This is what we can do for each other. We can help staff members focus on the tensions and the unanswered questions ... and [leave them] at the hospital instead of taking the stuff home."

•

Mr. Swanson, an American Baptist, now is developing a pastoral-care program at the Fox Chase Cancer Center in Philadelphia, training church-based pastors from the area to work not only with staff members, but also with patients.

In an interview, he said that pastoral care, in its finest sense, "extends hope beyond cure, beyond alleviation of pain. It's to help patients find meaning for what they're going through, to give substance to the idea of hope. 'I have time to hear your story, to listen, to affirm your individuality.'"

Can't the family be a source of support for the patient?

"Sometimes those closest to the patient are the least able to offer support at the time. They're devastated too. The whole family gets the diagnosis of cancer. The whole schedule is affected; financial security may be shaken. Many times, family members are not primary—or even good—resources for support. A surrogate person is needed for that, and this person can be an understanding pastoral person."

Does the support from pastors tend to be theological or humanistic? Both. Here are four types of pastoral work in hospitals:

• Pastoral visit. "You go to the patient and say, 'These are the services we offer.' You let him know what is available to him as a patient-parishioner. The presence of a pastor speaks. He's here, a representative of God, the church, the spiritual dimension of life. There's a sense of calmness, peace, purpose, and love—a symbol of the institution's ability to cure and care."

• Pastoral care. "You listen to the story of the patient, as the patient tells you about the hurt, about what's going on. As you listen, you are showing care. We can't cure everybody, but we can care for everybody."

• Pastoral counseling. "Here, the trilogy is at work—patient, pastor, and religious tradition. This is when religion is part of what's going on" at the request of the patient.

• Psychotherapy. "The purpose here is to effect change, when we're talking of family, relationships, dreams." But psychotherapy is limited to those pastors with special training.

•

Mr. Swanson said cancer patients frequently ask, "Why did this happen?" He lets them know that he has no answer and that "pat Sunday-school answers are not sufficient.... Often patients are angry and hostile, but this generally is a secondary response. Usually it comes out of 'I've been hurt'—and that's what we want to talk about, the hurt....

"Just to get the person to express hurt goes a long way toward defusing the destructive power. The person often is so angry—at everybody, from God to the family to himself. In the hospital, he may be pigeonholed as an angry person. But our position is that he is a whole person whose anger is his way of relating right now."

Mr. Swanson said cancer patients often ask, "How could a just God do this to me?" How does he handle that one?

"I understand that the patient is asking for communication, that it's not necessary for me to answer that question. What the patient really is asking is, 'Will you remain with me with this unanswerable question? Will you listen to my searching, to the foolish answers I come up with?' I welcome the question ... because it's a preface to communication that will take place....

"I let the patient know that I hear what he's saying. I repeat it. I say that I, too, have raised the question many times. I ask if he possibly is finding some direction already, finding some answers that don't fit or are not traditional answers....

"I try to find a good God in the midst of what we traditionally say is a bad God. Good things happen in the loss of a spouse, of a child, in a disease. 'Why does a good God do bad things?' The question is, 'Where is the goodness of God in the tragedy of this event?' Out of tragedy can come beauty and goodness," the discovery of meaning and increased openness to those who are suffering.

Often people ask, "Why is this happening to me?"

"I think the question is, 'Why not?'" Mr. Swanson said. "It's a cliché, but it's true. I'm not sure I really understand it all, but I think it needs to be addressed after we've looked at other matters."

It's all right for the clergy to say they don't have answers, he said.

"It's OK to put it in prayer: 'I don't know what to say. Lord, this is true chaos.' Chaos is the state between uselessness and order. All of the parts are there, but they're scattered, like in a puzzle. You start to create a picture out of the pieces, to address the chaos. It's what God did at Creation. It's what we do in counseling—so the person won't flounder in chaos. We try to make some order out of it, some sense, some direction."

Clergy and therapist
December 18, 1986

I was telling Stephen R. Treat about my long-held prejudice against clergymen who, even though they're not qualified by training or intellect, continue to dispense what they generously describe as therapy to the troubled folks in their congregations.

Mr. Treat, an ordained minister in the United Church of Christ, agreed with me. "The majority of counseling in the United States is done by the clergy, most of it by poorly trained people who look at it purely through a theological basis," he said. "In some cases, they create more harm than good."

I recalled a story that a woman once told me about going to see her minister when things were especially rough with her husband. "He asked me if my husband beat me. Did he drink too much? Did he run around with other women?' When I told him 'no,' that the problem was that—well, my minister wouldn't even let me finish. He told me that my husband didn't sound like such a bad guy and that I should go home, try to be a better wife, and be thankful for what I had."

I recalled another story that a man once told me about the time he and his wife went to see their minister—because his wife had found out that he'd been involved with another woman. "My wife said to the minister, 'Tell my husband that he's got to stop sinning.' And that's exactly what the minister told me. He never asked anything about our relationship, about how we hadn't had sex for six months because she thought it was dirty."

Says Mr. Treat: A lot of unlearning has to take place before some members of the clergy can become competent therapists. "There has to be a transition from theological to systemic thinking.

"A preacher gets a couple where one has had an affair, and if he uses only theology, he goes after the person who had the affair.... With systemic thinking, he understands there's two sides to every story. He realizes that nothing happens in a marital relationship without both playing a part.... This is the biggest unlearning that has to take place, getting away from looking at everything" solely through the prism of theology.

•

Mr. Treat knows a lot about unlearning because, you might say, that's what he is in charge of as director of clergy training at the Marriage Council of Philadelphia, which trains family therapists through its affiliation with the University of Pennsylvania's psychiatry department. The Marriage Council, in cooperation with the Eastern Baptist Theological Seminary, is offering a four-year program—one day a week—for parish clergy who want to improve their skills as therapists.

Mr. Treat, who is a senior clinical therapist and supervisor, said the training program for clergy is the same program that psychiatrists and psychologists go through but "with additional courses and supervision. Most of the clergy we accept would not be accepted into our regular training program because they don't have the credentials."

The current class of 26 is a "nice ecumenical group" that includes rabbis, sisters, and ministers from many Protestant denominations. Almost half are women.

All members of the clergy are eligible to apply for the program, said Mr. Treat, but he added, "We might shy away from somebody so fundamental that he was not open to new thinking.... We want to mold their theology as well as their psychology, to allow their theology to evolve," to be open to new ideas, to get away from black-and-white thinking.

Is there something about religion that attracts people who think in black and white?

No, said Mr. Treat, the makeup of the clergy is a "good reflection of society at large. In the world today, there are more black-and-white thinkers, and so we get more black-and-white thinkers into the clergy."

Blending theology and psychology is a critical part of the unlearning process, said Mr. Treat. "It's difficult to blend the two if you're a literalist," he said, but essentially, theology and psychology toil in the same vineyard—dealing with forgiveness, hope, suffering, pain, and everything else that makes us human.

"There's nothing in systemic theory that I can't find basis for in the Bible.... If you read the Bible in the context of the time in which it was written, there's no issue at all" in connecting it with modern psychology.

The training can make those in the program not only better therapists but also better preachers, said Mr. Treat.

"Good preaching is telling good stories; touching the hearts, minds, needs of people; telling the truths of human relationships. We work on the notion of moving toward what is more true in human relationships, rather than less true. If you and I have an argument, we're both pieces of it.... We teach the clergy to work with concepts," and, as a result, the preaching tends to be more down-to-earth and less pie in the sky.

Those who make it into the program tend to "self-select," said Mr.

Treat. They must be able to make the transition to new ideas, or they can't be marital therapists. "If you approach things as who's right and who's wrong, your therapy is far more destructive than constructive.... Also, if you go in with the idea that one's a sinner and one's good, you're not quite theologically sound. The Bible makes statements about judgment as well as adultery....

"If you deal with issues rigidly, you'd have trouble here. You would be confronted strongly. We're not in the business of helping views become more narrow. We're in the business of reconciliation."

1989–1992

On lifetime goals
February 23, 1989

It's not a new exercise. Over the years I've done it perhaps half a dozen times, but it never fails to stimulate my thinking, to force me to confront some of my ambivalences, to try to figure out who I am and what I want.

The exercise is this:

Write on a piece of paper your lifetime goals—how you'd like your scorecard to read after the third out in the ninth inning of your life.

Now shorten up the time frame and list your goals for the next three to five years.

Finally, put down your goals for the next six months, assuming that's all the time you have left on the planet. How would you want to play out your life if you had just six months to go?

The exercise, which is used by many life planners and career planners and even some therapists and philosophers, was brought out and dusted off not long ago by Gardner Yenawine, who was speaking to a by-invitation-only group of businesspeople who had just enough gray in their hair to confirm middle age. Yenawine, whose Boston-based career-development firm markets a program called LifeDesign, was introducing his work in the Philadelphia area under sponsorship of Millard Consulting Services Inc. of Fort Washington, Pa.

Yenawine gave members of the group about two minutes for each of the three parts of the exercise, and then he asked what surely was the jackpot question: "What did you learn about yourself from listing your goals?"

What people usually find out, he said, is that they "may not be using their time now on the things that they say are really important."

He asked the members of the group how their goals had changed when the frame was shortened from lifetime to six months. Everybody, just about, had the same response: Give up monetary goals and focus on relationships. In the words of one man: "I would change from things to people."

A woman said that in her final six months, she would "go to the seashore and invite all my friends to be with me."

•

What would you write as your lifetime goals?

Let me share with you some of what I wrote.

"At the end, I want to be as far along the road toward self-actualization as it's possible for me to be. I want to have a better understanding of who I am, what my role has been. I want to know what tranquillity feels like, not as a fleeting, transitory experience—I already know that—but as a permanent state. To know tranquillity may be what actualization really is all about. . . .

"I want to have completed what my friend Peter Koestenbaum calls an 'immortality project,' the way I want to be remembered. Now I have only a vague idea of what this will be. That vague idea stemmed from a game that I played some years ago with an after-dinner crowd that posed this question: 'If you could write the inscription on your tombstone and if you were limited to three words, what would you write?' That's a tough one, isn't it? What I wrote—and what has become my fuzzy immortality project—was 'He helped people,' which obviously is tied into the kind of writing I do and the speeches I make. . . .

"I'd like to be able to have more fun, a continuing kind of fun that erupts spontaneously, when I'm least expecting it. I make a lot of speeches about the need for adults to get in touch with the child who resides within them, the child who intuitively knows how to have fun. At times I feel I lose touch with my child, and I find myself too serious, even grim, about myself and my work and my schedule. I hope I can learn to laugh more. I heard somebody on the radio talking about how unfortunate it is that some people go a whole day without laughing. That stopped me and made me think. I have too many days in which I don't laugh.

"I want to experience as many different things as possible, keep my unfinished business to a minimum, put more of myself into the personal relationships that really matter to me."

•

What would you write as your goals for the next three to five years?

Here is part of what I wrote:

"I want to come to terms with my internal critic. When I do that, the laughter will come much more easily—and much more often. . . . I want to set a pattern of completing a book every 18 to 24 months. . . . I want to spend more time at the beach. . . . I want to be competent in the highest sense of the word as a catamaran sailor. . . .

"I want to stay healthy, keep my cholesterol level down, become a good-enough cook, read more novels, get back into golf on a regular basis. . . . I want to bury the hatchet with my older son, Jay, and construct a relationship that works for both of us. I want to get even closer to my younger son, Grant, who in some ways is so much like me that I'm both delighted and scared.... I want to go to the Caribbean more often in the wintertime—and stay longer."

•

What would you write as your goals for the final six months of your life?

Here is part of what I wrote:

"I want to write a book on what life is all about, what matters, how to find out sooner rather than later what matters.... I want to be at peace with myself, with what I've done with my life, with so few regrets that they won't be worth mentioning.... I want to watch sunrises, sunsets, moonrises.... I want to sail a catamaran right out to the edge, where at sunset the orange sky meets the silver sea. I wonder how it will look, when I'm on the edge. Will it still be so orange, so brilliant? Will it be like finding the end of the rainbow? Maybe there'll be a jackpot, floating on a raft.... I hope Jay and Grant will be able to tell me something like: 'Well, we had some rocky times with you, but we did OK—and we're glad you're our father.'

"Finally, I want to be able to tell myself that I'm proud of the person I became."

•

I look forward to hearing from you about your goals.

Humility is overrated
April 17, 1989

hum-ble (hum'bel) adj. Marked by meekness or modesty in behavior, atti-tude, or spirit; showing deferential or submissive respect.

self ef-fac-ing (self i-fa' sing) adj. Not drawing attention to oneself; humble.

The American Heritage Dictionary

A personal opinion: If there's one thing that well-intentioned parents do to make life more difficult than it should be for their children, it is to preach—by word and deed—the unlimited virtue of humility. Don't push and shove, children are taught, and, for heaven's sake, don't call attention to yourself. Be humble. Stand in the back of the line, keep quiet, don't make waves. Whatever you do, don't toot your own horn, and never—repeat never—act as if you're special. Nobody likes people who are too big for their britches. If you walk this straight and narrow line, you'll eventually be rewarded ... because good things come to those who wait ... and wait ... and wait.

As adults, some of us have a hard time shaking this early training—even though, on some level, we may know better. We continue to be invisible, to melt into the wallpaper. But the funny thing is, we still get praised for it—not by our parents but by peers.

Not long ago, I was attending the funeral of a friend, a businessman who had died unexpectedly at what seemed to be the peak of his life. We were standing around talking outside the church, a group of us, and a man who wore the collar of a clergyman was attempting to heap the ultimate praise on our mutual friend: "He was the most self-effacing person I ever knew."

My immediate response surprised me. I said to the clergyman: "I thought he was a nice guy who knew how to ask for what he wanted."

I don't think there's much virtue in self-effacement. I think there's quite a lot to be said for announcing your presence.

•

Jack Erdlen is president of Management Dimensions Inc., a placement and career-counseling firm in Wellesley, Mass., and when I heard from him the other day, I thought back to the funeral, and the early parental messages, and the whole matter of what I consider the essential nature of letting people know who we are and what we stand for.

Said Erdlen: "Many of today's workers have found their careers stalled or disrupted because of inadequate parental training. Most of us have not been prepared to cope with the modern work environment. The values with which we have become ingrained in our formative years don't go far enough."

Translation: Being humble has its limitations.

Erdlen said that when we were young, our parents instructed us to work hard, listen attentively, never question authority. This philosophy was complemented by an emphasis on humility in which it was never acceptable to brag about our abilities under any circumstances. Although such an approach may be commendable and may build character for some people, Erdlen said, it "will not further your ambitions in today's work society. You must take a pro-active stance in promoting your career....

"While not meaning to be cynical or disrespectful, I can honestly say that good things do not usually happen to the person who waits. It's unrealistic to believe that promotions, salary increases, interesting assignments, and other significant rewards will automatically come your way" simply because you're an above-average performer or even an excellent performer.

The problem, said Erdlen, is that we're hampered by our own modesty and all of the taboos—real or imagined—about promoting ourselves.

Erdlen said that the way we behave at work is not unlike the way we behaved in earlier times when we were hooked up with a blind date. "During the first conversation on the telephone, one person eventually asked, 'What do you look like?' And the other person invariably replied, 'Well, my friends say that I'm attractive.' To answer otherwise was always considered to be a sign of conceit and lack of humility, even though it might mean losing a date. The truthful response to this question could have been 'I'm attractive or handsome, certainly more than acceptable, and you'll be doing well in going out with me.'"

The same thing holds true in business, said Erdlen. "We can't be bashful about blowing our horn."

Some of the things that Erdlen suggests:

• Prepare for your annual performance appraisal by making a list of your contributions and accomplishments so that you can recite them to your manager.

• Retain a file that contains highlights of recognized performance achievements such as complimentary letters, commendations, awards, citations.

• Volunteer for undesirable short-term assignments that will demonstrate your flexibility and willingness to be a team player.

Erdlen said that "job security is being good at what you do and making certain that other people know about it, both inside and outside the organization. Don't be overconfident and obnoxious. However, you must learn to make that extra effort while being your own public-relations agent. Mother might be embarrassed by your boldness, but she will be proud of the results it brings."

●

A 30-year-old man stopped by the office to see me the other day. He was struggling in his career, and a big part of the struggle was his difficulty in standing up for himself and asking for what he wanted. How could he assert himself, he wondered, without making his boss think that he lacked humility?

I suggested that he not worry about that. It was more important that the boss recognize him as somebody who thought enough of himself to be willing to give more and to expect, in return, to get more. He should announce his presence, exhibit some boldness. The humble are not going to inherit the corporate towers.

What do you think?

"What are you willing to give up?"

October 24, 1989

It was a memorable evening, full of sharing and self-disclosure—at a level that's possible only with a friend you trust and respect.

We were at dinner, he and I, and I was talking about some of my stuff, what I thought I had contributed to some outcomes that were not satisfactory to me, what I thought others had been responsible for.

My friend, a therapist, was telling me about the time when he, agonizing over a personal dilemma, had a discussion with his own therapist: "God, I want some peace and tranquillity in my life. I'd give anything for peace and tranquillity right now.... He looked at me, this therapist, for a long time, and then he said: 'Oh, really? What would you be willing to give up for peace and tranquillity?' I thought about that, and I wasn't sure if the price was too high or not."

Later, when my friend was in a therapy session with one of his patients, he posed the same question: "What would you be willing to give up to make your life happier?" The patient settled back in his chair and reflected, then answered with stark honesty: "I'm not sure I'm willing to give up that much."

•

What are you willing to give up to get what you say you want—whether it's a more fulfilling life, a better relationship with your children, greater intimacy with your spouse, a more thorough understanding with your boss, increased self-acceptance?

It is, I believe, the deepest question that I ever have heard:

What are you willing to give up?

We live in a world that turns on trade-offs. For everything we get, we must surrender something. We can't have it all. The cake that we eat today isn't going to be in the cupboard tomorrow. Intellectually, most of us understand this, accept it as a fact of life, don't go out of our way to fight it.

Yet when we deal with things that strike at the very core of who we are and what we hope to become, we can get gun-shy. "I want to be happy.... I want my children to respect me.... I want my spouse to love me.... I want the world to appreciate me."

These are things that we have come to accept almost as rights. Some of us carry a heavy sense of entitlement. Somehow it doesn't seem fair that we should have to barter for that which rightfully should be ours. In this context—which we most fully appreciate at 4 A.M., when our defenses are down and our skin is flooded with the sweat of anxiety, we are forced to come to terms with life as it is, a life of compromise.

What are you willing to give up?

If you and I and everybody else want to be more satisfied, more loving, more capable of accepting love, we may have to give up quite a lot.

We may have to turn loose of our anger. How can others love us if we're angry and nasty? Yet, we protest, we have a right to be angry. Haven't we been victimized? Yes, maybe, but is anger going to lead to resolution of the problem?

We may have to stop blaming others for the bad things that have happened to us. When we stop blaming others, we have to take the frightening step toward recognizing and accepting our role in what happened. It's so much easier to blame everybody else. It's so hard to look at ourselves, so incredibly painful.

We may have to give up being right all the time—even when we're wrong. For many of us, this is the ultimate defense because if we are right, why must we back off and give benefit of doubt to those who tormented us? Answer: Because being right doesn't have anything to do with being happy.

We may have to give up our arrogance, our haughtiness, our self-righteousness, our quick-on-the-trigger inclination to look elsewhere—instead of at ourselves—for solutions.

We may have to admit that we've goofed. The devil didn't make us do it; we did it all on our own. We may have to own up to our mistakes, our shortcomings, the times we have cut corners at somebody else's expense. We may, heaven forbid, even have to say, "I'm sorry." We may have to ask for forgiveness.

We may have to become humble. For many of us, this is a big mountain to climb. If I ask you to forgive me, I may feel that I have lost control, that I am dealing from a position of weakness, that I am carrying my hat in my hands. We have to rise above this kind of thinking if we truly want to humble ourselves. The more I think about it, the more I am convinced that the strongest people in the world are those who can say, without feeling weak or second-class, that they are sorry, that they'd like another chance, that they acknowledge the pain that they have inflicted on another, that they, themselves, feel that pain.

We may have to give up our seemingly endless quest for money, power, fame, recognition, adoration. We may have to stand there, naked in the world, and present ourselves as we are—without the embellishments behind which we have hidden for so many years. We may have to ask, " Why am I afraid to tell you who I am?" That was the title of a bestselling book a number of years ago—a book that eloquently answered the question: I'm afraid to tell you who I am because, if you really knew me, you wouldn't like me. We have to be willing to take our chances—because we can't for very long be happy, satisfied, fulfilled if we don't remove our masks and let other people see our warts. After that, it's up to them.

We may have to stop taking ourselves so seriously—if we expect others to take us seriously enough. We may even have to learn to laugh at ourselves.

What are you willing to give up?

I telephoned my friend the day after our dinner and thanked him for introducing me to the question. Since then, I've done a lot of thinking. My sincere hope is that what I've written today will start you thinking, too.

How much is enough?
June 7, 1990

I was talking to some cardiologists in Laguna Beach, Calif., about stress in the workplace and how this stress is sometimes translated into physical illnesses—everything from headaches to high blood pressure, from ulcers to heart attacks.

The cardiologists agreed that stress could be a killer—figuratively and literally—and they were interested in how they could help their patients reduce their daily stress. Could they sell patients an idea that most of us intellectually know is true—that nothing is worth everything, that it's prudent and necessary to slow down at times, to back off, to smell the roses and savor the moonrises?

My opinion was that many people of high achievement have only one speed at which they work: fast. They have only one speed because they are driven by the fear, conscious or unconscious, that if they gear down, they will stand still or lose ground in the competitive world. Even worse, from their standpoint, is the concern that if they gear down, even for a little while, they won't be able to get back up to speed when they think that it's essential to gun it again.

This, in my judgment, is the heart of the problem—and why it's so difficult to help people to help themselves. If somebody could figure out a way to deal with this, he or she could make a major contribution to health in the business world ... and in the family world, too.

•

How do you get people who are on the fast track to move, at least temporarily, into a slower lane?

For some people, it takes trauma to awaken them to reality.

A spouse walks out, announcing that he or she can't take it anymore, can't deal with a person who is so wrapped up in achievement that there's no time, energy, or inclination for anything else—especially intimacy.

A child acts out, from alcohol to drug abuse, from wrecking a car to failing at school. It's the child's way of saying, "Please recognize my existence"—after years of being treated like nobody because the high achiever was too busy achieving.

Serious illness intervenes where humans have been unable to. An achiever lies in a hospital bed, stares at the ceiling, cries not in pain but in shame, and vows to try to undo the damage that has been done—to self and to those he or she professes to love.

Many of these people, because their eyes have been opened by cold splashes of reality, are relatively willing to listen to reason, at least for a while—until memories of their trauma fade. They may return to the fast track, but many of them are forever sensitized by the experience—and in the future they are able to recognize danger signs before crisis time and modify their behavior so that odds are reduced that lightning will strike twice.

These people are not the major problem for physicians who are committed to stress reduction. The major-problem group is made up of those high achievers who haven't yet been traumatized and who, when urged to slow down, ask a not-unreasonable question: Why?

It is a difficult question to respond to, almost impossible without getting into philosophy, the meaning of life, our reason for being. The question that needs to be asked, in response, is this:

How much is enough?

The question raises other questions with which we ultimately need to deal: Why do we work so hard? Why do we try to achieve so much? What would happen if we didn't work so hard or achieve so much? Why don't we take all of our vacation and even steal some extra days? What would happen if we didn't check in daily at the office when we're away? When was the last time we really had fun? Do we remember what fun is?

Why *do* we work so hard? We tell ourselves that we do it for our families, to provide them with security and the good life, but late at night, when we pull the covers up over our heads, we know that it's a lie. We do it for ourselves—for our own neurotic reasons, the most common of which is that we're trying to compensate for real or imagined deficiencies. The game that we play with ourselves is ultimately cruel because, no matter how hard we work or how much we achieve, we can't ever shake the monkey off our backs. We're still not successful enough—which we translate into our being not good enough. So we work harder.

How much is enough?

It's enough when we reach *some* of our goals.

It's enough when we can do *some* of the things that are important to us.

It's enough when food tastes good ... because we take time to eat properly.

It's enough when those we love enjoy our companionship, want to be with us, talk with us, tell us about their wins and losses and their hopes and fears.

It's enough when we can have fun on the golf course even if we shoot 10 strokes over our handicap—because we're tuned into the joy of being outdoors and spending time with people we want to be with.

It's enough when we don't feel guilty about working a four-day week—instead of seven days—and when we can savor the time away from work as much as the time on the job.

It's enough when Sunday night comes and, instead of settling in and getting ready to resume the rat race, we can say—and mean it—that we wish that the weekend had another day or two to go.

•

For people who manage to figure out how much is enough, life can be sweet. In the long run, they may achieve more than those who stay in the fast lane all the time—and they'll surely be healthier and happier. They won't clog the offices of cardiologists everywhere with angina and rapid heart beats and sweaty palms.

How do we get the word out to people that there is a better way to live? I don't know. I couldn't give the cardiologists the answer that they asked for.

Could you?

Seasoning optimism with realism
January 10, 1991

A few years ago, I had an opportunity to make a speech that, on the surface, looked like a good deal: Lots of money and a trip to Puerto Rico, where the organization's annual sales rally was being held.

There was only one problem.

The top brass invited me in for a meeting to make certain that I was the right man for the job. What they wanted, they said, was a speaker who could fire up the sales force by helping them to understand how lucky they were to work for this corporation, how no sacrifice—including time with the family—was too great, how they should feel obligated to give the corporation their last drop of blood.

"You want me to say that?"

"Yes. That's what you believe, isn't it? That's why you're successful, isn't it?"

I invited them to send somebody to hear me make a speech a few days later—to a group of business executives. My topic was balancing work with the other important parts of your life. Translation: Save that last drop of blood for where it will do the most good, and almost never does it do the most good when it's shed for the corporation.

Two-thirds of the way through the speech, the corporation's representative walked out.

Was I surprised when they told me that they had decided to continue their search for somebody to speak to their sales force?

No, I wasn't surprised. I try to be optimistic, but I also try to be truthful and realistic. They didn't need me. They needed somebody who would deliver the message they prescribed. They needed a motivational speaker.

•

I've never believed the messages that so many motivational speakers preach—that you should dare to be great, that nothing is beyond reach, that no price is too high for attaining the goals that you set. The truth, as I see it, is that we are limited in what we can do, and recognizing realistic limitations and knowing when to quit and try something else are marks of maturity and wisdom.

About the best that motivational speakers can do, in my judgment, is temporarily inspire people to try harder. By the time the people crash in disillusionment, the motivational speakers are long gone, inspiring another crowd in another city. In that way they bear a striking resemblance to some evangelistic faith healers I have encountered, but that's another story.

Because of the hard line that I have chronically taken against motivational speakers, I was grabbed by a section of Alan Loy McGinnis's new book, *The Power of Optimism*—the part that deals with some of the qualities usually found in optimistic people.

Wrote McGinnis: "Successful people do not talk about how wonderful things are when, in fact, they're bad. Certain people try to smile in the face of difficulties and declare that if everyone will be patient, things will turn out fine. But things usually do not turn out fine ... because small problems, when ignored, have a way of turning into bigger problems....

"At sales meetings, one often hears a standard motivational talk intended to pump up the troops. It runs something like this: 'You are wonderful in every way, your mind is a powerhouse, and if you will believe strongly enough, you can do anything.' We've all heard that sort of thing many times. From the story of *The Little Engine That Could* to the latest self-help books, we've been told that if we have enough faith we can move mountains."

McGinnis wrote that there is "enough truth in these pep talks to make them attractive, but it is easy for motivational speakers to get so carried away that they become absurd.... Napoleon Hill, in his book *Think and Grow Rich*, says: 'Whatever the mind of man can conceive and believe, it can achieve.'

"This is claptrap, and such overstatements give faith and hope a bad name. Many of our patients who must be confined to a locked psychiatric ward would subscribe to such nonsense, and it is their grandiosity that helped get them into trouble.... A phony pep talk is usually the last thing a group needs. What it may need is a leader who says: 'We've got a mess on our hands, but if we all roll up our sleeves, we can do something about it'"

•

I've known McGinnis for a long time. He's an interesting fellow—a former Presbyterian minister who became a psychologist and now is director of the Valley Counseling Center in Glendale, Calif., near Los Angeles. His new book on optimism represents his best work, I think. And that's saying a lot, because some of his other books, including *The Friendship Factor* and *Bringing Out the Best in People*, have been extremely successful.

At lunch not long ago, McGinnis, accompanied by his wife, Diane, who runs an interior-design business, picked up on my doubts about motivational speakers. Let's listen:

"We always hear about tenacity, about the miner who dug to 5,000 feet, got discouraged, quit—and then how somebody came along, dug deeper, and hit pay dirt. Now what does that story mean? If you drill to 5,000 feet and find nothing, should you keep going? What about 10,000 feet? It was W.C. Fields who talked about the virtue of trying again if you don't succeed the first or second time, but the third time? Said Fields: 'It's time to quit. Don't be a damned fool.'

"Obviously tenacity is a virtue ... but I don't know where the boundary is—the line at which it stops being a virtue. Usually we quit too soon," and, said McGinnis, maybe this is what the motivational speakers have in mind when they urge people to keep trying.

McGinnis said that "a lot of businesses fail because they're too optimistic, not realistic. They don't think of the worst-case scenario and prepare for it. ... A basic quality of what I call the tough-minded optimist is that he looks for ways that what he's doing can fail. Some say they never think of failure, but I think the opposite is true for successful people. Without expecting to fail, they figure out what to do if it doesn't work. ...

"Speakers tell you that there is opportunity without limit, that with enough faith you can accomplish anything. ... But reality is that it's a big world, with imperfections, with some major flaws. A tough-minded optimist expects trouble. This is different from what you hear from motivational speakers, some of whom will tell you to stand in front of a mirror and repeat: 'I love myself.'"

What is needed, said McGinnis, is a realistic appraisal of the situation and some plan—and alternative plans—for dealing with it: "Optimistic people look at the bad stuff, but, instead of pretending it's not there or getting buried in it, they say, 'Well, it's going to be tough, but I've faced tough situations before, and I've made out all right.' This is what is needed—not a mirror."

Growing up poor
February 12, 1991

I was writing a column about Christmas 1945, when I was 14, when my father's financial resources were so diminished that his gift to me was a pair of argyle socks—accompanied by tears and apologies that he was unable to give me anything more.

In that column, I was telling the story of the argyles to the Rev. James L. Shelton, a longtime friend, and I wrote this line:

"Jim Shelton grew up poor, too."

At the instant I finished that line, I stopped and read it, then read it again:

"Jim Shelton grew up poor, too."

While I've always been aware that we had fewer material things than many families, I'd never really thought of us as poor—yet there it was, like an ink blot, making a statement that I had to deal with.

What does it mean to grow up poor? What is the residue that forever stays with us?

•

After that column, I heard from many readers, most of whom shared stories about the Christmases that they most vividly remembered. But one letter writer made no mention of Christmas. What he wanted to know, because he had grown up poor, too, was what it meant to me, the ways in which it had shaped my philosophy and my actions, the residue.

I read and then reread that letter, and then I thought and thought some more. Without question, growing up poor had left its mark on me. What I want to do in this column is try to define the many forms that this mark has taken.

Maybe you'll find something that reminds you of a mark that you carry—whether or not you grew up poor.

•

I was interviewing a Beverly Hills psychologist, Lee Hausner, who wrote the book *Children of Paradise*, which is about the perils of growing up rich, of getting too much too soon, of appreciating nothing, of feeling entitled, of being perpetually bored.

As I listened to her recite a litany of disadvantaged wealth, I thought anew about the many ways in which I had grown up lucky.

My parents gave me virtually unlimited time and undivided attention, and maybe one of the reasons, aside from their being loving, tuned-in people, was that it was what they had to give—the most precious gift of all.

We had few of the distractions that can accompany money, and the result was that we spent much of our time together, the three of us, reading, listening to the radio, talking, sharing dreams, and exposing wounds.

I knew from an early age that I was valued and loved. And from as far back as I can remember, I felt important, worthy of the space that I was occupying, committed to doing with my life something that would be meaningful not only to me but also to my parents—and others, too. This is not to suggest that a person can't grow up in a wealthy family with these same values, but my judgment, after considerable thought, is that there's something about being poor that, if we're lucky, can light a fire that glows forever.

I grew up knowing that there is no free lunch, that we work for what we get, that the harder and smarter we work, the higher it is possible for us to climb. Entitlement was not a word that I understood.

Growing up poor was not a bad deal at all for me, yet it has left me with some baggage:

• Because we lived back then in so many places that weren't very nice, I have today a tendency to spend a disproportionate amount of money on housing. In a sense, I have been "house poor" for most of my adult life, yet I have elected not to do anything about it—because I understand that it fills a deep need that I have.

• Although I have held memberships in six country clubs as I moved around the country, I am sometimes uncomfortable in that setting, as if I shouldn't be there. It goes back, of course, to when I was growing up, as a financial have-not, with the mindset that country clubs were only for the financial haves. A few years ago I was playing in a member-guest golf tournament at an exclusive club in the Philadelphia area, and, as I was lining up a putt, my inner voice said to me: "You don't belong here."

• I am disdainful of people who inherit wealth and do nothing with it to try to make the world a better place. On the other hand, I admire those who cash in their ideas for wealth—but I don't feel the same urgency for them to spread around their money. Why? I'm not sure, but it must have something to do with making the most of what we have to work with.

• Because we never took vacations, I have had to learn, as an adult, how to enjoy vacations without feeling guilty and without feeling a need to justify spending the money.

• I invest more time than I realistically can justify with people who want to bounce ideas off me, talk about their problems, use me as a reality check. Why? Probably because of indebtedness I feel to a world that has been generous enough to me over the years. Growing up poor offers a contrast that probably exaggerates my sense of indebtedness—but I'm not sure that's all bad.

Finding friendship after 65
February 14, 1991

For people in the so-called "golden years"—65 and beyond—the most critical factor in good mental health is "having friends and having the ability to make friends."

When psychologist Matti Gershenfeld told me that, I wasn't surprised. It seems to me that having friends and making friends may be the most valuable asset that any of us ever will have, regardless of age. But, said Gershenfeld, it's especially important for older people, because friends can be a primary buffer against loneliness, depression, and many of the other things that society routinely—and without much compassion—accepts as inevitable components of aging.

Gershenfeld is president of the Couples Learning Center, an educational nonprofit corporation in Jenkintown, Pa., that offers many workshops that deal with problems of aging—from being a happy "golden girl" to enjoying retirement.

Is the ability to make friends something that can be taught and learned?

Yes, said Gershenfeld. "In the 'Golden Girl' workshop, I ask women where they stand with their friends now. What kinds of problems are they having? They have a lot of roadblocks," which include:

- "She used to be my friend, but we have nothing in common now."
- "They live too far away."
- "Since the kids grew up, we have no shared interest."
- "I like her, but my husband doesn't like her husband."

Gershenfeld asks those in the workshop to identify the obstacles to making new friends. Again, people see lots of difficulties.

- "If I approach somebody, it makes me sound as if I have no friends, as if I'm desperate."
- "Everybody seems to have their own crowd and they don't need any more friends."
- "I'm interested in the theater now—I wasn't before—so how can I possibly find friends?"
- "At my age, I'm embarrassed to say I need a friend."

Said Gershenfeld: "They make it seem as if their reasons are insurmountable, as if there's no way for them to make new friends, but ..."

Gershenfeld has a plan, a way to tear down the obstacles, smash through the roadblocks.

"I ask them to 'think of somebody you once knew and liked and telephone that person.' If you haven't called somebody for 15 years and then you call, it's reasonable to assume that they'll want to know why. Somebody always asks what is the answer to that question, and I tell them to be honest. 'I'm taking a course on making friends, and the first assignment was to think of somebody I once liked and telephone her. I thought of you.' Every time this happens, the person reports back that the person she called begins to laugh and says, 'Hey, you made my day. Being the person you picked makes me feel good.' After that, you make plans to get together—and your shared history with the other person tends to make the reunion very comfortable.

Gershenfeld's next assignment: Pick somebody in this workshop group, meet for lunch, discuss some of the items on this list:

- "How I'm different now than 10 years ago."
- "The most important thing I've learned about children."
- "How marriage is different than I thought it would be."
- "If there was one interest I could pursue, it would be ..."

Discussing these questions, said Gershenfeld, is a major step toward getting away from superficial talk that too often leaves us with nothing to say after we've mentioned the children and what we've been doing lately.

And the next assignment is ...

"Make a list of where you typically interact with other people—at church, playing tennis, in a parents' group, wherever. Pick somebody you like in each group and ask, 'Can we get together for coffee?' The trick is to go beyond the setting and tap into the individual's personal interests. You can play tennis with somebody for 20 years and not really know the person."

Does this same approach apply equally to men and women?

No, said Gershenfeld, this works better for women. "The way men make friends is different and more difficult. It generally involves legitimacy of interests—somebody you work with, see at political rallies or business meetings. There's usually a connection through some activity—not through talking, which works for women. . . .

"Men don't have 'permission' to make friends—so they need an activity. A common way is to say, 'Let's meet for a drink after work.' This creates a legitimacy for getting together. . . . What works best is something that provides an opportunity to see the other person on an ongoing basis—cards, racquetball, something like that."

What about handling rejection? This seems to me, I told Gershenfeld, to be a big barrier to making friends. What if the other person responds to your overture by saying, in effect, "No, thanks. I already have all the friends I need"? Doesn't this fear keep many people from aggressively seeking friends?

Yes, it's a factor, all right, said Gershenfeld, but it should be approached in the same way that we approached dating so many years ago. "If you ask for a date Friday, and she says she's busy, it's possible that she really is busy. But if you ask 10 times and she's always busy, you get the message: She's not interested. So you think, 'What the heck, it's the wrong connection ... or the wrong time,' and you try other people.

"It's this way with friendships, too. Sometimes you won't connect," but usually it's nothing personal. And remember: Nothing ventured, nothing gained.

"Act your age!"

February 21, 1991

The boy looked to be about 4 or 5, and in the grocery store he was acting like the legendary bull in a china shop. He was into this and that, toppling some cereal boxes off a shelf, trying to rip open a plastic bag of potato chips.

At first, his mother seemed to try very hard not to be aware of what was going on, but finally she couldn't take it anymore. She turned with what seemed to be a full measure of fury toward the boy and screamed, "Act your age!"

The boy flinched and pulled back—as if he'd been burned—and obediently followed his mother toward the checkout counter. I watched them go, with a feeling of sadness that I didn't immediately understand. It wasn't until later in the day, as I replayed the scene in my mind, that the reason for the sadness became apparent to me.

The boy was acting his age. He was doing what little boys—and little girls, too—are prone to do: get into things because of their broad curiosity and high energy.

What his mother was telling him was to grow up, to behave as she wanted him to—as a sober adult, not as a free-spirited little boy.

That, I believe, is ample reason for sadness.

•

This doesn't happen only to 5-year-olds. In one way or another, it happens to most of us, for most of our lives. Always we are told—directly or by implication—what is expected of us, what is appropriate. We are told to act our age, and society will be the judge of what that means.

At this or that age, this or that kind of bathing suit is appropriate, this kind of business suit, this kind of shoe. Plaid pants are out because they make you look like a child, irresponsible, unworthy of your station in life. So, with heavy heart, you put away the plaid pants you love so much and put on something that is appropriate for somebody your age.

You want to go back to school, but at your age, what would people think? You wouldn't have anything in common with anybody. They'd think you were silly. Better to be safe than sorry. Forget about school. Stay home and read important books.

You want to buy a convertible, a two-seater, very much like the one you had in college, but the salesman looks you over and asks if you're really sure that this car is right for you. After all, this is a car for kids, almost a toy, and at your age you don't need a toy. No, you need a sedan, probably black or dark gray, sedate, dignified, like the one over there on the showroom floor. He'll be glad to show you the car that's right for you.

When you reach a certain age, you can't act like a child anymore—without paying a price, which is that people will think that you're irresponsible. You can't be goofy. You can't play with your teddy bear, figuratively or even literally. You can't have much fun. You must be grim—because grimness is a mark of maturity, of success. The more grim you are, the stronger is the signal that you send out announcing to the world that you've made it, that you're a person to be reckoned with.

How sad it is that so many of us buy into this—and act not as we feel like acting but as we think is appropriate—for people our age.

I speak to a lot of business groups, which generally contain more than their share of grim people, and I ask them to consider two questions: What is fun for me? Why don't I do more of it?

For the most part, these grim, successful people can't answer the first question. It has been so long since they've had fun, since they've behaved like kids, that they don't remember what it feels like. Even if some of them do remember, they struggle with the second question: Why don't they do more of it? Well, you see, they don't have the time and, even if they did, they'd feel guilty, because fun is for children, not successful adults. It just wouldn't be appropriate.

•

A while back I came into possession of a self-inventory exercise put out by Ginger Swain & Associates of Old Lyme, Conn.—a list of sentences to be completed by those who want to find out more about who they are, their values, what they stand for. Some of the questions:

I appreciate about myself—. I thought about that one a long time before I answered: "The willingness to march to my own drumbeat, to be my own person, to be unconventional if I feel like it, to be more concerned about what I think of me than what others think of me."

One example of my ability to feel joy is—. "The unbridled, childlike elation that comes when the catamaran is flying across the bay, when the wind is whistling through the sails, when the sun is hot on my back and the salty air is melting in my mouth."

One of the happiest periods of my life was—. "When I realized, finally, that I belonged, that I had paid my dues, that I didn't have to apologize, didn't have to play a role, that it was OK to cry if I felt like it—although others might be laughing."

I need to spend more time with—. "People who enjoy life, who know how to have fun, who are rugged but not crude in their individuality, who like themselves even when others are critical of them."

I need to spend less time with—. "People who are overly concerned about fitting in, being appropriate, being accepted—people who are phony because they aren't true to themselves, who don't know who they are because they're in lockstep with everybody else."

Before I die, I want to—. "Regress—or progress—to childhood again, to feel the same freedom and lack of constraints that I felt as a child, the same sense of being carefree, the same confidence that things will work out in ways that are reasonable."

•

Does the time ever come when we really need to act our age? I don't think so. I hope not. What do you think?

Mastering the fear of death

March 28, 1991

It was 8 o'clock on an already warm July morning, and the grass was drenched with dew. In an hour, I would meet a friend from high school—he's a lawyer now—for breakfast at his house, and then he and I would drive 50 miles into south-central Missouri, to the sprawling Lake of the Ozarks, and spend the day on his yacht. Yes, a real yacht.

But now it was private time—for me and Mom and Dad. It was the first time that I had visited their side-by-side graves since Mom's death earlier that year. I parked my rental car beside where they rested and left open the door so that the big-band music from the radio would wash over me—and them.

It was appropriate because they had taught me to appreciate that kind of music, which Dad once described to me as "the only real music I know."

Harry James was blowing "Trumpet Blues" as I sat down at the foot of the graves, talked to them about my life, about Marilyn, about Jay and Grant, about triumphs and defeats, about love, about being thankful, about...

"You both died the way you lived—full of joy," I said. "I hope I can do as well."

•

The letter was from a New Jersey woman who had read my column on the importance of confronting the inevitability of death—because avoiding the confrontation necessarily meant missing many of the joys of living. Here is part of what she wrote:

"It seemed as though you wrote that just for me.... I am 66, and just recently began thinking of my mortality, and I'm having a problem with it. I heard about a woman last year who was prearranging her funeral because she was dying and didn't want her family to have that burden. I thought she must be a wonderful person to be so considerate of others....

"I decided to do the same thing, but I didn't realize how traumatic it would be for me. For the last six months, I have been in turmoil. Where do I want to be buried? I come from the seashore. Should I be there? Or should I be in the city where I am now? These are decisions that I don't really need right now—because of some overwhelming problems....

"I know I must make a decision and then get on with my remaining years.... I'm trying to change, to make peace with things, but it's difficult for me. Maybe it's better not to know where I'll be when the time comes. What do you think?"

•

Psychiatrist Barry Schwartz is a longtime friend with a sense of humor. He once described to me the most elusive patient he ever tried to work with. "The guy said he might be late for the next session and, if he was, I should go ahead and start without him."

But there is also, as you would expect, a serious, insightful side to Schwartz, who, after he read the column on confronting death, told me about a book that he had read not once, not twice, but three times.

The book: *Zen in the Art of Archery*, by Eugen Herrigel, published originally in German 50 years ago. It's just 105 pages long, but, said Schwartz, those are 105 incredible pages.

"There is the story of a lance-carrier in the emperor's guard who one day prostrates himself before the imperial sword-master and says, 'Oh, great sword-master, I implore you to teach me the art of the sword.' The sword-master seems embarrassed and tells the lance-carrier to stand up. He tells him that he's been watching him for 10 years and there is nothing he can teach him, because he knows he already is a sword-master....

"What follows is disbelief by the lancer. 'I know nothing of the sword. How could you be noticing me for 10 years? I'm only a humble lance-carrier in the palace guard. You must have me confused with someone else.' The sword-master is adamant. He has been watching him for 10 years and he, the sword-master, knows that the man already is a sword-master. More confusion. More denial.

"Finally the sword-master scratches his head and says, 'You say you are not a sword-master. Well, have you mastered anything?' And the lancer says 'Yes, master, I have mastered the fear of death.' And the sword-master grins and says 'Ah, then there is nothing I can teach you.'

"It's a powerful little book," and he suggested that I read it three times.

•

When we have mastered our fear of death, we are free to make decisions without the gnawing worry that whatever we decided might not have been right. Or best. Or most appropriate. Or what was expected. To the New Jersey woman who wrote the letter to me, I would say that location is far less important than the love that is conveyed by the very act of prearranging burial, which may be one of the most selfless deeds that anybody can perform.

Mom and Dad prearranged their burials, and, as was their custom, they were upfront with me about their reasons. They wanted me not to be burdened with that decision when the time came because I'd have enough other things to tend to.

They wanted it to be less difficult for me—because they loved me. That was what love was all about, they said—looking out, as best they could, for those who mattered to them.

•

Harry James had finished "Trumpet Blues" and had been followed by Benny Goodman, Artie Shaw, Jimmy Dorsey, and some of those other guys. Now Glen Gray's Sonny Dunham was blowing the car doors right off the hinges with "Memories of You."

It always had been one of Dad's favorites—"the way a horn should make a song sound," he said. It was time to leave ... until fortune brought me back to our little town in mid-Missouri.

"Goodbye," I said, and I repeated, "I hope I can do as well."

That's the lofty goal at which all of us can aim—trying to emulate those who have done it the very best, the masters.

Finding the real stuff
August 18, 1991

A while back, I wrote a column about a conversation I had with an old friend, Los Angeles psychologist Melvyn Kinder, who talked about shifting downward from materialism, about finding where the real stuff was, about discovering that although money could buy a lot of things, it couldn't buy happiness.

In fact, said Kinder, he had found in his patients almost an inverse relationship between money and happiness: More money equaled less happiness. This was because people had invested so much in the pursuit of money that the "reward" they unexpectedly found was emptiness—not the joy they had anticipated.

I received many letters in response to that column, and I want to share with you part of the letter that I found most interesting.

•

"Money can't buy happiness? For many years I have repeatedly said, 'Money can't buy me anything but happiness.' To me, happiness is all that is worthwhile in life. Without it, one is lost. I am essentially a very happy person who has lived some of his dreams, but the one ingredient that would make me totally happy is enough money to be independent.

"In 1983, my wife and I sold our home and bought a 42-foot sailboat. Two years later, we both quit our jobs and went cruising for a year. It was something we had planned for all our married life, and it was a unique kind of therapy that I would recommend to all who are even mildly afflicted with wanderlust. Upon our return, we had no choice, financially, but to sell our beloved boat.

"Now that we're back to work, we're often asked if we would go cruising again. If we could afford it, you bet we would. There are some aspects of that life for which we will never find a satisfactory substitute: being outdoors all the time; feeling the wind and sun and salt-water spray and rain; the communion with nature; the sights and sounds of animals; the smell of marsh and beach and imminent rain; the sunsets and sunrises, and the magnificent clear, starry nights....

"But above all, we miss our freedom—and freedom is an essential ingredient to our being totally happy. Sufficient money could supply that vital need....

"The people for whom money can't buy happiness never have really understood what it takes for them to be happy. Money can't buy happiness until one has clearly determined what will really make them happy. Most people I know, rich or poor, have never figured it out.... Your friend Kinder has, however. He wants 'more time.' He wants the freedom to enjoy 'the best things in life.' But that freedom is only available to those with sufficient money."

•

Well, what about that? Do you agree that money can't buy anything but happiness if people know what it would take to make them truly happy? It's an interesting question, isn't it?

I think that money can buy happiness only if happiness is tied directly and exclusively to lifestyle. For many people, I would guess, this is their benchmark for happiness and, for them, enough money would be—well, enough, because it would enable them to live the way they want to live.

But what about those people for whom happiness goes beyond lifestyle?

Money can't buy happiness if our definition of happiness is good health. Money can buy the best medical care available, but sometimes the best medical care isn't enough. We're paralyzed after an automobile accident, or we're told that we have inoperable cancer or an eye disease that ultimately will cause blindness. In this situation, money doesn't count for much.

Money can't buy happiness if our definition of happiness is having well-adjusted, successful children. We can give them "things," including money, but if we haven't given them enough of ourselves at the right times, we may never be able to help them fill their emotional gas tanks—something that money can't buy.

Money can't buy happiness if our definition of happiness is having a loving relationship with our spouse and the other significant people in our lives. If we've burned our bridges down to the water line, we sometimes can't ever rebuild them—no matter how hard we try, no matter how much money we spend.

Money can't buy happiness if our definition of happiness is making it big in a career for which we essentially have no aptitude. If I want to be a writer but simply can't write, money can't help me. If I want to be a physician but can't master science, money can't help me. If I want to be a teacher but can't communicate, money can't help me. Perhaps money can soothe my anguish, but I'll still be disappointed—and unhappy.

•

What it comes down to, I think, is that, for some people, happiness is on the inside—and for them what's happening on the outside doesn't matter too much.

I remember a conversation with my father in his final years. He and my mother lived what I consider a frugal life, without many of the things that many of us take for granted—eating out, taking some trips, going to a show now and then. Mostly they stayed at home and talked, and read, and worked in their little garden, and tended their lawn and shrubs.

I asked Dad why he and Mom didn't do more things—since they had the means to travel, to do about anything they wanted. Dad smiled and told me that they were doing about anything they wanted.

"The way we live may not look like much to some people," he said, "but for us, it's plenty. It's everything we want."

That's the key, I think. For us, it's plenty. And no amount of money can buy that kind of inner peace. When we're filled up on the inside, there's less need for us to spend money for things on the outside.

Ultimately, the quest for happiness may have to do with only this one thing—finding peace with ourselves.

What do you think?

The satisfaction of doing new things

October 29, 1991

I can't think of a greater challenge, or more fun, than doing new things. It's important at any age, but it's especially important as we get into middle age and beyond, when many of us invest too much energy in hanging on to what we have and not enough energy in growing.

We grow when we try new things, when we're open to new ideas, to new ways of looking at things. We grow when we're willing to climb out of our ruts.

It's what psychiatrist Spurgeon English had in mind when he talked about the necessity to continue to expand our lives—rather than fall victim to contraction, which becomes a way of life for many people in their later years.

It's what anthropologist Ashley Montagu had in mind when, in his book *Growing Young*, he spoke against falling victim to "sclerosis of the mind," a hardening that shuts the door to adventures that can come when we're willing to get off the expressway and wander down side roads.

When I talk about doing new things, I don't necessarily have in mind major events such as career change or around-the-world trips. What I'm talking about is within reach of all of us, little things that can teach us and entertain us—and enlarge our world.

I try to practice what I preach.

A few years ago, Marilyn and I took a winter vacation to Antigua, and as I sat in the sand and watched the colorful sails of the catamarans, I asked myself, "Why not?" Why couldn't I learn to sail? Marilyn and I took lessons the next summer, and catamaran sailing has exposed me to a world I never knew was out there—a world of excitement that can be alternately exhilarating and terrifying. There's nothing quite like the scream of the wind when it's rushing between the sails during a high-speed run.

Early this spring, I decided I was going to design and have made up in a variety of colors my very own chambray golf shirt—with button-down collar, oversize sleeves, deep placket, four-inch locker loop, and nightshirt-length tail. I even created my own logo for the left chest. Satisfying? You bet.

I'm now recording 55-second thoughts for the day for a Philadelphia radio station, and this is something new for me. I sit in the booth, read my script, watch the digital clock counting off the seconds, and edit as I go along to finish on time. It's challenging—and it's fun.

Last month, I wrote the first of the quarterly newsletters that I've committed to produce as president of the condominium council at our beach place. I'm an old hand at condominium newsletters, but what makes this new venture fun and challenging is that the condominium is a second home for most of the owners, and they miss the day-to-day contact that keeps them up to date on what's going on. The newsletter is an attempt to create a dialogue between absentee owners and the council so they'll know as much as we do about how things are going. If we ask for money, I want everybody to anticipate it.

A few weeks ago I asked a friend to teach me how to regrip my golf clubs. We spent an hour putting grips on 12 clubs that I keep in my big bag. It was so much fun I went back two days later and regripped seven clubs I keep in my carry bag. I can't overemphasize the satisfaction I felt when I teed off with my very own regripped clubs. I also hit the ball longer and straighter than I have in years. Was that because of my grips or because of my head? I'm not sure it matters.

The friend who taught me to regrip is Ray Adams. Now there's a guy from whom we all can learn something.

●

By anybody's definition, Ray Adams would deserve a spot on the list of all-time unforgettable characters. He's an electrical engineer—he once taught as an adjunct professor at Drexel University—and he retired after 38 years at Philadelphia Electric Co., where he was manager of employee relations. He once was a professional musician, playing drums, bass, piano, and trumpet. He holds dual citizenship in the United States and Ireland, and he writes regularly for Irish publications, often under pseudonyms.

He has a contract for a book he's working on now, and he tinkers endlessly with new programs for his three computers. He designs some of his own programs, and he's even preparing a program that will greet my wife with "Hi, Marilyn" when she punches up her word-processing format.

After Adams left Philadelphia Electric, he went to school to learn to make golf clubs, and he developed his own business, building custom clubs and repairing clubs for a number of golf shops in the Philadelphia area. He sold off the business because it was keeping him so busy he didn't have time for some of his other interests—like painting with watercolors.

For many years, he has been rated one of the region's foremost watercolor artists, and his house looks like an art gallery. His colors are bright and true—despite his being color-blind. How does he do it? "I'm not sure," he said. Sometimes he paints lefthanded—"to get an angle" that can't be achieved properly with the right hand.

You think this is a lot of activity? Well, hang on. There's more. Every winter, he goes to a South Florida club where, as an assistant golf pro, he teaches putting and chipping.

Is there anything Ray Adams can't do?

"I like to think that I can do about anything I want to do."

What drives him to be so active?

"There's so much to do and it would be a shame not to get around to things that are interesting. Besides, it's fun."

I asked Adams if he missed the corporate scene. After all, 38 years is a long time.

His answer was brief and to the point: "No, not in the least."

He is in many ways the healthiest person I ever met, a role model for the ages, forever young because that's the way he's decided it's going to be.

Besides that, he helps me with my putting and chipping.

The reason for the wind-up toys

January 2, 1992

It's been almost nine months since I went to Betsi Smith's kindergarten at Abington Friends School in Jenkintown, Pa.—a kindergarten designed to help adults get back in touch with the little child who lives within. I spent four hours there on a Saturday morning, and, yes, my little child did emerge and, yes, my little child was reluctant to go back inside when it was time for me to leave.

It was a marvelous experience, and I've written two columns about it. Other people regard it as a marvelous experience, too, hundreds of people who in the weeks after my first column appeared flooded Smith with queries about what they had to do for admission.

It started as an occasional program on Saturday mornings, and then, because the response was so great, Smith began classes at night. The longer it continues, the more momentum it generates.

People magazine did a three-page spread on the kindergarten a month ago under the headline "School of Soft Knocks." ABC sent a television news crew a few weeks ago. What started as Betsi Smith's personal adventure has become a national phenomenon.

Why? What's the attraction?

The more I talk about it with people and the more feedback I get, the more I'm inclined to think the appeal is every bit as simple as I thought in the beginning:

Structure and bureaucracy are the defining experiences of adulthood, and kindergarten is a dramatic change. It has no structure, no bureaucracy. People are free to make choices. They can model with clay or paint with their fingers. Nobody dictates what they should do, how they should do it, when they must be finished. Nobody gives them a grade, symbolically or literally.

The thing that most sharply impressed me was the supportive nature of the other "children" with whom I went to kindergarten. They applauded during show-and-tell when I read a passage from my Zane Grey baseball book. They liked my model airplane and my fingerpainting. The whole experience was marked by support and enthusiasm. Nobody could do anything wrong.

Contrast this with the way many people work in business today. They're told exactly how to do their jobs, with little room for any creativity—because too many bosses come from the old military model of leadership, which holds that people should be herded like sheep.

Too many people in business are constantly criticized—because too many bosses believe people work harder when their feet are held to the fire, when they're fearful of losing their jobs. They're told that their attitude is inappropriate, that somebody else could do their job better, and the threat, of course, is that they'll be out in the cold if they don't shape up.

The reality, quite obviously, is that most people don't work better when they're constantly under fire. Not long ago, I interviewed Ross Webber, professor of management at the Wharton School of the University of Pennsylvania, who wrote the book *Becoming a Courageous Manager*. He told me that one of his great concerns today was that organizations were squeezing creativity out of people by their constant demands for more output.

Smith's kindergarten gives people a break from all of this, a chance to be stroked, to let their hair down without the fear that they'll be criticized, that their best won't be considered good enough. Whatever somebody does is plenty good enough.

Part of the impact of the kindergarten experience on me has been that I'm more open to doing things I once might have regarded as silly, things for which "responsible" people shouldn't have time.

I now have a batch of wind-up toys—they cost $1.99 each—that I keep at work and at home. There's a purple gorilla holding a golden banana, a green kangaroo with pink boxing gloves, a red mouse with a triangle of cheese. I wind them up and they do flips, moving across the desktop at speeds that are rather remarkable. Whenever I need a reality check, I wind up one of them and watch it flip. I find myself laughing. I find myself paying more attention to the teddy bears I keep in my office, asking them if they want me to get the red mouse to teach them how to do flips. They never answer, but I believe they will—eventually.

That's the great thing about being a little kid—you learn how to believe again. And when you believe, anything is possible.

The agency that books my speaking engagements sent me for Christmas a desktop calendar that has a cartoon for every day of 1992. The first one I turned to showed groups of sheep and cattle, clustered separately, at a cocktail party, sipping drinks and talking with great animation. Two cowboys sit on their horses nearby, and one says to the other: "Well, what have I always said? Sheep and cattle just don't mix."

Now that's funny.

In years past, I might have trashed the calendar, and my rationalization would have been that I've already got two wall calendars, and I don't have enough room on my desk for anything else. All that is true, but now it doesn't matter. I just push everything over a few inches and put the calendar down on the desk between the red mouse that flips and the Garfield cat whose paws hold my business cards.

That's growth, I think, because I've discovered, finally, that it's impossible to put too much kiddie stuff on a desk—anybody's desk, but especially mine.

I've bought a Mickey Mouse sweatshirt that's absolutely dazzling—the best $28 I ever spent. It goes so well with my Mickey Mouse wristwatch. Now I'm thinking about—well, I'll share that with you later.

And to think, all this came about because of four hours in kindergarten.

When tales of sex abuse aren't true

January 5, 1992

Just before Thanksgiving, I wrote a column about therapists who assume that their adult female patients may have been sexually abused as children. These therapists believe that because the patients may have repressed memories of such abuse, the therapists have a responsibility to help them recall it.

Through interviews, the column made the point that some patients now are "remembering" sexual abuse that apparently never happened—and families are being torn apart by what Philadelphia psychiatrist Harold Lief called "a social phenomenon" and what UCLA psychiatrist Richard Green described as "the new sex-abuse industry."

One therapist told Lief that with her help, 70 percent to 80 percent of her patients remember childhood sexual abuse—a figure that was deemed beyond comprehension by Lief, who has been in practice for 40 years and is recognized as one of the nation's foremost sex therapists.

The increase in the numbers of women who, with the help of their therapists, remember childhood sexual abuse has been tied by some critics to the book *The Courage to Heal*, which urges troubled women to consider the possibility of sexual abuse and which, on page 21, tells them, "If you are unable to remember any specific instances [of childhood sexual abuse] but still have a feeling that something happened to you, it probably did." Some therapists routinely give this book to patients to sharpen their will to remember sexual abuse.

Lief said that the horrors and consequences of legitimate sexual abuse "should never be minimized, but there is another side to this situation"—false allegations that destroy innocent families.

After the column appeared in newspapers around the country, I received a response that was larger and more passionate than anything that has come to me in more than a decade. About 25 percent of the response was negative and outraged—from people who felt that I and those I interviewed didn't believe that childhood sexual abuse ever happened. About 75 percent was positive and appreciative—from parents and family members who said they had been falsely accused, and also from some "victims."

•

Here is part of a letter from one woman whose story is not too dissimilar from what I heard from many other women—about therapists who won't take "no" for an answer.

"I consulted a counselor for help in dealing with having grown up in a home with an alcoholic parent.... My mother, who from all accounts did not have an ideal childhood, turned to alcohol to alleviate her problems. When that didn't work, she became verbally and emotionally abusive toward me and my father. Life in our house was a constant verbal battle.... After I married and put some emotional distance between us, I tried to salvage some of the relationship."

The woman entered therapy. "During my first session, [the therapist] asked me if I had been sexually assaulted during my childhood," she said. "He seemed very unhappy when I answered that I hadn't been.... There was no physical abuse involved. The counselor wouldn't accept this. He could only help me if I recognized and admitted to having been sexually abused as a child. He claimed that I had blocked this abuse out and was in deep denial."

They talked about other things, but always the therapist returned to sexual abuse and continued to demand that the woman acknowledge it. "I wondered what happened to other people who had gone to this man for help and had been put under similar pressure by him," she said. "If I had been less certain of the events of my childhood or more vulnerable to suggestion, I would have simply caved in. Instead, I was almost tempted to laugh."

She left therapy after the second session. "I have begun to suspect that this sexual-abuse theory is the psychologists' placebo for the '90s," she said. "People who are confused and uncertain look for any answer to explain why their lives didn't turn out like the storybooks. Many of these will latch on to anything to explain away the pain."

From another woman:

"I must say that I have long possessed the gravest suspicions of these long-delayed accusations, because my sister and I were sexually abused by our father, and we never forgot. I have always had the most vivid memories of my experience, even of the words exchanged on the occasions when it took place....

"No intelligent human being is unaware of the fact that the mind works in astounding ways to protect itself from trauma. I must point out, however, that even when a memory has been long suppressed, when it returns through responsible therapy, the patient will recall details and specific incidents....

"When I entered therapy, my therapist viewed her task as helping me to deal with the abuse and then to put it behind me, so I could get on with my life.... I was looking for a way to lead a full and satisfying existence despite my history. This is what therapy should be about.... My therapist was extremely blunt and realistic about a great many truths having to do with being an adult—taking personal responsibility, meeting your obligations to others, accepting the fact that there are things you cannot change.... In accepting her statements I also accepted the fact that I could not expect the world's corners to be padded for me, simply because I had suffered sexual abuse as a child....

"What on earth is the point of therapy that encourages you to go through life as a victim who is always looking for excuses? What intelligent, properly trained therapist could possible countenance such an attitude, let alone listen to it week after week?"

•

I talked with psychologist Ralph Underwager, who is clinical director of the Institute for Psychological Therapies in Northfield, Minn., a pioneer in advocating rights for parents who claim to be falsely accused of sexual abuse by their children.

A while back, Underwager, who has gained a reputation for parental advocacy, appeared on a national TV talk show with three women who claimed to have remembered, with the help of therapists, childhood sexual abuse from many years past.

The show's host, Geraldo Rivera, asked Underwager: "Don't you believe these women are victims?"

Answered Underwager: "Of course, but they're victims not of parents but of misguided, mistaken mental-health professionals."

The audience broke into applause.

Underwager said he and staff members are "working with a group on research about this whole phenomenon. It's a rare opportunity to be involved in gathering data about a social phenomenon while it's actually happening, not years later."

He said the "phenomenon" of false accusations now is appearing in New Zealand, Australia, and the Netherlands. "It seems that the United States is exporting it to the rest of the world." He predicted that "it will get worse before it gets better because when these proponents are confronted with disconfirming evidence they strengthen their proselytizing."

I told Underwager that I was hearing from some women who claimed not that they had been sexually abused as children but that they had been forced to participate in satanic rituals. Was there a connection?

Yes, said Underwager, and the connection often is this: If the therapist believes that all bad things can be traced to childhood sexual abuse, the patient tends to recall sexual abuse. But if the therapist believes that satanic ritual is the culprit, then this is what the patient remembers.

The influence of the therapist can be awesome, he said, and it must be taken into account whenever adult patients "remember" events.

•

Psychiatrist Harold Lief told me that he received 23 telephone calls from parents on the day after my column appeared in *The Philadelphia Inquirer.* In the weeks since, he has received dozens and dozens of calls and letters. Parents are confused and dispirited, he said, and wonder how this could be happening to them.

He said that the problem must be dealt with nationally "to bring to the attention of the therapeutic community what is happening." He is submitting to the American Family Therapy Association an abstract for a seminar on false accusations that are the result of what he described as "unfortunate" action by some therapists.

"Families are being destroyed," he said. "The difficult thing is that there is sexual abuse. We have to have a balanced approach. There can be the danger that we'll go too far and miss real, genuine cases of abuse.... But the whole business of so many therapists jumping on this bandwagon, this social movement, is really disquieting. Some highly credentialed people are involved, not just people on the fringes.... They start with the premise that 50 to 70 percent of women have been abused, and they reason backward and find evidence to support abuse. I regard this as a false premise."

Lief said that one woman, now 33, told him that she had been raped repeatedly by her father for a year when she was 15 and 16 but that she had no memories of it. "She can't remember it, but she knows it happened," he said. "She's convinced that she's repressed it and that memories will return eventually." How can she be so certain? It was her therapist who told Lief that she finds abuse in 70 percent to 80 percent of her patients.

Said Lief: "It's possible, I suppose, to be raped by your father at 16 and forget it, but I rather doubt it. You could forget an isolated event perhaps, but not a series of events. You'd have to be in a dissociated state when it happened, like an automaton.... People with multiple personalities could do that, but it's very rare.... I'd like to see evidence, professionally, that you can repress events in your late teens, especially events that are repeated. I don't know of any evidence to support this."

I asked Lief to comment on therapists who look for sexual abuse in every female patient.

"A therapist who insists on the sexual abuse theory—or any kind of bias—will tend to pick up cues to substantiate that frame of reference and overlook things that don't fit. The selection process reinforces the bias," he said.

Is it appropriate for a therapist to drive hard at the patient to remember sexual abuse?

"When the therapist is taking a general history, it's OK to ask the patient, 'Do you have any knowledge of sexual abuse as a child?' But if the answer is 'no,' you don't persist," Lief said. "You don't say, 'Oh, come on, you must have some memories.' You just leave it, and the memories, if they're real, may come up later in association with other things in therapy."

Some therapists who help patients "remember" sexual abuse encourage patients to tell everybody about it, including their children and their children's schoolteachers. I asked Lief how he felt about that.

"There's a fine line here," he said. "You want the patient to overcome denial, to sense that she's not so terrible that she can't be accepted by society. Part of making things known to others is to achieve some kind of sanction. But on the other hand, if you bring harm to your children and other family members, what good have you done?"

What about confronting parents?

"You bring your mother and father into therapy," he said. "You do it with a competent therapist.... The therapist should have some detachment, but the problem we have here is that these people, those who see sexual abuse everywhere, have this great fervor to demonstrate criminality. They're advocates, overcommitted to the process, instead of being detached therapists."

Meeting a childhood hero
January 12, 1992

The name of the book is *Country Hardball*, and it's the autobiography of Enos "Country" Slaughter, who played the big-league game of baseball for 19 seasons, hit for a lifetime average of .300, and in 1985 was elected to the Hall of Fame.

When I grew up in Missouri in the 1940s, I idolized the men—some of them were boys—who played for the St. Louis Cardinals, guys who were bigger than life. One of them was Enos Slaughter, No. 9, the right-fielder. They called him "Colonel Clutch," because when the game was on the line, they wanted him at the plate, standing motionless with the bat on his left shoulder until the pitch rode in high and tight and ...

Crack!

"It's way back there! Way back! It might be!" The Cardinals' broadcaster in those days was Harry Caray. "It could be!" The roar of the crowd almost blotted out his voice. "It's off the top of the screen! One run! Two runs! Cardinals win! Cardinals win!"

More than any player, Slaughter typified for me what big-league baseball was all about—playing hard when you were hurt, banging into the wall for a game-ending catch, and knocking in the winning run in a September game when the pennant was hanging in the balance.

As a kid, I once got his autograph at the ballpark, my most treasured possession—until a few years later when my mom, who worked retail, asked him to sign a baseball for me when he visited her store in the off-season as a representative of Bee Hats.

Anybody remember Bee Hats? Well, that's how long ago it was.

I grew up—as we all do, if we're lucky—but one thing that I didn't grow out of was my affection for the Cardinals and my boyhood heroes, especially Slaughter.

As a newspaper editor in North Carolina, I interviewed Slaughter when he was baseball coach at Duke University. And then, a few years after that, I discovered one more benefit to the many that I already knew about when I married Marilyn Oakley. Her father's farm is just down the road from Slaughter's 150-acre farm in Roxboro, N.C., and her father, Osborne Oakley, played high school baseball with Slaughter. To this day, they're friends, and it was Big Oz who some years ago helped me arrange an interview with Slaughter for a book I was writing about farm families.

I consider myself very fortunate. Few people ever have the opportunity, as adults, to get to know their heroes of childhood.

●

Reading Slaughter's *Country Hardball* was for me like climbing into a time machine and returning to the halcyon days of youth—names and faces from yesteryear, long gone but never to be forgotten: Lon Warneke, Coaker Triplett, Don Padgett, Billy Southworth, Jimmy Brown, Terry Moore.

Slaughter elegantly makes the point that much of his success as a baseball player was because others touched his life in everlasting ways. One of those was Eddie Dyer, who was his manager in 1936 in Columbus, Ga., in the South Atlantic League and who later would be his manager in St. Louis. Slaughter was 20, homesick, and playing so poorly that he thought his career might be doomed.

One night in Savannah, Ga., he struck out with the bases loaded, and Dyer screamed at him: "You jumped a foot in the air trying to hit that last pitch! That's why you're hitting .220."

Slaughter stood in right field, head down, and when the inning was over, "I trotted back toward the dugout, then slowed down to a walk. When I reached the dugout steps, there to greet me again was Dyer, with an even angrier expression on his face. 'What's the matter, son? Are you too tired to run all the way? If so, then I'll get you some help.' That changed my life right there. From that moment on, Enos Slaughter never loafed on a baseball field."

After the game, Slaughter returned to his rooming house and spent a sleepless night, mentally preparing himself for what he thought was next: being sent deeper into the minor leagues. He went to the ballpark early to apologize to Dyer for his poor play.

"Eddie just smiled, motioned for me to sit down and told me something that floored me. 'Son, if you can overcome just two things, you have a good chance to go to the major leagues.' I couldn't believe what I was hearing.... I had never even dreamed of being a big-league ballplayer before."

The two things: learning the strike zone and hitting the relay man on throws from the outfield.

But there was still more help needed, and it came from one of the big-name stars of the game, pitcher Lon Warneke. In 1938, with the Cardinals, Slaughter was terrified by ground balls, and after he'd misplayed a couple that cost games, Warneke took matters into his own hands.

"He noticed my discomfort with ground balls and apparently decided he didn't want that fear in anyone fielding behind him," Slaughter writes. "During that first year, he hit fungoes to me every day. Two or three would be fly balls, but the rest were grounders. This went on day in and day out, at home and on the road. I finally got to where ground balls were like anything else coming to me out there. Having mastered what I had once feared, I realized the importance of practice, practice, and more practice."

•

Some other stories that bring back names—and memories:

"There will never be another Pepper Martin.... Pepper would play with nothing on under his uniform. No jock strap, no sweat socks, nothing. He didn't care how much he sweated in those big wool uniforms. If he was going good, he didn't want his uniform washed."

"Terry Moore became my best friend on the club and ... my best friend in baseball. As a rightfielder, I felt fortunate to have him play alongside me in the outfield. When I had to go back deep for a long fly ball, he would run to the wall and yell 'Careful!' if I was getting too close. He was the best defensive centerfielder I ever played alongside."

"Joe Medwick tried to get in with the young guys when they first came up to the big leagues.... He wanted to let you know that he was the star and if everything wasn't just the way he wanted it, he would be bitter about it. Eating out with him wasn't a whole lot of fun because he liked to show off and talk nasty to the waitresses.... Joe and Terry Moore had been playing alongside each other in the Cardinals' outfield for six years when one day a ball was hit high and deep into left center. As Terry went charging toward the fence in pursuit, he relied on Medwick to warn him if he was in any danger. Medwick was hollering that Moore had plenty of room as the ball sailed 20 feet into the stands. Terry crashed into the concrete wall, and, when he came to, he told Medwick that if he ever ran him into the fence again, he'd break Medwick's neck."

•

I talked to Slaughter a few weeks ago when I was in North Carolina. He's 76 now, and he plays in celebrity golf tournaments all over the country. He still makes appearances at old-timer baseball games, but, he said, "they only pay me $1,100, and I can get twice that for a baseball-card show."

He is not a wealthy man—by the usual standards that society applies to wealth. In 1942, when the Cardinals beat the Yankees in the World Series, he was paid $9,000, and his highest salary in 19 seasons was $22,000. But in other ways, Enos Slaughter is very wealthy—because he has spent a virtual lifetime doing what he loved, a man who played a boy's game as well as anybody and better than most.

Slaughter, himself, summed it up after his election to the Hall of Fame:

"My life is complete."

How many people do you know who can say that?

About the authors

Darrell Sifford was born in 1931. From 1964 to 1974, he was executive editor of *The Charlotte News*. In 1973, he began writing a column with the intention that it be a feature with which readers could identify on a personal level. The column was soon syndicated as part of the Knight-Ridder News Service. In 1976, he joined the staff of *The Philadelphia Inquirer*, where his column appeared several times a week. The strength of the bond between him and his readers may be without parallel in the newspaper industry.

He died in a drowning accident while vacationing in the Caribbean on a month-long trip that was a gift from his wife to celebrate his 60th birthday.

•

Marilyn Sifford was born in 1948. For more than 20 years, she has been involved in human-resources development in the private sector and in not-for-profit organizations. She established her own business, S.T.A.R. Consulting, in 1989. In May 1994, she married Bob Butera.